KWIK·SEW® currently publishes the following books
by Kerstin Martensson:

KWIK·SEW®S Method for Easy Sewing

KWIK·SEW®S Swim and Action Wear

KWIK·SEW®S Beautiful Lingerie

KWIK·SEW®S Sewing for Baby

KWIK·SEW®S Sewing for Toddlers

KWIK·SEW®S Sewing for Children

KWIK·SEW®S Sweatshirts Unlimited

Appliqué the KWIK·SEW® Way

Dear Customer:

This book is not related in any way to publications and patterns produced and distributed by KWIK•SEW® Pattern Co., Inc., Minneapolis, Minnesota, under the registered trademark "KWIK•SEW®".

KWIK•SEW® Pattern Co., Inc. produces and distributes patterns and sewing instruction books for home sewing.

Each book includes a master pattern in multi-sizes. The patterns are printed on a quality white paper using a different color ink for each size. The books have easy-to-follow instructions using time-saving techniques, many illustrations and color photographs.

Please see reverse side for book titles.

Contact KWIK•SEW® for more information and to order books, patterns, or a Home Pattern Catalogue.

KWIK•SEW® *Pattern Co. Inc.*

3000 Washington Avenue North • Minneapolis, MN 55411-1699 • U.S.A.
Phone: 612/521-7651 • Toll Free: 1-888-KWIKSEW
Fax: 612/521-1662 • e-mail: info@kwiksew.com

www.kwiksew.com

BEST–LOVED DESIGNERS
C O L L E C T I O N

QUICK-SEW CELEBRATIONS

Decorative Creations for Festive Occasions from America's Top Designers

Edited by Marjon Schaefer

BEST-LOVED DESIGNERS COLLECTION:
QUICK-SEW CELEBRATIONS
Copyright © 1998 by Landauer Corporation

This book was designed and produced by
Landauer Books
A division of Landauer Corporation
12251 Maffitt Road, Cumming, Iowa 50061

President and Publisher: Jeramy Lanigan Landauer
Vice President: Becky Johnston
Editor in Chief: Marjon Schaefer
Art Director: Tracy DeVenney

BEST-LOVED DESIGNERS COLLECTION:
QUICK-SEW CELEBRATIONS
Editor: Mary V. Green
Art Director: Stan Green
Graphic Designer: Stan Green/Green Graphics
Photographers: Craig Anderson; Scott Little
Technical Illustrator: Stan Green/Green Graphics
Printed in Hong Kong

Published by Martingale & Company
PO Box 118, Bothell, WA 98041-0118 USA

Library of Congress Cataloging-in-Publication Data Available.

This book is printed on acid-free paper.

1 2 3 4 5 6 7 8 9 10

**Sally Korte &
Alice Strebel**
Kindred Spirits

Kris Kerrigan
Button Weeds

**Janet Carija
Brandt**

Lynette Jensen
Thimbleberries

**Patrice
Longmire**
Patrice & Co.

McKenna Ryan
Pine Needles

Cheryl Jukich
*Threadbare Pattern
Company*

Sandy Belt
Town Folk Designs

Margaret Sindelar
Cottonwood Classics

Suellen Wassem
Pieceful Heart Designs

INTRODUCTION

Just for the fun of it, discover the magic of make-it-quick projects, designed to help you celebrate holidays, birthdays, and other special-occasion days throughout the year! These easy-to-make fabric favorites that make special days memorable are featured in 10 quick-sew country and folk art collections created by America's Best-Loved Designers.

To help you celebrate, each leading fabric artisan contributes an exciting new special-occasion collection, including a wide range of forever-favorites from homespun hearts, folk art angels and stars, to whimsical snowmen and Santas. For a special event, unique decoration, or a last-minute gift, make-it quick with fresh new inspirations, from decorating Dad's den for Father's Day to warming hearts on the bride's special day. Best of all, the projects are easy and fun to make—and they're special remembrances family and friends will anticipate and enjoy throughout the year!

For fast, fun results we've provided several pages of General Instructions and comprehensive Sources for helpful product information. Also included are the company names and addresses of the contributing designers so that you may contact each for special patterns, fabrics and trims, and if you find a design inspiration that makes your celebration just that much more special, it's your opportunity to let the designers know they've made your day. After all, that's what makes them some of America's Best-Loved Designers!

Marjon Schaefer
Editor-in-Chief

Friendship in Bloom   pg. 8

A Busy Hen's Kitchen   pg. 22

From Heart to Home   pg. 32

Make a Christmas Wish   pg. 52

TABLE OF CONTENTS

Catching Memories   pg. 74

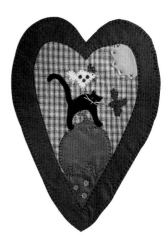

Pumpkin Patch Treats   pg. 104

Christmas With a Twist   pg. 118

Wildflower Wedding   pg. 130

Autumn Rose   pg. 42

GENERAL INSTRUCTIONS

FOR EVERY PROJECT

As you gather your materials and begin each project, here are some guidelines you may find helpful:

- The fabric called for in the materials list is 44"-wide lightweight to medium-weight cotton unless otherwise specified.
- Scraps of fabric are intended to be those you have on hand. If you don't have a particular color or pattern in your scrap basket, you'll only need to purchase ⅛ yard pieces or fat quarters.
- Since many of these projects are decorative items, it's not necessary to prewash the fabrics. Prewash fabrics for any piece that will be laundered.
- Cut strips and rectangles with a rotary cutter for speed and accuracy.
- Sew all seams with a ¼" seam allowance unless noted otherwise. After stitching, press seam allowances to one side, usually toward the darker fabric.

QUICK-SEW APPLIQUÉ
TRACE, APPLY FUSIBLE WEB, CUT, AND FUSE

- Use regular-weight fusible web unless directed otherwise in the materials list. Regular and lightweight fusibles have a lighter coating of adhesive, and the appliqué pieces should be hand- or machine-stitched after fusing. Heavyweight fusible web is for projects where the appliqué pieces are not stitched.
- Place the fusible web, paper side up, over the appliqué patterns. Trace the patterns. (The patterns are the reverse of the finished project.) Cut the fusible web about ⅛" outside the traced line (Diagram A). To save time, trace all patterns to be cut from one fabric about ¼" apart from each other on the fusible web. Cut around the outside of the grouped patterns.
- Fuse the pattern to the wrong side of the fabric. Cut out on the traced lines (Diagram B). Transfer any dashed placement lines to the fabric.
- Peel off the paper backing. Position the appliqué on the background fabric, overlapping the pieces at the dashed lines; fuse in place (Diagram C).

FINISHING THE WALLHANGING OR QUILT
LAYERING

- Cut the backing and batting several inches larger than the quilt top.
- Lay the backing wrong side up on a flat surface. Secure the edges with tape. Center the batting over the backing, smoothing it flat. Position the finished top on the batting.
- Hand-baste or safety-pin the layers together about every 4", beginning in the middle and working to the edges. Trim the batting and backing even with or ¼" beyond the edges of the quilt top.

DIAGRAM A

DIAGRAM B

DIAGRAM C

QUILTING

BY MACHINE

- Sew with a fairly long straight stitch. A walking foot attachment helps keep layers even and makes quilting easier. To change direction, stop with the needle in the fabric, lift the presser foot, and pivot the fabric on the needle.
- For intricate designs, use an embroidery foot attachment and lower the feed dogs. Use an embroidery hoop to help keep the fabric stretched.

BY HAND

- Thread the needle with an 18" length of quilting thread and tie a small knot at the end. Insert the needle through the quilt top and into the batting, about 1" from where you will begin quilting. Bring the needle up at the beginning of the quilting line, giving the thread a gentle tug to pull the knot through the top and hide it in the batting.
- Take several small, even running stitches at a time. To end a line of stitching, make a small knot close to the fabric. Insert the needle into the fabric and bring it out again about 1" from the end of the stitching. Pop the knot through the top layer into the batting, and cut the thread.

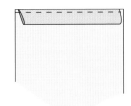

DIAGRAM D

ADDING A HANGING SLEEVE

- The sleeve is added after quilting is completed but before the binding is added. Follow these instructions to make a 2½"-wide sleeve, a good size for most wallhangings. First, cut a strip of fabric 5½" inches wide and 1" shorter than the width of the quilt.
- Press under ½", then ½" again on each short end; machine stitch the hem. Fold the strip in half lengthwise, wrong sides together, and press. Pin the strip to the top back edge of the quilt, with raw edges even (Diagram D). Stitch with a ¼" seam allowance. The raw edges will be covered by the quilt binding.
- After the binding is stitched to the quilt, smooth and pin the hanging sleeve. Whipstitch the sleeve's folded edge in place.

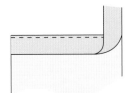

DIAGRAM E

DIAGRAM F

BINDING

- Sew the binding strips together into one long strip. Fold the strip in half lengthwise, wrong sides together, and press.
- With raw edges even, pin the binding to the quilt top, leaving several inches loose at the beginning. Sew with a ¼" seam allowance.
- At the corner, fold the binding up at a 45° angle (Diagram E), then down at a 90° angle. Sew from the top (Diagram F), continuing along the edges to 6" from the beginning. Overlap; trim ends to ½". Open the binding, sew the ends together, refold the binding and finish sewing to the top.
- Turn the binding to the back so it just covers the stitching. Whipstitch the folded edge in place, making mitered corners on the back (Diagram G).

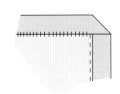

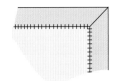

DIAGRAM G

Sally Korte & Alice Strebel

FRIENDSHIP IN BLOOM

There are probably as many different types of friendships as there are reasons for forming them. We develop relationships with neighbors, business colleagues, garden group members, etc.

Then there are friendships that are deeper, and longer-lasting. These are friends with whom you share not only an interest or an activity but a way of life and a system of values. These are kindred spirits—and who better to design a collection celebrating friendship than two women who named their business for their own relationship?

Sally Korte and Alice Strebel have been friends and business partners—Kindred Spirits—for over ten years. Their business developed, in part, because friends asked them to create patterns for their distinctive clothing. They continue to meet people who share their outlook on life. "When we teach we always find immediate friends in our classes," Sally says. "They already feel they know our hearts because of our work." This comes as no surprise to Sally and Alice, who describe kindred spirits as "those people who are friends even if they don't know each other yet, and who will remain friends even if they never see each other again."

Let your friends know how much they mean to you by creating one of these friendship gifts. Vary the embellishing, making each one a personal token of affection.

MATERIALS

- ¼ yard of burlap or light tan fabric for background
- Assorted large scraps for pocket, pieced borders, heart appliqué, and ruched flower
- ⅜ yard of fabric for backing
- Gray, green, black, gold, blue, and red embroidery floss
- 13" x 21" piece of thin cotton batting
- ⅝" button
- Fade-away fabric marker

Finished size 12" x 20"

CUTTING

1. From the burlap or tan fabric, cut the following rectangles: 4½" x 10½" (A), 2½" x 4½" (B), 3½" x 4½" (C), 4½" x 6½" (D), 5½" x 8½" (E), and 4½" x 5½" (F).

2. From the assorted scraps, cut two pockets (one will be the lining) and one heart using the patterns on page 17. Cut one 1¼" x 12" strip for the ruched flower.

   For the pieced border, cut 1½"-wide strips ranging from 3½" to 6½" in length. (You will need approximately 101" of pieced border.)

3. From the backing fabric, cut a 13" x 21" rectangle.

ASSEMBLY

1. Using the fade-away marker and referring to the photo as needed, write the phrases "Friends, Like Flowers, Bloom Longest in Our Memories," "Forget Me Not," and "Rosemary for Remembrance" on the appropriate rectangles. Transfer the bee, ladybug, beehive and flower designs from pages 17-18. Use three strands of floss to satin-stitch the bee and lady bug bodies and to make the flowers with a lazy

daisy stitch. Use four strands of floss to backstitch all remaining stitching.

2. Blanket-stitch the heart to the C rectangle, leaving the edges raw.

3. To make the ruched flower, press under ¼" on both long edges of the 1¼" x 12" strip. Sew loose running stitches from fold to fold at a 45-degree angle, as shown in Diagram A. Gather the thread up as tightly as possible as you go. Evenly distribute the gathers and knot the end. Form a tight circle at one end, and curl the strip into a tight spiral, overlapping the edges, and tacking it as you go along. Stitch the flower in place on the D rectangle.

DIAGRAM A

4. Place the pocket and pocket lining right sides together and stitch around the outside edges, leaving an opening for turning. Trim the seam allowances and turn right side out through the opening. Press the flap toward the front of the pocket, and stitch the button in place to hold the flap down. Position the pocket on the E rectangle so that it is centered from side to side and ¾" from the bottom edge. Blanket-stitch in place using three strands of floss.

5. Lay out the completed rectangles, referring to Diagram B for placement. Sew the 1½"-wide strips together end-to-end, and add these pieced borders between the rectangles as shown. Sew border strips to the top and bottom edges, and then to the sides.

6. Trim the backing and batting to match the completed quilt top. Place the quilt top right sides together with the

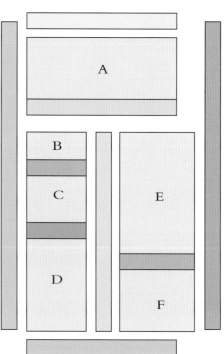

DIAGRAM B

backing, and then place the batting on top; pin. Sew the three layers together, leaving an opening for turning. Trim the seam allowances, and turn right side out through the opening. Sew the opening closed.

7. Quilt through the center of the pieced borders using three strands of floss and long running stitches.

Forget-Me-Not Pillow

10" x 16"

MATERIALS

- ½ yard of print fabric for pillow
- ¼ yard of burlap for sleeve
- Assorted scraps for ruched flower and pieced binding
- Green, gold, blue, and gray embroidery floss
- Polyester stuffing
- Fade-away fabric marker

CUTTING

1. From the print fabric, cut a 16" x 20" rectangle. From the burlap, cut a 7½" x 20" rectangle.

2. From the scraps, cut a 1¼" x 12" strip for the ruched flower. Cut fourteen 1¾" x 3½" pieces for the binding.

ASSEMBLY

1. Fold the print fabric in half crosswise, right sides together, so that it measures 16" x 10". Sew the long seam, leaving a 3" opening near the center. Sew the two side seams. Trim the seam allowances and turn

right side out through the opening. Stuff the pillow and sew the opening closed.

2. Sew seven binding pieces together end to end to make one long strip. Fold the binding in half lengthwise, wrong sides together, and press. Repeat with the remaining seven binding pieces.

3. Pin the binding strips to the right side of the 7½" x 20" burlap rectangle, aligning the raw edges. Sew with ¼" seam allowances, and press the binding toward the edges. Handstitch along the outside edges with embroidery floss and long running stitches.

4. Fold the rectangle in half crosswise, right sides together, so that it measures 7½" x 10". Stitch the seam, and turn right side out.

5. Using a fade-away marker, transfer the embroidery design onto the pillow sleeve and write the words "Forget Me Not." Backstitch the stems, leaves, and words using six strands of floss. The forget-me-nots are lazy daisy stitches and the flower centers are French knots, both stitched with three strands of floss.

6. Make the ruched flower following the directions in Step 3 of the Quick-Sew Wallhanging Assembly instructions. Stitch the completed flower at the top of the stem. Slip the sleeve onto the pillow.

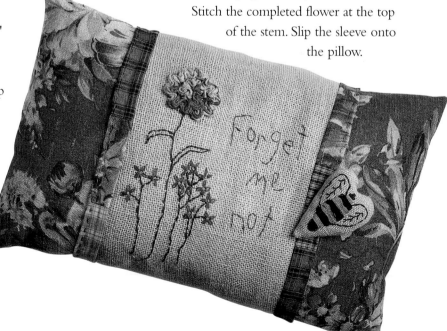

Busy Bee Doll

6" x 10" sitting

MATERIALS

- ▪ ⅜ yard of black check fabric for arms and legs
- ▪ ¼ yard of gold plaid fabric for body
- ▪ ⅛ yard or scrap of black fabric for head
- ▪ Polyester stuffing
- ▪ Black embroidery floss
- ▪ Two ½" gold buttons
- ▪ Four ½" black buttons
- ▪ Straw hat
- ▪ Black paint
- ▪ 2¼ yards of dark wire

ASSEMBLY

1. Using the patterns on pages 19-21, trace and cut out two heads from black fabric. Cut one body front and two body backs from gold plaid fabric.

2. Fold the black check fabric in half, right sides together. Trace the arm and leg patterns twice onto the doubled fabric. Sew on the traced lines, leaving the straight ends open.

3. Cut out the arms and legs and turn right side out. Stuff the hands and feet to the line indicated on the pattern. Tie black floss knots at the wrists and the ankles.

4. Place the two back pieces right sides together, and sew the center back seam from the neck edge to the dot marked on the pattern.

5. Place the back right sides together with a head piece, aligning the straight edges at the neck. Sew together across the neck edge. Repeat with the front and the second head piece.

6. Position the arms 1½" below the neck seam on the body front, gather the fabric slightly and baste. Position the legs approximately ¼" on either side of the center front; gather slightly and baste.

7. Pin the back and front right sides together, matching the neck seams. Place the arms inside, out of the seam area, but leave the legs dangling out the bottom. Sew around the body from one leg, up around the head and down to the other leg. Leave open at the bottom where the legs protrude.

8. Turn right side out and stuff firmly. Sew the opening closed. Sew on the gold button eyes, and sew a black button at each wrist and ankle.

9. Cut a 9" length of wire and set aside.

To make the wings, bend the remaining length of wire back and forth into three loops on each side of the bee, making each loop about 6" long. Pinch the loops together in the center and stitch to the back of the bee about 1¼" below the neck seam.

10. Paint the hat black and "scrunch" it to make it look old. Poke the 9" piece of wire through the top of the hat and curl the ends to make antennae.

Gardener's Tote Bag

Approximately 10" x 14" x 5"

MATERIALS

- ⅞ yard of burlap for bag and lining
- ⅜ yard of print fabric for large pockets
- ⅛ yard each or large scraps of two black plaid fabrics for straps
- Assorted scraps for pocket trim, small pocket, and ruched flowers
- Green, black, and light gold embroidery floss
- Seven assorted buttons
- Fade-away fabric marker

CUTTING

1. From the burlap, cut two 20" x 26" rectangles.
2. From the print fabric, cut two 5½" x 10½" rectangles for the pocket fronts and two 7" x 12" rectangles for the linings.

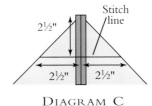

2½"   2½"   2½"

Stitch line

DIAGRAM C

3. From each plaid fabric, cut two 1¾" x 44" strips.
4. From the scraps, cut two 1¼" x 12" strips for ruched flowers, and one pocket and pocket lining from the pattern on page 17. Cut four 1" x 10½" and four 1" x 7" strips for the trim on the large pockets.

ASSEMBLING THE BAG

1. Fold a 20" x 26" burlap rectangle in half crosswise, right sides together, so that it measures 20" x 13". Stitch the two sides using a ½" seam allowance.
2. At one lower corner, fold the bag as shown in Diagram C, centering the seam on the folded corner. Measure 2½" in from the corner and mark a stitching line. Pin, then stitch along the marked line. Repeat on the opposite corner. Turn the bag right side out.
3. In the same manner, fold and stitch the second rectangle, but leave an opening in one side seam for turning. Stitch the corners as described in Step 2. This will be the bag's lining.
4. With right sides facing, tuck the bag inside the lining, aligning the top edges. Stitch around the top of the bag. Turn the bag and the lining right side out through the opening in the lining. Tuck the lining inside the bag and stitch the opening closed. To keep the lining from shifting, tack the bag and lining together at the bottom corners.
5. To make the straps, sew each pair of 1¾"-wide strips end-to-end to make two 84"-long strips. Place the strips right sides together, and sew both long sides with a ¼" seam allowance. Turn the tube right side out and press.
6. The straps begin and end at the bottom of the bag. Pin one end of the strip to the flat bottom of the bag,

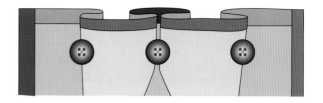

with the outside edge of the strip approximately 3" in from the edge of the bag. Pinning as you go, bring the strip up the side of the bag, leave a 17" loop for the handle, and come back down the same side, making sure the strap is again 3" from the outside edge. Take the strip across the bottom of the bag and up the other side, allow a 17" loop, and bring it down the same side, back to the starting point at the bottom. Fold in the raw edges on both ends, and stitch in place. Make any necessary adjustments and make sure the handles are exactly the same length. When you are satisfied, blanket-stitch both edges of the straps using three strands of floss.

FINISHING

1. Make the small pocket as described in Step 4 of the Quick-Sew Wallhanging instructions. Position the completed pocket between the straps on one side of the bag, and blanket-stitch in place.

2. Accent the bag with embroidery as desired, referring to Step 1 of the Quick-Sew Wallhanging Assembly instructions. On the bag shown, the words "Rosemary for Remembrance" along with two ruched flowers and a bee were added between the straps on one side. "Friends, Like Flowers, Bloom Longest in Our Memories" was stitched around the top edge.

3. To make the large pockets, begin by sewing the 1" x 10½" strips to the top and bottom edges of the pocket fronts, using a ¼" seam allowance. Sew the 1" x 7" strips to the sides. Place the pocket fronts right sides together with the linings, and stitch with a ¼" seam allowance, leaving an opening for turning. Turn right side out and stitch

the opening closed. Position a pocket on each end of the bag, and blanket-stitch in place using three strands of embroidery floss.

4. Pleat the fabric at the top of each pocket as shown in Diagram D, gathering the fabric as much or as little as desired, and sew a button at each pleat. The pleats will have the effect of gathering the sides of the bag.

Friendship Card & Envelope

4½" x 7"

MATERIALS

- ¼ yard each of two print fabrics for envelope
- Large scraps of light and print fabrics for card and tag
- Scraps of red, blue, and gold fabric for flowers
- Green and brown embroidery floss
- Fabric stiffener
- 6" piece of wire
- One ⅝" and two ½" buttons
- Fade-away fabric marker

CUTTING

1. From the print fabrics, cut two 5¾" x 17" rectangles.

2. From the scraps, cut one 4" x 6" piece and one 1¾" x 3" piece of light fabric, and two 5" x 7" pieces of print fabric.

ASSEMBLY

1. Place the two 5" x 7" rectangles right sides together. Sew all around the outside edges. Trim the seam allowances. Carefully cut a small slit through the front layer of fabric. Turn right side out and press. Set aside.

2. Using the fade-away marker, transfer the design from page 18 onto the 4" x 6" rectangle. Backstitch the words and stems using two or three strands of floss. Cut the flower circles and attach them with green floss French knots.

3. Using two strands of floss and long running stitches, sew the stitched piece to the print background. Poke two small holes at the top and insert the wire; twist the ends to hold it in place. Stiffen the greeting card following the manufacturer's directions.

4. To make the envelope, place the two 5¾" x 17" rectangles right sides together. Place the pattern for the envelope point at one end of the fabric and cut around it. Sew around the edges, leaving an opening for turning. Trim the seam allowances. Turn right side out through the opening. Press.

5. Cut a 1" x 7" strip of any fabric. Turn in ¼" at each end, and pin to the lining side of the point, right sides together and raw edges even. Stitch with a ¼" seam allowance. Fold the binding to the outside, turn in the raw edge, and blindstitch in place.

6. Fold the envelope right sides together, bringing the bottom end up just to where the point begins. Pin the sides together, and machine-stitch very close to the edge. Turn the envelope right side out. Make a buttonhole in the pointed end and sew the ⅝" closure button in place.

7. Transfer the design for the words and flower onto the 1¾" x 3" rectangle. Backstitch the words and flower stem using two strands of floss. Cut a tiny circle of fabric for the flower, and attach in place with a French knot. Sew the buttons near the bottom of the envelope. Cut a buttonhole slit on each side of the patch, and button it onto the envelope.

2" x 3"

MATERIALS

- Two 4" x 5" pieces of burlap
- Scrap of fusible web
- Polyester stuffing
- Black and gold embroidery floss
- Pinback
- Fade-away fabric marker

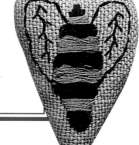

ASSEMBLY

1. Trace the heart pattern, below, onto the center of both burlap pieces. Transfer the bee design onto the center of one of the traced hearts.

2. Using three strands of floss, satin-stitch the black and gold stripes of the bee's body. Backstitch the wings in black.

3. Cut out the two hearts. Place the front and back right sides together and sew all around the outside edge. Carefully cut a slit through just the back layer of fabric, and turn right side out. Stuff.

4. Iron a small piece of fusible web onto a scrap of fabric. Cut a small heart from the fabric and fuse it onto the back of the stitched heart to cover the slit. Sew on the pinback.

RUCHED FLOWER

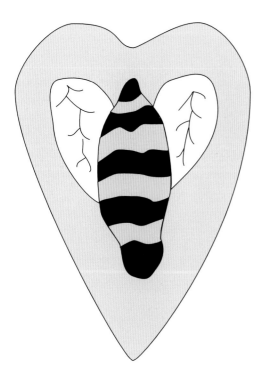

BEE PIN PATTERN

SMALL HEART

RUCHED
FLOWER

Fold line

WALLHANGING
POCKET

Cut 2

you're so thoughtful you're so kind A truer friend I'll never find

To you from Me

ENVELOPE POINT

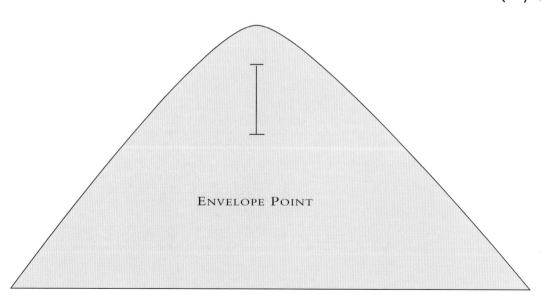

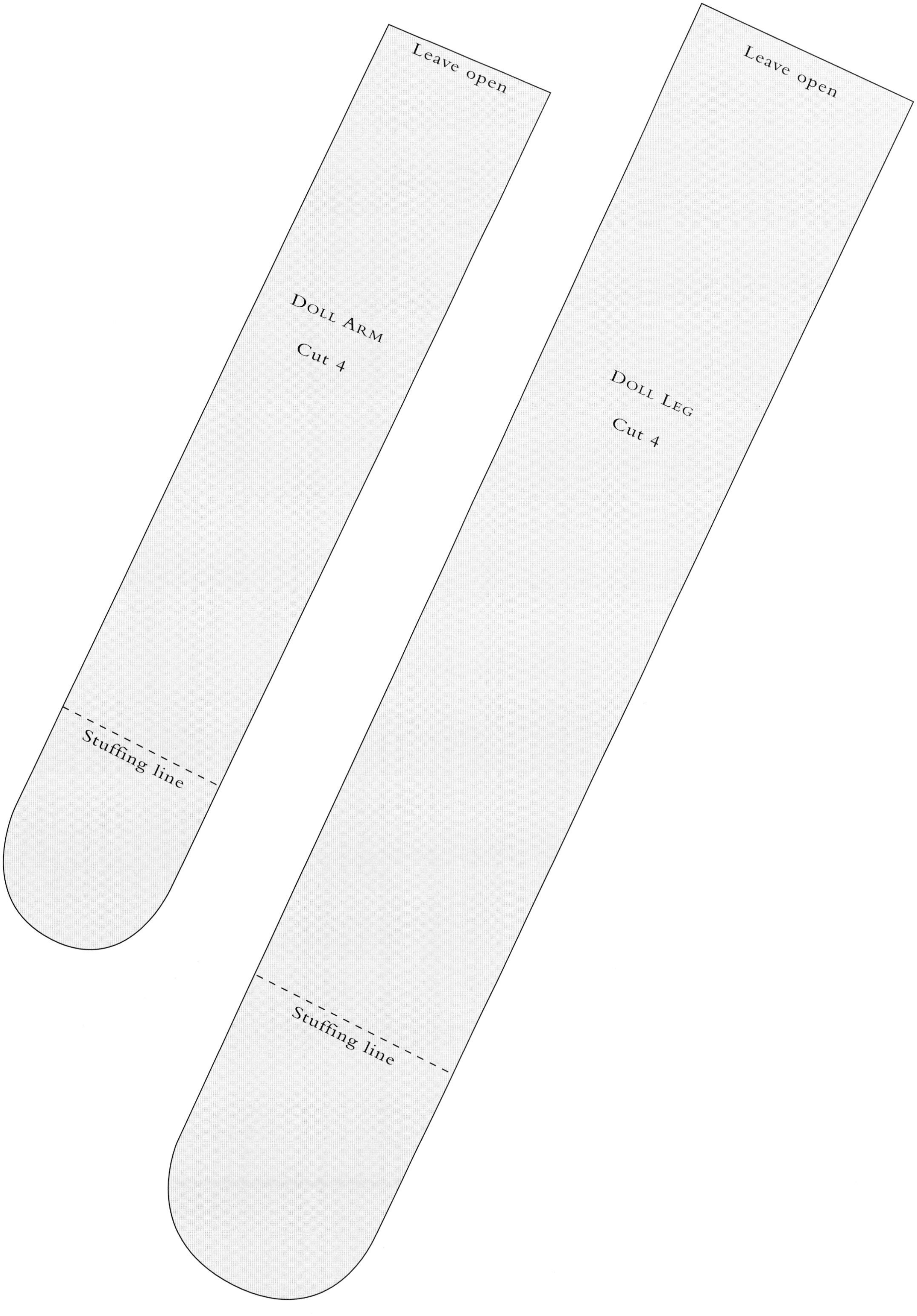

Leave open

Leave open

Doll Arm

Cut 4

Doll Leg

Cut 4

Stuffing line

Stuffing line

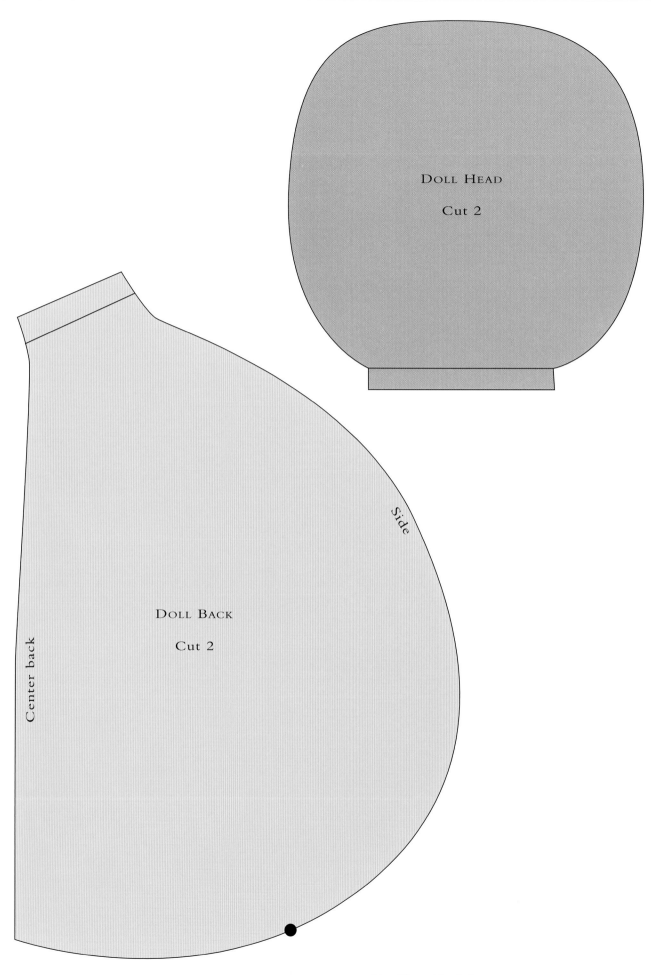

DOLL HEAD

Cut 2

Side

DOLL BACK

Cut 2

Center back

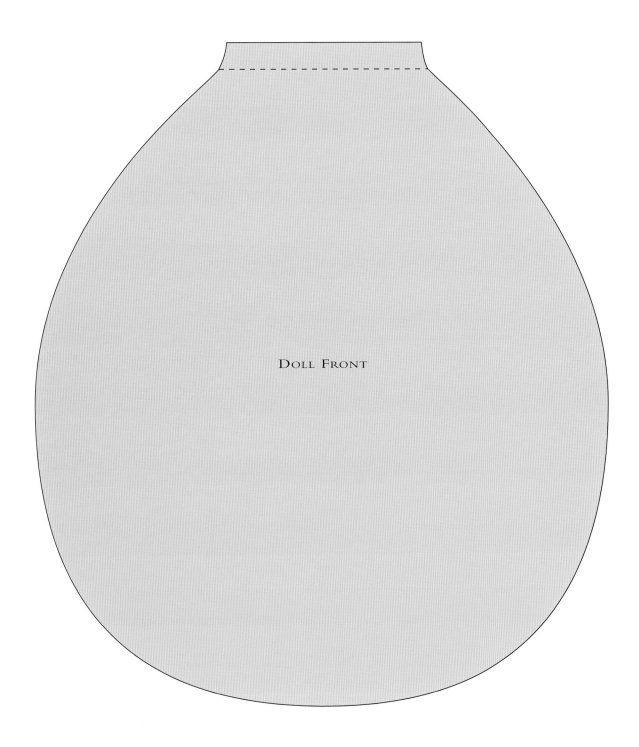

DOLL FRONT

Kris Kerrigan

A BUSY HEN'S KITCHEN

Easter at the Kerrigan's begins at dawn when their roosters crow, announcing the start of the traditional egg hunt! When the children were young, Kris explains, a note to the Easter Bunny asked that the egg hunt take place in two rooms, with the boys in one and the girls in another. Even now that they're older, this competition is still keen.

Dinner is the major event of the day, and preparations begin after church services. Everyone helps dye the eggs—boiling and shelling and dipping them in mugs of dye. Kris devils yolks and arranges the colorful halves on a platter, making a beautiful presentation. Her grandfather was a chef and her mother enjoyed creating unique dishes, so preparing a special holiday meal is a family tradition.

That tradition, and Kris' own hens, inspired her to create the Busy Hen's Kitchen collection. Kris and her daughter, Rachel, raise chickens on their Iowa farm. One breed, the Araucanas, lay eggs in shades from turquoise to deep olive. Collecting their eggs, Kris says, "is like celebrating Easter every day!" She hopes the Busy Hen's quilt, with its personalized eggs, will become a keepsake in your family.

MATERIALS

- 1½ yards of green solid fabric for backing, large background, and appliqués
- ½ yard of yellow plaid or print fabric for borders, wings, and appliqués
- ⅓ yard of striped fabric for borders, aprons, and appliqués
- ½ yard of blue print fabric for binding, background, and appliqués
- ¼ yard each of one blue and three green print fabrics for backgrounds
- ⅛ yard of blue check fabric for background, binding, and appliqués
- ⅛ yard each or scraps of cream, blue, pink, and yellow solid fabrics for pieced eggs and appliqués
- ⅛ yard or scraps of pink print fabric for nests
- 36" square of batting
- Fusible web
- White, pink, yellow, blue, and green embroidery floss
- ⅝ yard of ¼" green ribbon
- Six ¼" buttons
- Fade-away fabric marker
- Black fine-point permanent marker

Quick-Sew Wallhanging

Finished size 32" square

CUTTING

1. From the green solid fabric, cut one 36" square for the back, one 14" square (A), and three 2½" x 3½" rectangles (F).

2. From the yellow plaid fabric, cut two 1½" x 29¼" strips (O), three 1½" x 27¼" strips (N), one 1½" x 19" strip (K), one 1½" x 15" strip (C), one 1½" x 14" strip (B), and three 1½" x 8¾" strips (M).

3. From the striped fabric, cut two 2" x 32¼" strips (Q), two 2" x 29¼" strips (P), and three 3¼" x 5" rectangles (aprons).

4. From the blue check fabric, cut one 1" x 18" strip (J), one 1" x 17½" strip (I), one 1" x 15½" strip (E), one 1" x 15" strip (D), one 2½" square (H), and forty 1" squares (G).

5. From the blue print fabric, cut four 2" x 44" strips for binding and one 8¾" square (L).

6. From the blue and green print fabrics, cut one blue and three green 8¾" squares (L).

7. From the cream solid fabric, cut one 1¾" x 9" rectangle ripped into eighteen ½"-wide pieces for straw. From the pink solid fabric, cut three 2½" x 3½" rectangles (F), and from the yellow and blue solid fabrics cut two 2½" x 3½" rectangles each (F).

8. Refer to the General Instructions on page 6 to trace, apply fusible web to, and cut the following appliqué pieces: From the cream solid fabric, cut nine small eggs from the pattern on page 31; one 4¼" square, cut diagonally for two hen bodies; one 2¼" square, cut diagonally for two wings; and one 1¾" x 2½" rectangle for Rapid Rabbit's note.

9. From the yellow solid fabric, cut two 4¼" squares, cut diagonally for four hen bodies; one 2¼" x 3¼" rectangle; one mug handle and one spoon handle from the patterns on page 31.

10. From the yellow plaid fabric, cut two 2¼" squares, cut diagonally for four wings.

11. From the pink solid fabric, cut one 2¼" x 3¼" rectangle; three 1½" squares, cut diagonally for six hen combs/wattles; and one mug handle and one spoon handle from the patterns on page 31.

12. From the pink print, cut three 2¼" x 5" rectangles for nests.

13. From assorted fabrics, cut 26 small eggs from the pattern on page 31.

APPLIQUÉ AND ASSEMBLY

1. Refer to the photograph and follow the instructions at right for placement of the appliqués. After fusing the appliqués in position, use embroidery floss to blanket-stitch by hand or machine around them.

2. Center and fuse the nests at the bottom

of the green L squares; blanket-stitch. Center and fuse a yellow print hen wing on three of the yellow bodies. Fuse a comb/wattle and a body by each nest. Place six pieces of straw on each nest and fuse three eggs on top to hold them in place. Stitch around the appliqué pieces, leaving the ends of the straw free. Sew on button eyes.

3. Position a mug handle ⅜" from the side of each blue L square, and place the mug so that it slightly overlaps the handle; fuse. Center and fuse the two white hen wings on the two white bodies. Fuse a comb/wattle and a body to each blue L square, placing the tail 3¾" and the beak 5¾" from the bottom of the square; stitch. Fuse and stitch the pink spoon handle at the top edge of the yellow mug, with the handle overlapping the hen's body and touching the wing. Repeat for the

yellow spoon handle above the pink mug. Fuse a print egg (matching the color of the mug) to the top of each mug, overlapping the spoon handle slightly; stitch.

4. Cut two 6½" lengths of ribbon and tie each into a bow. Tack the bows below the chicken wings. To make the aprons, press under ¼", then ¼" again along one long edge of the two 3¼" x 5" striped rectangles. Gather this edge with running stitches of embroidery floss. Tack one end to the hen's breast just below the spoon handle and the other end beside the bow. Embroider tail feathers, legs, and toes in long stitch or back stitch. Add button eyes.

5. Repeat instructions above for the yellow hen on the large background with one change: this hen holds an egg slightly tucked under her wing. Fuse this egg to the body before fusing the wing. With the black permanent marker, write "Call Rapid Rabbit's Delivery Service 555-1234" on the 1¾" x 2½" rectangle of cream fabric. Fuse to the right side of the background above the hen; stitch. Long-stitch a pin shank and add a French knot for a pin head. Fuse and stitch the pile of eggs to the left side of the background, placing colors randomly.

6. To make the name eggs, place four squares (G) on the corners of each rectangle (F) as shown in Diagram A; stitch as indicated by the dotted lines. Fold each G toward the corner and press; trim the excess seam allowance. Sew the eggs into two rows of five eggs each. Sew the H square to the end of one row.

7. Assemble the quilt top following Diagrams B (below), and C (next page), and these instructions: Sew B to

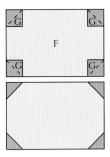

DIAGRAM A

the right side of A, then sew C to the bottom of the A unit, D to the right side, then E to the bottom. Sew the row of eggs without the H square to the bottom of the A unit, then sew the other row of eggs to the right side. Sew I to the right side of the A unit, J to the bottom, then K to the left side.

8. Stitch a horizontal M sashing between two L blocks; add to the left side of the A unit. Sew vertical M sashings between the remaining L blocks, and sew N sashings to the top and bottom of this row. Sew this section to the top of the L/A unit, and add another N sashing to the bottom of the L/A unit. Sew the O sashings to the sides. Add the P borders to the top and bottom, and the Q borders to the sides.

FINISHING

1. With the fade-away marker, write your family members' names centered on the name eggs. Embroider the

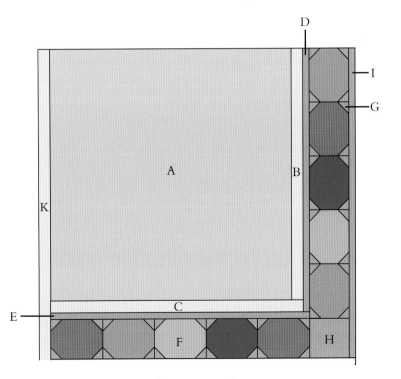

DIAGRAM B

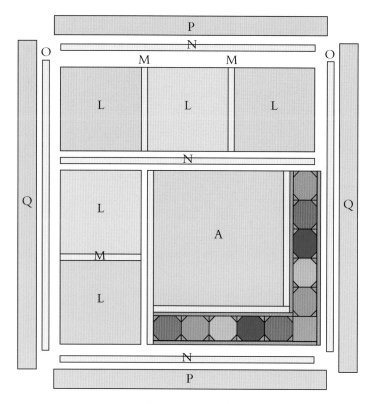

DIAGRAM C

names in backstitch or chain-stitch. In the same manner, add the color names on the mugs.

2. Refer to the General Instructions on page 7 to layer the wallhanging, then quilt as desired. Trim the edges of the layers even.

3. Prepare the binding strips and a hanging sleeve as directed on page 7. Referring to the General Instructions for mitered corners, sew the binding in place using a ¼" seam allowance. Turn the binding to the back and whipstitch in place.

Finished size 12½" x 40"

MATERIALS

- ¾ yard of yellow plaid fabric for backing, hens, and inner border
- ⅜ yard of blue print fabric for outer border
- ¼ yard of green solid fabric for background
- ¼ yard of yellow print fabric for hen wings
- Assorted scraps or ⅛ yard each of pink, yellow, and blue fabrics for eggs, combs, wattles, and beaks
- 14" x 43" piece of batting
- Fusible web
- Pink, white, blue, green, and yellow embroidery floss
- Fade-away fabric marker
- Two ½" buttons

CUTTING

1. From the yellow plaid fabric, cut one 13" x 29½" rectangle for runner back, two 9⅜" squares for hen bodies (front and back), two 1" x 24½" strips and two 1" x 9½" strips for inner border.

2. From the blue print fabric, cut two 2¼" x 25¾" strips and two 2¼" x 13" strips for outer border.

3. From the green fabric, cut one 8½" x 24¾" rectangle for the background.

4. From the yellow print fabric, cut two 6" squares for wings and two 2½" squares for beaks.

5. From the pink fabric scraps, cut two 2½" squares for combs, and two

2" squares cut diagonally for four wattle triangles.

6. Refer to the General Instructions on page 6 to trace, apply fusible web to, and cut the following appliqué pieces: From pink, yellow, and blue prints, cut 11 medium eggs from the pattern on page 31.

ASSEMBLY

1. Position and fuse the eggs randomly in the green background. Stitch around the eggs with embroidery floss and blanket stitches.

2. Sew the long 1" inner border strips to the sides of the background, and sew the shorter 1" strips to the ends. Sew the long 2¼" border strips to the sides, and sew the shorter strips to the ends.

3. With a fade-away marker, mark the two 2½" beak squares with a diagonal line. Place each square right sides together with a body square, as shown in Diagram D(1). Sew on marked line. Trim seam allowance to ¼" (2). Press beak toward corner (3). Cut each square diagonally, forming four body triangles (4).

4. Sew two wattle triangles right sides together on the short sides as shown in Diagram E. Turn right side out and press. Sew the wattle triangles near the

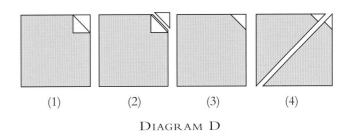

(1)   (2)   (3)   (4)

DIAGRAM D

DIAGRAM E

beaks as shown in Diagram F.

5. Fold each of the 6" wing squares in half diagonally, then in half again to form prairie points; press. Repeat for each 2½" comb square. Center each wing on a body triangle and stitch across the top. Sew a comb to the top of the body between the beak and the wing as shown in Diagram F.

6. Sew a completed hen front to each short end of the runner top. Sew a hen back to each short end of the backing.

7. Place the runner top wrong side down on the batting. Lay the runner backing, right sides together, on runner top. Pin all layers together. Trim the batting to the shape of the runner. Sew around the outside

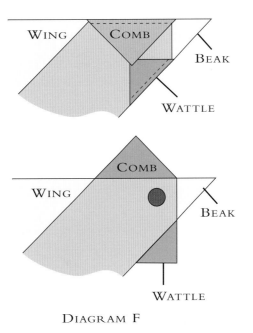

DIAGRAM F

edges, leaving a 5" opening on one long side for turning. Turn right side out and press; hand-stitch the opening closed.

8. Quilt around the eggs, in the borders, and on the hens' bodies, below the wing and midway between the wing and the body's bottom edges. Sew on buttons for eyes.

Chicken Place Mat

Finished size 10" x 20"

MATERIALS

- ¹⁄₂ yard of yellow plaid fabric for hen body
- ¹⁄₄ yard of yellow print fabric for hen wings
- Scraps of pink fabric for comb and wattle and yellow striped fabric for beak
- 15" square of batting
- One ⁵⁄₈" button
- Fade-away fabric marker

CUTTING

1. From the yellow plaid fabric, cut one 15" square for hen body.
2. From the yellow print fabric, cut one 8³⁄₄" square, cut diagonally for two wing triangles.
3. From the pink fabric, cut one 3¹⁄₂" square for comb, and one 2¹⁄₂" square, cut diagonally for two wattle triangles.
4. From the yellow striped fabric, cut one 2¹⁄₂" square for beak.
5. Cut the batting square diagonally in half for two triangles, though only one will be used.

ASSEMBLY

1. Referring to Step 3 of the Table Runner instructions and Diagram D, sew the beak to the body square. Refer to Step 4 of the Table Runner instructions and Diagram E for the wattle and comb construction. Sew the wing in the same fashion as the wattle, centering and stitching it to the top of the body front.
2. Place the body front wrong side down on a batting triangle. Place the body back right sides together on the body front. Stitch around the edges, leaving a 4" opening for turning. Turn right side out and press. Sew opening closed.
3. Quilt the hen body below the wing, and midway between the wing and the body's bottom edges. Sew on a button eye.

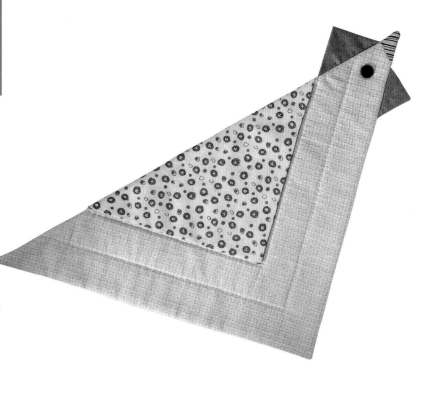

MATERIALS

For one napkin and ring

- ½ yard of yellow plaid fabric for napkin
- Scraps of blue, green, and solid cream fabrics for napkin ring
- Fusible web
- Pink and yellow embroidery floss
- ½" hook-and-loop tape
- Black fine-point permanent marker

CUTTING

1. From the yellow plaid fabric, cut one 15" square for the napkin.
2. From the green fabric, cut one 3½" x 7" strip, one 1¾" x 4" strip, and one 4" square for the napkin ring.
3. From the blue fabric, cut one 1¾" x 4" strip for the napkin ring.
4. From the solid cream fabric, cut one 1½" x 4" strip for the napkin ring.

ASSEMBLY

1. Press under ¼", then ¼" again, on each napkin edge; hem. If you prefer, serge the napkin edges.
2. Fold the 3½" x 7" strip right sides together lengthwise and sew, making a long tube. Turn right side out, center the seam on one side, and press. Turn the ends under ¼" and hem.
3. Using the black marker, print the name centered on the cream strip. Sew the strip between the two 1¾" x 4" strips. Fuse webbing between this pieced

front and the 4" square back piece.
4. Trace the large egg pattern onto the front and cut out the egg shape. Blanket-stitch around the outside edges of the egg.
5. Center the egg on the napkin ring. Using floss, sew the egg to the ring with running stitches close to the seam lines, as shown on the pattern. Cut a ½" square piece of hook-and-loop tape, and sew one side to each end of the napkin ring.

Towel

Finished size 17" x 29"

MATERIALS

- ½ yard of yellow plaid fabric for towel
- ⅛ yard each of pink and green fabrics for towel bands and appliqués
- Scraps of pink, blue, cream, and striped fabrics for appliqués
- Fusible web
- Green, cream, blue, yellow, and pink embroidery floss
- 6½" length of ¼"-wide green grosgrain ribbon
- One ¼" button
- Fade-away fabric marker

CUTTING

1. From the yellow plaid fabric, cut one 18" x 32" piece for the towel.
2. From the pink fabric, cut one 2½" x 18" strip for the towel band. From the green fabric, cut one 2" x 18" strip for towel band.

3. From the striped fabric, cut one $3\frac{1}{4}$" x 5" rectangle for the apron.

4. Refer to the General Instructions on page 6 to trace, apply fusible web to, and cut the following appliqué pieces: From the pink fabric, cut one $1\frac{1}{2}$" square, cut diagonally for one comb/wattle, and one spoon handle from the pattern on page 31; from the blue fabric, cut one $2\frac{1}{4}$" x 3" rectangle, one mug handle, and one small egg; and from the cream fabric, cut one $4\frac{1}{4}$" square, cut diagonally for one hen body, and one $2\frac{1}{4}$" square, cut diagonally for one hen wing.

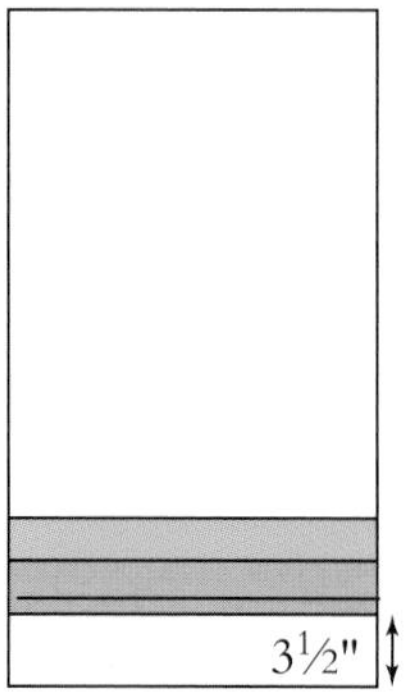

$3\frac{1}{2}$"

DIAGRAM G

ASSEMBLY

1. Place the pink and green strips right sides together and sew along one long side. With fade-away marker, mark a line on the yellow plaid fabric $3\frac{1}{2}$" from the bottom of the towel. See Diagram G. Pin the towel band right sides together to the towel, aligning the pink strip with the marked line. Stitch with a $\frac{1}{4}$" seam allowance. Press the band down toward the bottom.

2. Press under $\frac{1}{4}$" on all edges (fold the band with the towel). Press under $\frac{1}{4}$" again and hem. Sew running stitches across the bottom of the pink band with green embroidery floss.

3. Refer to the Quick-Sew Wallhanging instructions as needed for help with positioning the appliqués and adding the apron, bow, and embroidery stitches. Center the appliqué pieces on the towel, fuse, and stitch. Construct the apron and tack on the bow. Embroider the color name on the mug, and add the hen's tail feathers and legs. Sew on a button eye.

POT HOLDER

Fuse the hen design from the wallhanging to an $8\frac{3}{4}$" square of fabric. Blanket-stitch around the appliqués and add a button eye. Layer the stitched square with two squares of cotton batting and a backing square. (Do not use polyester batting; it will not protect your hand from heat.) Quilt the layers together and bind the edges. Sew a plastic cabone ring to the back of the pot holder at the center top.

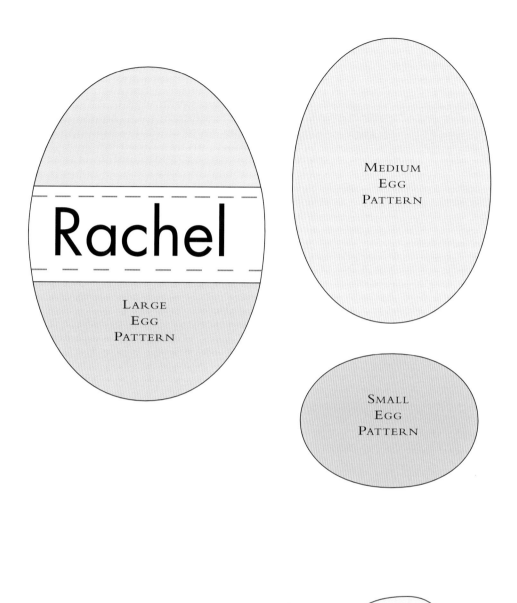

Rachel

LARGE
EGG
PATTERN

MEDIUM
EGG
PATTERN

SMALL
EGG
PATTERN

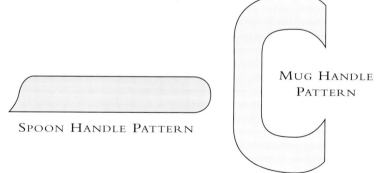

SPOON HANDLE PATTERN

MUG HANDLE
PATTERN

Janet Carija Brandt

FROM HEART TO HOME

There's something very special about coming home. Whether it's revisiting a childhood home or settling into a new one, there's a feeling of comfort, security, and belonging. Janet Brandt remembers a particular homecoming during her college years, and it was that memory that inspired her collection. "We were heading home for the holidays," Janet recalls. "It was late at night and snowing like crazy. There were several of us packed into the car, sharing the ride home, having a great time. It was hot and noisy, with the radio blaring and everyone talking at once. When I was dropped off at the foot of our long driveway, I was suddenly struck by how cold and quiet it was. As I walked up the driveway in the falling snow, I could see Christmas lights twinkling through the window. There were lights on throughout the house, and I knew everyone was home, waiting for me to arrive. It made me feel so warm and welcome, and I never forgot that special feeling. That's what coming home means to me."

Make someone you know feel special with a heartfelt gift from Janet's charming collection. Her quick wallhanging and pillow set make an ideal housewarming gift or a reminder of home for a college-bound student. Add the clever footstool for an easy, whimsical accent.

MATERIALS

- ⅝ yard of hand-dyed purple fabric for background and backing
- ¼ yard each of hand-dyed blue, green, pink, and yellow fabrics for appliqués
- ⅛ yard of pink print fabric for binding
- 20" x 21" piece of thin batting
- Lightweight fusible web
- Blue, green, pink, and yellow embroidery floss

Finished size 18" x 19"

CUTTING

1. From the purple fabric, cut one 18" x 19" rectangle and one 20" x 21" rectangle.
2. From the pink print fabric, cut two 1½" x 44" strips for the binding.
3. Refer to the General Instructions on page 6 to trace, apply fusible web to, and cut out the following appliqué pieces from the patterns on pages 38-41: Three large hearts, one bird and one bird reversed, one banner 1 and one banner 1 reversed, three fleur-de-lis, two large flowers, one adult bear and one adult bear reversed, one baby bear, one table, two adult chairs, one baby chair, two adult bowls, one baby bowl, one banner 2 and one banner 2 reversed, one medium heart, letters to spell "Home Sweet Home," five small leaves, and assorted flowers and flower centers as desired. Note: For this project, the baby bear's body and head are cut and fused separately.

ASSEMBLY

1. Arrange the appliqué pieces on the 18" x 19" background rectangle. For best results, remove the backing and position all the pieces, checking their placement, before fusing any of them. Make any needed adjustments, then fuse in place.

2. Using two strands of floss, blanket-stitch around the edges of all the appliqué pieces. Blanket-stitch the arms of the adult bears as indicated by the

dashed lines on the pattern—this gives the arms the appearance of being separate pieces.

3. Layer the backing, batting, and quilt top, and baste. Using two strands of floss, echo-quilt around the shapes with rows of stitching ¼" apart.

4. Trim the backing and batting even with the edges of the quilt top. Prepare the binding strips and a hanging sleeve as directed in the General Instructions on page 7. Sew the binding to the quilt with a ¼" seam allowance. Bring the folded edge to the back and whipstitch in place.

14½" x 17", 11½" x 14", 8½" x 11"

MATERIALS

- ½ yard each of hand-dyed pink and green fabrics for background, backing, and appliqués

- ¼ yard of hand-dyed purple fabric for background, backing, and appliqués

- Large scraps of hand-dyed blue and yellow fabrics for appliqués

- Heavyweight fusible web

- Polyester stuffing

- Variegated acrylic yarn for twisted cord

- Blue, green, orange, and purple fabric markers

HOME IS WHERE THE HEART IS PILLOW

1. Cut two 15" x 17½" rectangles from the pink fabric.

2. Refer to the General Instructions on page 6 to trace, apply fusible web to, and cut out the following appliqué pieces from the patterns on pages 38-41: Two banner 1 and two banner 1 reversed, two large flowers, two large hearts, two small hearts, and letters to spell "Home Is Where The Heart Is."

3. Arrange the appliqué pieces on one of the pink fabric rectangles. For best results, remove the backing and position all the pieces, checking their

placement, before fusing any of them. Make adjustments, then fuse in place.

4. Using the fabric markers, carefully outline the appliqué pieces just inside the edge of the fabric. Add "stitches" just outside the pieces.

5. Place the pillow front and back right sides together and stitch with a ¼" seam allowance, leaving an opening for turning. Turn right side out through the opening and stuff. Stitch the opening closed.

6. Measure around the outside of the pillow. Referring to the instructions on page 36, make a twisted cord to this length. Slip stitch the cording in place over the seam.

HOME SWEET HOME PILLOW

1. Cut two 12" x 14½" rectangles from the green fabric.

2. Refer to the General Instructions on page 6 to trace, apply fusible web to, and cut out the following appliqué pieces: One bird and one bird reversed, one large heart, one small heart, two leaves, one banner 1 and one banner 1 reversed, and letters to spell "Home Sweet Home."

3. Appliqué, assemble, and finish the pillow according to the instructions in Steps 3 through 6 for the "Home Is Where The Heart Is" pillow.

I LOVE YOU PILLOW

1. Cut two 9" x 11½" rectangles from purple fabric.

2. Refer to the General Instructions on page 6 to trace, apply fusible web to, and cut out the following appliqué pieces: One baby bear reversed, one small heart, one baby bench, two fleur-de-lis, letters to spell "I Love You," and assorted flowers and flower centers as desired.

3. Carefully cut just the baby bear's arms

along the dashed lines on the pattern, and slip the small heart under his paws. Fuse these pieces to the background as a unit.

4. Appliqué, assemble, and finish the pillow according to the instructions in Steps 3 through 6 for the "Home Is Where The Heart Is" pillow.

TWISTED CORD

The handmade twisted cord adds a great finishing touch to the pillows and footstool. To make the cord, measure the length you'll need (around the outside of a pillow, for example) and multiply this measurement by four. Cut three pieces of yarn to that length. Hold the three lengths together and knot one end. Secure to a sturdy object. Insert the other end into the head of a Fiskars hand drill. Stand back and start to turn the crank. The yarn should be gently stretched, but not taut. Continue to crank until the yarn starts to turn back on itself. Keeping the yarn gently stretched, fold it in half, then let go. The yarn will twist back on itself, making the cord. Knot each end to hold the twist.

Approximately 11" x 13" x 9"

MATERIALS

- 1 yard of gold wool flannel
- ¼ yard of purple wool flannel
- ⅛ yard each or large scraps of blue, green, and pink wool flannel
- 40" square of batting
- Blue, pink, purple, and yellow embroidery floss
- 60" of twisted cord
- 10" x 12" x 7" plastic step stool
- Hot-glue gun and glue sticks

ASSEMBLY

1. Machine-wash and -dry the wool flannel.

2. From the gold wool flannel, cut a 28" x 32" rectangle. From the purple wool flannel, cut a 9" x 12" rectangle.

3. Trim each corner of the gold rectangle as shown in Diagram A. Measure in 5½" from the corner and mark the fabric. Measure 11" along the two sides and mark. Lightly draw a line joining the three points; cut the fabric along the line. The corners will be gently curved, resulting in an oval shape.

4. Center a 9" x 12" rectangle of purple wool on the oval; pin in position. Cut assorted flowers, flower centers, and large leaves from the patterns on pages 38-41. Arrange the appliqués around the purple rectangle as desired, overlapping the edges of the rectangle all

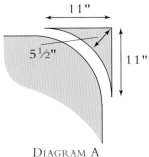

11"

5½"

11"

DIAGRAM A

around. Pin the appliqués in position.

5. Using two strands of floss, blanket-stitch the appliqués, then chain-stitch around the inside of the appliqués (on the purple wool) and around the outside of the design. Stitch around the outside edge of the gold wool oval using two strands of floss and a long blanket stitch.

6. Cut a strip of batting 12" x 40". Fold crosswise in half, then in half again so that it measures 12" x 10". Hot-glue the batting to the top of the step stool. Cut a 22" x 25" piece of batting. Center this piece on top of the folded batting. Gently pull the edges of the batting down, between the legs, to the underside of the step stool; hot-glue to secure. Hot-glue the batting to the outside of the legs to secure the corners.

7. Center the appliquéd oval on the step stool. Wrap the twisted cord around the stool, adjust the folds of the skirt, and pull the cord snug to hold the folds in place. Tie the cord in a bow.

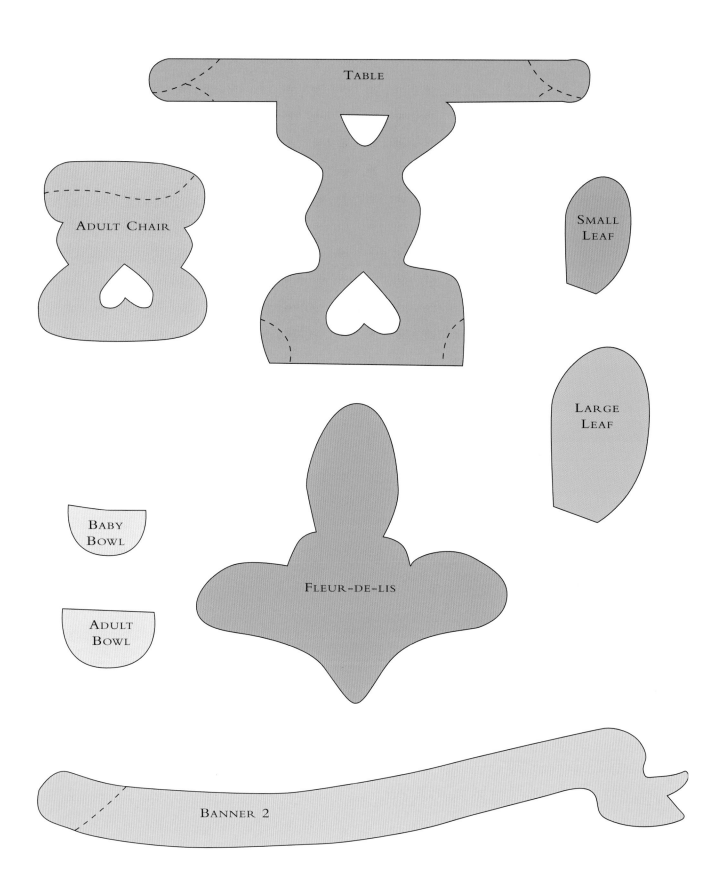

TABLE

ADULT CHAIR

SMALL LEAF

LARGE LEAF

BABY BOWL

ADULT BOWL

FLEUR-DE-LIS

BANNER 2

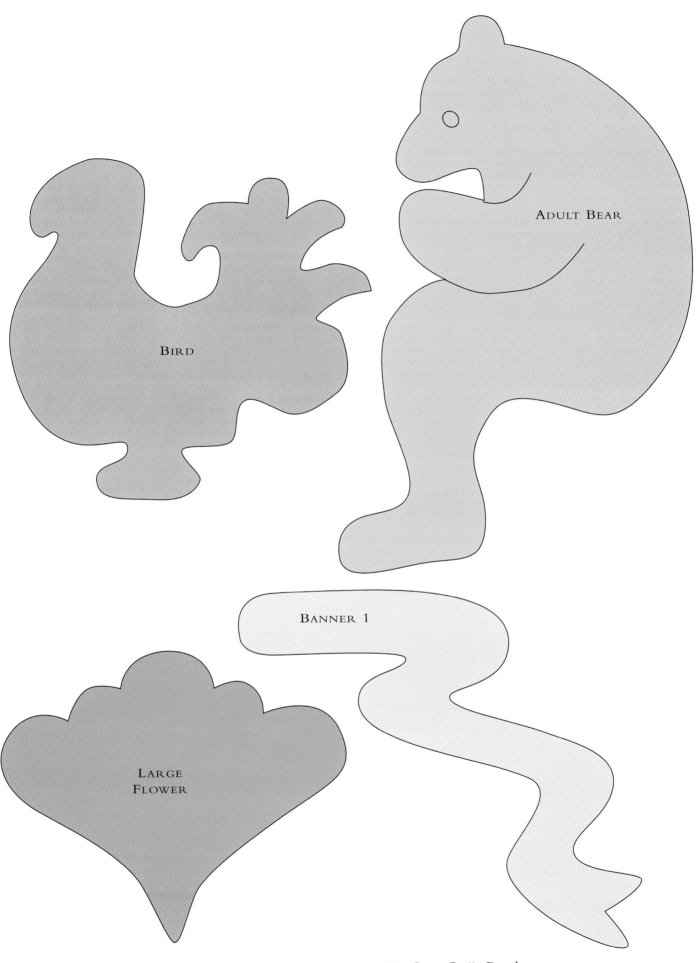

BIRD

ADULT BEAR

BANNER 1

LARGE
FLOWER

BABY BENCH

BABY BEAR

BABY
CHAIR

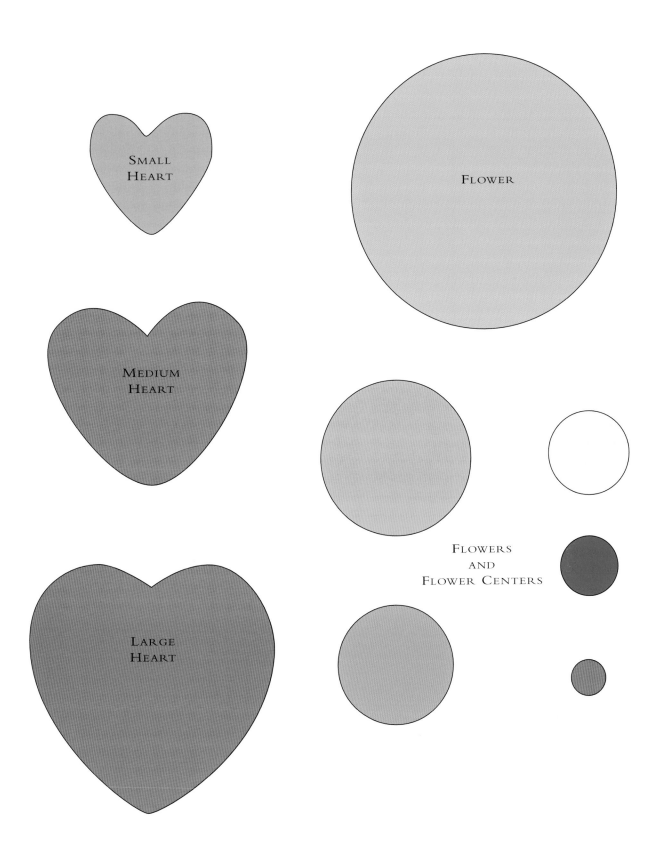

SMALL
HEART

FLOWER

MEDIUM
HEART

FLOWERS
AND
FLOWER CENTERS

LARGE
HEART

Lynette Jensen

AUTUMN ROSE

T he end of summer brings with it more than just cooler temperatures and changing leaves. It brings about a change of pace, a return to routine, a time when thoughts turn inward, toward home. For Lynette Jensen, it marks the beginning of her favorite season. "I love the autumn," Lynette says. "Everything has a different look, a different feel. I think of it as a time of gathering in—of family, immediate and extended, of friends, of the harvest."

With the season as her inspiration, Lynette designed a collection that's perfect for Thanksgiving, but could easily be used throughout the fall season. "Thanksgiving is the introduction to the holiday season," she says, "and I always do special things to make my home inviting. In these projects I used warm harvest colors to create a sense of comfort and abundance."

One of Lynette's goals as a designer is to create heirlooms: She wants to inspire quiltmakers to make items their families will treasure for years. She uses warm colors and simple, timeless patterns that are fun and easy to make, as in these charming pieces. The generously sized wallhanging can double as a cozy throw. And the chair pad, pillow, and coordinating table topper are sure to make any dining area a special, welcoming place.

MATERIALS

- 5 yards of brown print fabric for blocks, inner border, and backing
- 2⅝ yards of red print fabric #1 for lattice and outer border
- 1 yard of gold print fabric for blocks, appliqués, and binding
- ⅝ yard of cream print fabric for blocks
- ⅝ yard of green print fabric for blocks and cornerstones
- ⅜ yard of red print fabric #2 for cornerstones and appliqués
- 66" square of batting
- Fusible web
- Black and gold embroidery floss

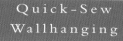

Finished size 62" square

CUTTING

1. From the brown print fabric, cut thirty-six 2½" x 6½" rectangles and seven 2½" x 44" strips.
2. From red print fabric #1, cut twenty-four 4½" x 10½" rectangles and eight 6½" x 44" strips.
3. From the gold print fabric, cut thirty-six 2½" squares and seven 2¾" x 44" strips.
4. From the cream print fabric, cut nine 4½" x 6½" rectangles, eighteen 1½" x 2½" rectangles, and seventy-two 1½" squares.
5. From the green print fabric, cut thirty-six 1½" x 2½" rectangles. Cut thirty-two 2⅞" squares, cut diagonally for 64 triangles.
6. From red print fabric #2, cut sixteen 3⅜" squares.
7. Referring to the General Instructions on page 6, trace, apply fusible web to, and cut out nine flowers from red print #2 and nine flower centers from the gold print.

ASSEMBLY

1. First piece the leaf sections. Place a 1½" cream square right sides together on a 1½" x 2½" green rectangle as shown in Diagram A (1). Stitch diagonally corner to corner on the cream square. Trim the seam allowance to ¼" and press toward the green fabric. Place a cream square on the opposite end of the rectangle. Stitch diagonally corner to corner, trim, and press. Repeat to make 18 left leaf units.

2. To make the right leaf units, position the fabrics as shown in Diagram A (2), and sew the diagonal line in the opposite direction. Make 18 units.

3. Sew the left leaf units together in vertical pairs. Repeat with the right leaf units. Sew a left leaf section to each right leaf section. Stitch the 1½" x 2½" cream rectangles to the sides of the nine leaf sections.

4. Sew a 4½" x 6½" cream rectangle to the top of each leaf section. Position the flowers on the background so that the bottom petals are just above the leaves; fuse. Position and fuse the flower centers. Blanket-stitch around the flowers using three strands of black floss. Blanket-stitch around the centers with three strands of gold floss.

5. Referring to Diagram B, sew a 2½" x 6½" brown rectangle to the top and bottom of each block. Sew a 2½" gold square to each end of the remaining brown rectangles. Sew to the sides of each block. The completed blocks should measure 10½" square.

6. Sew a green triangle to two opposite sides of a 3⅜" red square; press. Sew green triangles to the remaining two

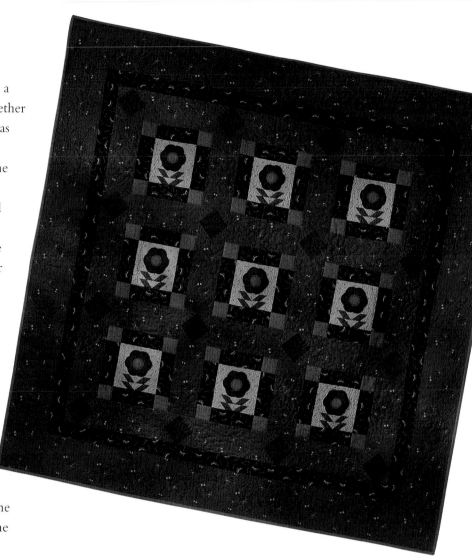

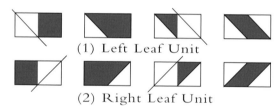

(1) Left Leaf Unit

(2) Right Leaf Unit

DIAGRAM A

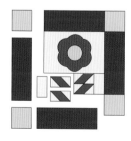

DIAGRAM B

sides, and press. Repeat to make 16 cornerstones.

7. Referring to Diagram C, sew the cornerstones and lattice strips into rows. Sew the blocks and lattice strips into alternate rows. Join the rows.

8. Measure the quilt top from left to right through the center. Cut two 2½"-wide brown strips to length. Sew

the strips to the top and bottom of the quilt. Measure the quilt from top to bottom through the center. Cut 2½"-wide brown strips, adding partial strips if necessary to achieve the required length. Sew the strips to the sides of the quilt top.

9. In the same manner, measure the quilt top and cut two 6½"-wide red print strips to length, piecing as necessary. Sew the strips to the top and bottom of the quilt top. Measure, cut, and sew the remaining 6½"-wide strips to the sides. Press the quilt top.

10. Refer to the General Instructions on page 7 to layer and quilt the wallhanging, prepare the binding strips, and make a hanging sleeve. Sew the binding to the quilt with a ⅜" seam allowance, mitering the corners.

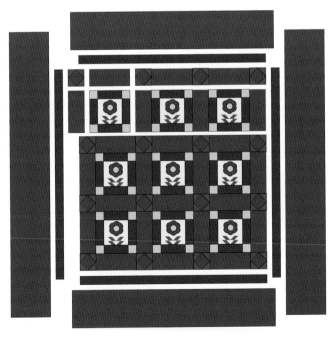

DIAGRAM C

Finished size 31" square

MATERIALS

- 1⅜ yards of green fabric for outer border and backing

- ¾ yard of cream print fabric for background

- ⅝ yard of tan fabric for corner squares and appliqués

- ½ yard of red print fabric #1 for outer border and appliqués

- ⅜ yard of red print fabric #2 for middle border and appliqués

- ⅜ yard of brown fabric for inner border

- Scraps of red, rust, and light, medium, and dark green fabrics for appliqués

- 35" square of thin batting

CUTTING

1. From the green fabric, cut one 35" square and twenty 2½" squares.

2. From cream fabric, cut a 18½" square.

3. From the tan fabric, cut four 2¾" x 44" strips and eight 2½" squares.

4. From red print fabric #1, cut four 2¾" x 44" strips.

5. From red print fabric #2, cut twenty-four 2½" squares.

6. From the brown fabric, cut four 2½" x 18½" strips.

7. Refer to the General Instructions on page 6 to trace, apply fusible web to, and cut out the following appliqué pieces: Six flowers, six flower centers,

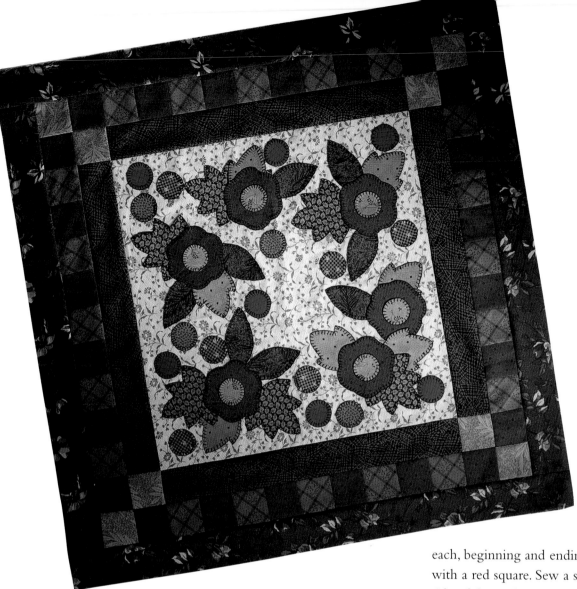

17 berries, six of leaf A, seven of leaf B, and eight of leaf C.

ASSEMBLY

1. Using the photo as a guide, position and fuse the appliqué pieces on the cream background square. Blanket-stitch around each piece using three strands of embroidery floss.

2. Sew a 2½" x 18½" brown strip to the top and bottom of the square. Sew a 2½" tan square to each end of the two remaining brown strips. Sew the strips to the sides of the background square.

3. Sew the red and green squares together in four strips of eleven squares

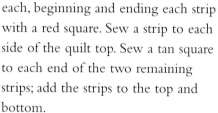

each, beginning and ending each strip with a red square. Sew a strip to each side of the quilt top. Sew a tan square to each end of the two remaining strips; add the strips to the top and bottom.

4. Measure the quilt top from side to side through the middle. Cut two 2¾"-wide red strips to this measurement, and add to the top and bottom of the quilt. Measure from top to bottom through the middle, and cut the two remaining red strips to length. Sew them to the quilt sides.

5. Refer to the General Instructions on page 7 to layer and quilt the table topper and prepare the binding. Sew the binding to the quilt with a ⅜" seam allowance. Bring the folded edge to the back and whipstitch in place.

Finished size 21" square

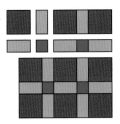

DIAGRAM D

MATERIALS

- 1¼ yards of dark green fabric for patchwork, ruffle, and backing
- ½ yard of brown print fabric for ruffle
- ¼ yard each of red print and medium green print fabrics for patchwork
- 16" pillow insert

CUTTING

1. From the dark green fabric, cut two 16½" x 18½" rectangles, four 3¾" x 44" strips, and four 2½" squares.
2. From the brown print fabric, cut four 2½" x 44" strips.
3. From the red print fabric, cut nine 4½" squares. From the medium green print fabric, cut twelve 2½" x 4½" rectangles.

DIAGRAM E

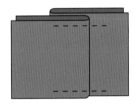

DIAGRAM F

DIAGRAM G

ASSEMBLY

1. Sew the red 4½" squares and the medium green 2½" x 4½" rectangles together in rows, as shown in Diagram D. Sew the remaining green rectangles and the 2½" dark green squares into alternate rows. Join the rows.
2. To make a mock double-ruffle, sew the brown strips together with diagonal seams, as shown in Diagram E. In the same manner, sew the green strips together. Sew the brown and green strips together lengthwise.
3. With right sides together, sew the short raw edges together with a diagonal seam, forming a loop; trim the seam allowance to ¼". Referring to Diagram F, fold the loop in half lengthwise, wrong sides together; press. Sew long gathering stitches ¼" from the raw edges.
4. Divide the ruffle into quarters and mark. Position the ruffle on the pieced top, right sides together and raw edges even, with the quarter marks on the corners. Pull the gathering thread so that the ruffle fits the pillow top. Pin, and sew a scant ¼" from the edges.
5. To make the pillow back, fold the two back pieces in half, wrong sides together, forming two 9¼" x 16½" double-thick pieces. See Diagram G. Overlap the two folded edges by 2". Sew across the top and bottom, a scant ¼" from each edge, to secure the folds. Layer the back and top right sides together, with the ruffle toward the center and out of the seam area. Sew around the outside edges. Trim the corner seam allowances, if needed. Turn right side out, fluff the ruffle, and insert the pillow form.

Approximately 16" x 16"

MATERIALS

- ⅞ yard of dark green fabric for appliqués, ties, and binding
- ¾ yard of tan fabric for front, back, and appliqués
- Scraps of light green, medium green, red, gold, and tan fabrics for appliqués
- Fusible web
- 18" square of fleece
- Black embroidery floss

ASSEMBLY

1. Trace the heart pattern pieces from pages 50–51 and join them to make a pattern for half a heart. Place the pattern on the folded tan fabric, trace, and cut out.

2. Refer to the General Instructions on page 6 to trace, apply fusible web to, and cut out the following appliqué pieces: Three flowers, three flower centers, three berries, three each of leaf A and leaf B, and one leaf C.

3. Using the photo as a guide to placement, position and fuse the appliqué pieces to the tan heart. Blanket-stitch around each piece using three strands of floss.

4. Cut an 18" square of tan fabric for the backing. Layer the backing, fleece, and appliquéd front, and baste the layers together. Quilt as desired. Trim the fleece and backing to match the front.

5. To make the ties, cut four 3" x 28" green strips. Fold each strip in half

DIAGRAM H

lengthwise, right sides together. Stitch along the raw edges of each strip using a ¼" seam allowance, leaving one end open for turning. Trim the seam allowances, turn right side out, and press. Pin the ties to the back of the heart as shown in Diagram H. Tie the pad to your chair, and make any necessary adjustments. The ties will be stitched on with the binding.

6. To make the binding, cut 2½"-wide bias strips from the green fabric. Sew the strips together with diagonal seams to make one strip approximately 52" long. Fold the strip in half lengthwise, wrong sides together, and press. Pin the binding to the heart, raw edges even, and stitch using a ¼" seam allowance, catching the ties in the seam as you go. Bring the fold to the back and whipstitch in place.

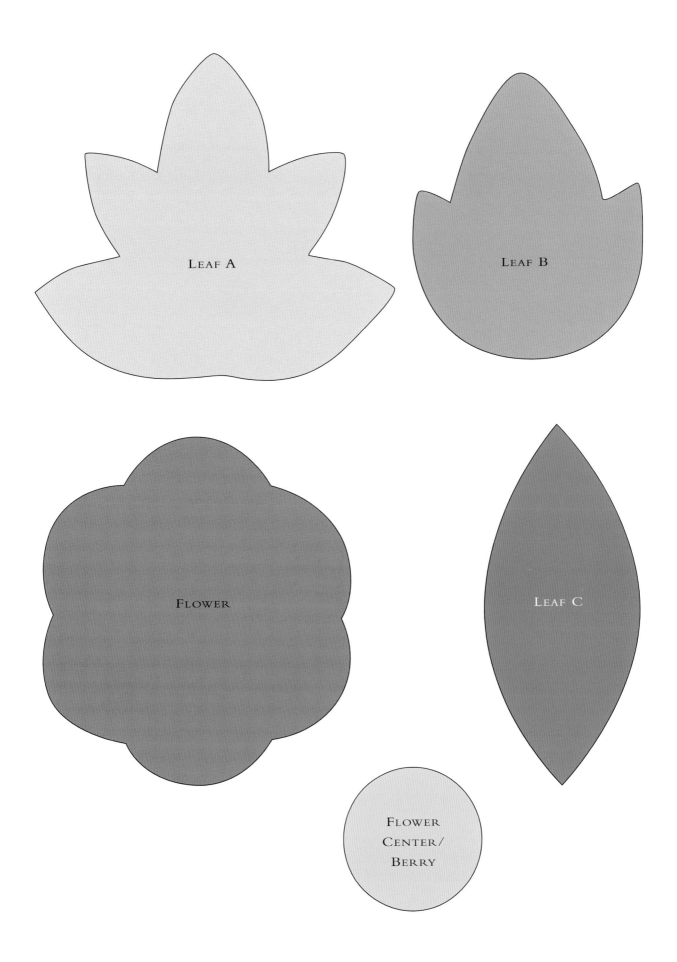

LEAF A

LEAF B

FLOWER

LEAF C

FLOWER
CENTER/
BERRY

Cut on fold

HEART 1

Connect at Heart 2

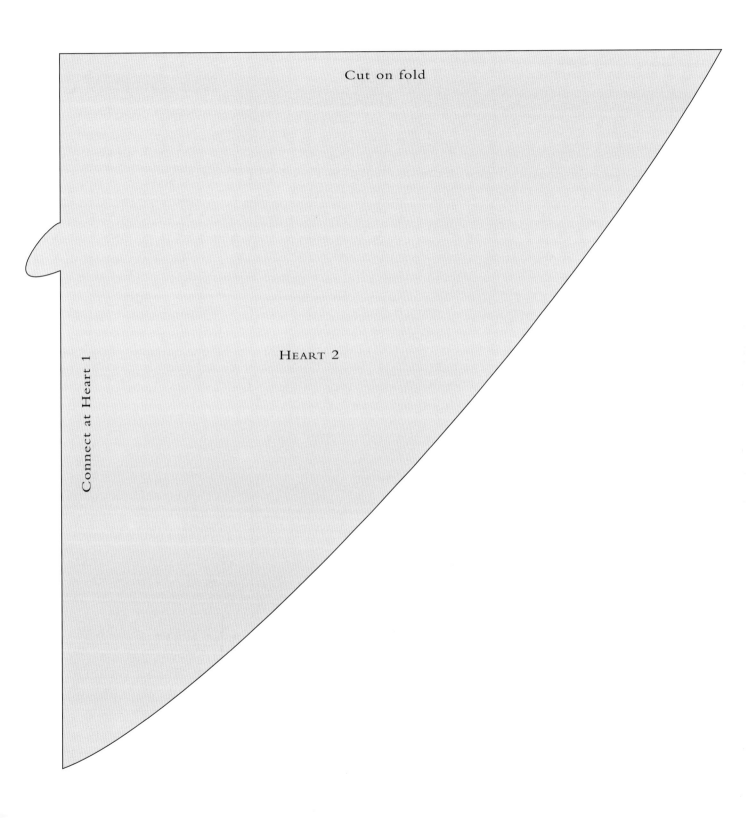

Cut on fold

Connect at Heart 1

HEART 2

Patrice Longmire
MAKE A CHRISTMAS WISH

Patrice states without hesitation that Christmas is her favorite time of year. In fact, she likes it so much, she keeps a bit of Christmas around her all year long. "The neighborhood kids have gotten used to hearing Christmas music coming from our house in July," she laughs. "I use it to inspire me when I'm designing holiday projects." Patrice also keeps a sign in her office which reads "Merry Christmas everyday!"

Holiday traditions at the Longmire home include making gifts for family and friends. "I have always sewn," Patrice says, and I've always enjoyed making things for others. My kids love to sew, too, so making gifts is a big part of our holiday pre-parations." Patrice is delighted that her children—including her 11- and 13-year-old boys—share her love of sewing. Patrice started her pattern company so she could spend more time with her family, and for more than six years, that's just what she's done.

Bring the spirit into your home with this charming collection. The wallhanging makes a cheerful greeting in an entryway, while the garland adds a unique accent to a mantel. The plump snowman and sweet angel look right at home on a table or tucked into a cozy corner.

MATERIALS

- ⅞ yard of red check fabric for Flying Geese blocks, backing, and binding
- ¼ yard of dark tan fabric for Flying Geese blocks and background
- ¼ yard each or large scraps of tan check, light tan check, olive green check, gold plaid, black plaid, dark tan, gold print, tan stripe, green check, and dark brown stripe fabrics for background blocks
- Assorted scraps for appliqués
- 22" x 36" piece of thin quilt batting
- Fusible web (optional)
- Black, ecru, gold, dark green, and red embroidery floss
- Powder blush
- Silver quilter's pencil

Quick-Sew Wallhanging

Finished size 18" x 32"

CUTTING

1. From the red check fabric, cut one 22" x 36" rectangle and three 2½" x 44" strips. Cut three 5¼" squares; cut diagonally both ways for four triangles (A).

2. From the dark tan fabric, cut one 4½" x 14½" strip (C). Cut twelve 2⅞" squares; cut diagonally for two triangles (B).

3. From tan check fabric, cut two 4½" x 7½" rectangles (D). From light tan check, cut two 3½" x 7½" rectangles (E).

4. From olive green check fabric, cut one 5½" x 8½" rectangle (F). From gold plaid, cut one 5½" x 6½" rectangle (G).

5. Cut one 5½" x 8½" rectangle (H) each from black plaid and dark tan.

6. From gold print, cut one 2½" x 14½" strip (I).

7. Cut one 6½" x 7½" rectangle (J) each from tan stripe and green check.

8. From dark brown stripe, cut one 4½" x 16" strip (K).

9. Refer to the General Instructions on page 6 to trace, apply fusible web to,

and cut out the appliqué pieces on pages 62–63. If you prefer, appliqué the pieces by hand, but be sure to add ¼" seam allowances when cutting out the pattern pieces. Cut two trees, one stocking, three mittens, one hand, two small hearts, one snowman, one angel body, head, wings, and two angel feet, twelve leaves, one basket and basket handle, two large stars, one small star, one flower stem, small leaf, and blossom, one moon, and one house and roof.

ASSEMBLY

1. Sew a B triangle to each side of an A triangle, as shown in Diagram A. Repeat to make 12 Flying Geese blocks.

2. Referring to Diagram B, assemble the quilt top as follows: Sew the D and E blocks together in a strip. Sew F and G together, and add to the bottom. Add C to the top.

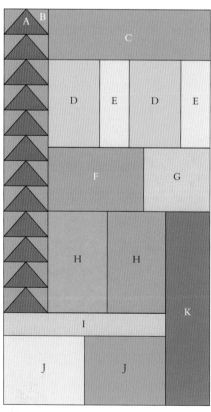

DIAGRAM B

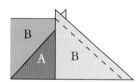

DIAGRAM A

3. Sew eight Flying Geese blocks together in a strip. Add to the left side of the pieced section.

4. Sew the two H pieces together. Sew the remaining Flying Geese blocks in a strip; add to the left side of the H blocks. Sew I to the bottom.

5. Join the two J pieces together, and sew to the bottom of I; add K to the right side. Sew the two sections together to complete the quilt top.

6. Referring to the photograph, position and fuse the appliqué pieces. Tuck the basket handle under the basket and the house under the roof. Place the angel's wing and feet under her body; rest the head on top of the body.

7. Use a silver quilter's pencil to mark the stocking, the snowman, and the phrase "Make a Christmas Wish." Backstitch the shapes and letters using three strands of embroidery floss. Stitch the toe and heel of the stocking and the heart on the snowman in a contrasting color using a running stitch. Stitch the snowmen faces, adding French knots for eyes. Sew three buttons down the front of the appliquéd snowman, and apply powder blush to the snowmen and angel cheeks.

FINISHING

1. Refer to the General Instructions on page 7 to layer the wallhanging. Quilt about ¼" outside all appliqué pieces. Add additional quilting as desired.

2. Trim the edges of the layers even. Prepare the binding strips and a hanging sleeve as directed in the General Instructions on page 7.

3. Referring to General Instructions for mitered corners, sew the binding in place using a ¼" seam allowance; turn to the back; whipstitch in place.

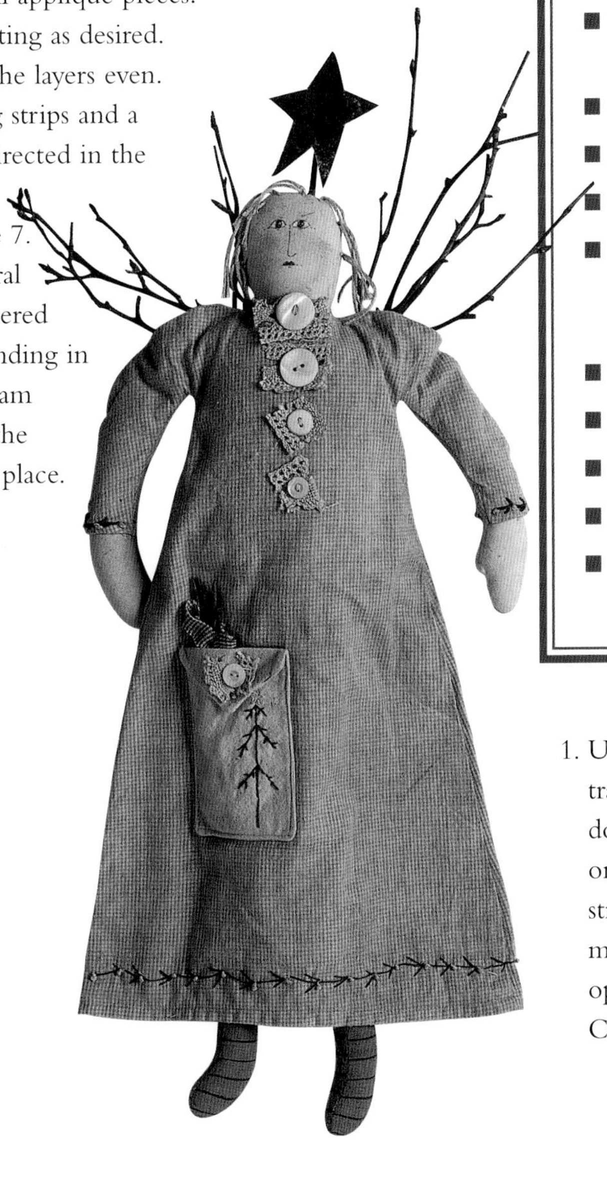

Approximately 18"

MATERIALS

- ½ yard of tan check fabric for dress
- ¼ yard of muslin for body and dress pocket
- ⅛ yard of brown stripe fabric for legs
- Polyester stuffing
- Yellow and green embroidery floss
- Assorted flat lace
- Assorted buttons
- Pink, red, and white acrylic paint
- Stencil brush
- Small paint brush
- Black Pigma .01 pen
- 3" square of scrap metal (.005 thickness) or cardboard for star
- White vinegar to rust star
- Sealer for star (optional)
- Assorted twigs
- Hot-glue gun and glue sticks
- Unsweetened instant tea

BODY

1. Using the patterns on pages 65-66, trace one body and two arms on a double layer of muslin. Trace two legs on the wrong side of a double layer of stripe fabric. With right sides together, machine-stitch on traced lines, leaving open where indicated on the patterns. Cut out ⅛" beyond stitching and turn

right side out. Stuff body, arms, and legs to within 2" of openings. Machine-stitch the openings closed.

2. Assemble the body with hot glue. Place glue on tops of arms, press on body, and hold until glue has cooled. Repeat with the legs, pointing toes forward.

3. Using the pattern as your guide, draw the angel's face lightly with pencil, then darken the pencil lines with the Pigma pen. Fill the eyes with white acrylic paint and let dry. Draw and fill in the pupils with the Pigma pen. Place a tiny white dot of acrylic paint inside the black pupils to add life to the eyes. For cheeks, brush on pink acrylic paint using a very dry stencil brush. Paint her lips with red acrylic paint.

4. To make the hair, thread a needle with six strands of yellow embroidery floss. Beginning at one side of her head, insert needle in front of the seam line and exit behind it. Tie the floss in a knot and trim to 2½" to 3". Repeat this about eight more times, until you reach the other side of her head.

DRESS

1. Trace the two dress pieces and join them to make the pattern. Fold the tan check fabric right sides together. Place the pattern on the fold and trace; repeat. Mark the neck opening as indicated on the pattern. Cut out the pieces, place right sides together, and machine-stitch from the sleeve edges to the neck opening. Clip and open out.

2. Press under a ¼" hem on sleeves and neck edge. Use six strands of floss to stitch a row of French knots around the edge of each sleeve. Use two

strands of floss to add straight stitches between each French knot.

3. With right sides together, machine-stitch from sleeve edge to bottom of dress. Clip the seam allowance under the arms and turn right side out. Machine-stitch a ½" hem along the bottom edge of the dress. About 1" up from the bottom, hand-stitch the same design as on the sleeves.

4. Trace the pocket pattern onto a double layer of muslin. Machine-stitch on the traced line, leaving an opening for turning. Cut out ⅛" beyond stitching. Turn right side out and stitch the opening closed; press.

5. Using the pattern as your guide, draw the tree design on the pocket. Backstitch the tree using two strands of green floss and add the star in yellow. Machine-stitch the pocket to the dress. Tack the flap in place by hand, stitching a small piece of lace and a button on the flap. Gather two or three small twigs and tie together with a thin piece of homespun fabric. Place the twigs in the angel's pocket.

6. Cut pieces of lace slightly larger than the buttons you have chosen. Hand-stitch the lace and buttons to the front of the dress, adding as many as desired.

7. If desired, tea-dye the angel to make her look aged.

WINGS

1. Gather a few thin twigs, 5" to 8" in length, and divide into two small bunches. Tie thin jute or embroidery floss around the bottom of each bunch. Criss-cross the tied ends of the bunches to form wings, and tie them together.

2. Hand-stitch the wings to the back of the angel's body.

STAR

1. Trace the star pattern onto thin metal or cardboard, and cut out on the traced line using regular household scissors. To rust the star, roughen the surface using light sandpaper or a kitchen scrubber, spray with white vinegar, and let stand overnight. If you want, spray a sealer over the rusted star to keep the rust from rubbing off on the angel.
2. Hot-glue the rusted star to the end of a twig. Insert the twig down the back of the angel's dress. Lift up the dress and glue or hand-stitch the twig to the angel's back to hold in place.

MATERIALS

- ¼ yard of flannel or muslin for body
- Scraps of brown and black wool fabrics for hat, scarf, and crow
- Scraps of fabric for patch and flower
- Polyester stuffing
- Brown, yellow, green, and white embroidery floss
- Assorted buttons
- Cat litter
- Pink acrylic paint
- Silver quilter's pencil
- Wooden birdhouse (optional)
- Craft glue

BODY

1. Trace the snowman patterns on pages 69-70 onto a double layer of flannel or muslin. Machine-stitch on the traced line around the entire body. Cut out ¼" beyond the stitching line.
2. Carefully cut a slit in one side of the body where indicated on the pattern. Turn the body right side out and fill the bottom with two cups of cat litter. Firmly stuff the remainder of the body with polyester stuffing. Hand-stitch the opening closed.
3. Using the pattern as your guide, write the word "Snowman" with a pencil or silver quilter's pencil. Backstitch the

letters using three strands of floss. Begin and end the stitching near the crow's position so the crow's body will cover the knots.

4. Trace and cut out the crow and the flower; stitch to the snowman using primitive stitches and one strand of floss. Backstitch the flower stem. Make a French knot in the flower center, and add a few extra French knots nearby. Make a French knot for the crow's eye, and use primitive running stitches to make his feathers and feet.

5. Cut a ½" x ¾" scrap of fabric and stitch it to the snowman with running stitches. Glue buttons to the patch.

FACE

1. Using the pattern as your guide, lightly draw the face onto the snowman. Add cheeks using a stencil brush and pink acrylic paint.

2. Make French knots for the mouth and eyes, and add a small straight stitch above each eye. Begin and end all stitching at the top of the head so the hat will cover the knots.

3. Cut out a scrap of fabric for the nose and stitch in place using regular sewing thread and small primitive stitches.

ARMS

1. Cut small slits in the snowman's side where indicated on the pattern.

2. Cut two twigs each about 5½" long. Place a small amount of glue in each slit, and insert a twig about ½". When the glue is dry, hang a small birdhouse from one twig arm if desired.

HAT AND SCARF

1. Trace two hat pieces onto a scrap of wool fabric and cut out. Machine-stitch the pieces together with a ¼"

seam allowance, leaving the straight side open. Trim the seam allowance close to the stitching line. Turn the hat right side out.

2. Fold the brim up ½", then ½" again. Hand-stitch the folds in place.

3. Stitch the buttons onto the hat. Place the hat on the snowman; tack in place.

4. Cut a 2" x 14" piece of brown wool fabric for the scarf. Use a silver quilter's pencil to lightly draw the cup and the words "Hot CoCo" on one end of the scarf. Backstitch using three strands of embroidery floss. Stitch across the other end of the scarf, alternating French knots and straight stitches. Tie the scarf around the snowman's neck.

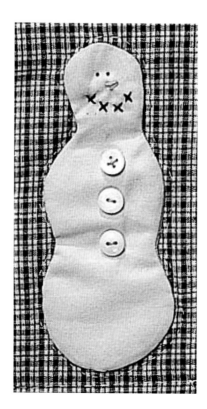

Approximately 70" long

MATERIALS

- 1 yard of muslin for garland and angel body
- ¼ yard of red check fabric for angel dress
- ⅛ yard each or scraps of green, red, and gold fabrics for mittens, stockings, hearts, and stars
- Scraps of fabric for stocking cuffs, angel wings, and appliqués
- ⅛ yard or large scrap of cotton batting for snowmen and stars
- Polyester stuffing; fusible web
- Yellow, red, brown, and tan embroidery floss
- Assorted buttons
- Gold and red acrylic paint

- One ball of 3-ply jute twine
- Black Pigma .01 pen
- Powder blush
- 2" square of metal or cardboard
- Small twig
- Unsweetened instant tea

ANGEL

1. Using the patterns on page 71, trace the body, arms, and legs onto a double layer of muslin. With right sides together, machine-stitch on the traced lines, leaving open where indicated on the pattern. Cut out ⅛" beyond stitching and turn right side out; stuff to within 1" of openings. Machine-stitch the openings closed.

2. Assemble the body with hot glue: Place glue on tops of arms; press on body and hold until glue has cooled. Repeat with legs.

3. Using the pattern as your guide, draw the angel's face lightly with pencil. Darken the pencil lines with the Pigma pen. Fill in heart-shaped lips

with red acrylic paint using a small paint brush.

4. To make the hair, thread a needle with three strands of embroidery floss. Beginning at one side of her head, insert needle in front of the seam line and exit behind it. Tie the floss in a knot and trim to 2½" to 3". Repeat nine more times, until you reach the other side of her head. The hair will hang down and look very primitive.

5. Trace two dress pieces on the fold and mark the neck openings as indicated on the pattern; cut out the pieces. Place the pieces right sides together, and machine-stitch from the sleeve edges to the neck markings. Clip the neck. Open out, and press under a ¼" hem in the sleeves and neck edge. Machine-stitch the hem in the sleeves; you will finish the neck later.

6. With right sides together, machine-stitch from the sleeve edges to the bottom of the dress. Clip the seam allowances under the arms and turn right side out. Hand-gather the neck edge with two strands of embroidery floss. Hand-stitch assorted buttons to the front of the dress. Place the dress on the doll; tighten the gathers around the neck, knot the floss, and clip.

7. Trace the small star pattern from page 62 onto thin metal or cardboard. Cut out on the traced line using regular scissors. Paint the star with gold acrylic paint and let dry. Hot-glue the star to the top of a twig. Insert the twig down the back of the angel's dress. Lift up the dress and hot-glue or hand-stitch the twig to the angel's back.

8. To make the wings, trace the pattern onto the wrong side of a double layer of fabric. Machine-stitch on the traced line all around the wing. Cut out ⅛"

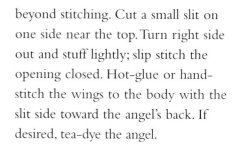

beyond stitching. Cut a small slit on one side near the top. Turn right side out and stuff lightly; slip stitch the opening closed. Hot-glue or hand-stitch the wings to the body with the slit side toward the angel's back. If desired, tea-dye the angel.

HEART

1. Trace the heart pattern from page 73 onto a double layer of fabric. Make as for the angel wings, Step 8.
2. Sew a button to the front of the heart. Repeat to make a second heart.

MITTEN

1. Trace the mitten pattern from page 72 onto a double layer of fabric placed right sides together. Cut out on the traced lines. Trace and cut out the heart appliqué.
2. Hand-stitch the heart to the front of one mitten piece. Place mitten pieces right sides together and machine-stitch. Press a ½" hem around the top of the mitten and hand-stitch in place using floss. Turn right side out. Sew a button to the top of the mitten. Repeat to make a second mitten.

STAR

1. Layer a thin piece of quilt batting between two pieces of fabric. Trace the star pattern from page 73 onto the top piece of fabric, and cut out all three layers at once.
2. Hand-stitch the layers together with running stitches. Repeat to make a second star.

SNOWMAN

1. Trace the pattern from page 64 onto a piece of quilt batting. Make French knots for his eyes using a double strand of floss. Sew the buttons down the center front, and brush on powder blush for cheeks.

2. Place the traced snowman on top of a second piece of batting, and cut on the traced line, cutting the two layers at once. Blanket-stitch the layers together around the raw edges. Just before completing the stitching, stuff lightly to plump him up a bit. Continue blanket-stitching to close up the opening.

3. Tear a thin piece of fabric and tie it around his neck. Repeat to make a second snowman.

STOCKING

1. Trace the pattern from page 73 onto a double layer of fabric placed right sides together; cut out.

2. Cut two 2½" squares of fabric for the cuff. Fold each square in half wrong sides together, and press. Align the raw edge of each cuff with the top raw edge of each stocking, right sides together, and machine-stitch. Press the cuff up and the seam allowance down toward the stocking.

3. Trace and cut out the tree appliqué; fuse or hand-stitch to the stocking front. Sew the button in place.

4. Place the stocking front and back right sides together and machine-stitch, using a ⅛" seam allowance. Clip the curves and turn right side out.

Add French knots around the cuff using three strands of floss. Press lightly. Repeat to make a second stocking.

GARLAND ASSEMBLY

1. Tea-stain the muslin before tearing to give it an aged look. Tear the muslin into long ½"-wide strips. Cut the strips into 4" pieces.

2. Cut a piece of jute twine to the desired length, and add an additional 8". (The garland shown is 70" long.) Make a small hanging loop at each end, and knot the jute.

3. Using a double knot, tie the fabric strips around the twine, beginning at one end and working along the twine until it is completely covered with strips.

4. Hand-stitch the accents to the garland in this order: One each mitten, heart, snowman, stocking, star, angel, star, stocking, snowman, heart, and mitten.

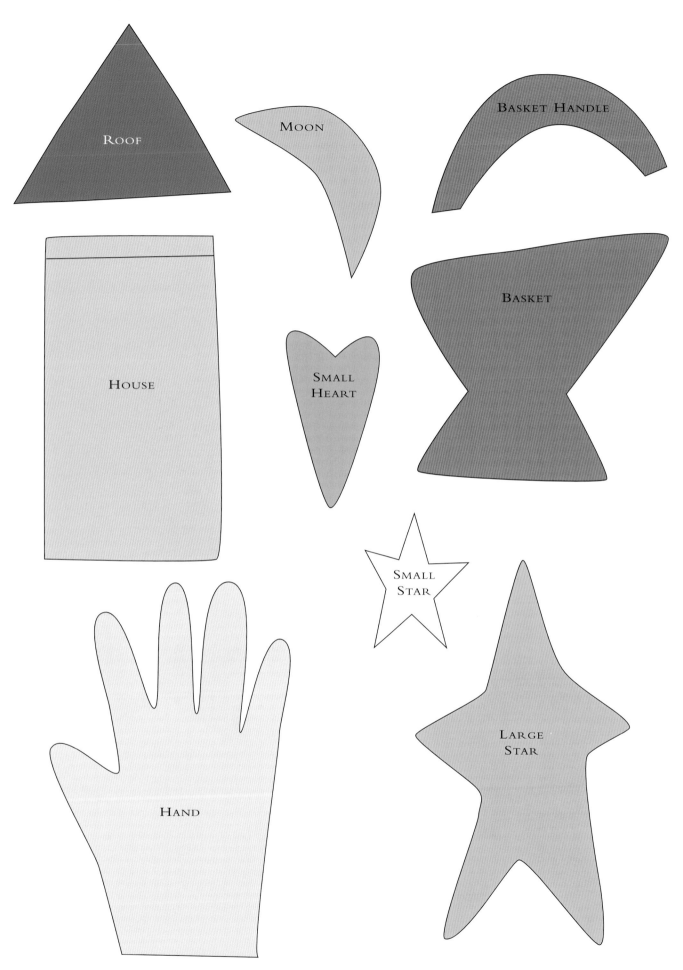

ROOF

MOON

BASKET HANDLE

HOUSE

SMALL HEART

BASKET

SMALL STAR

LARGE STAR

HAND

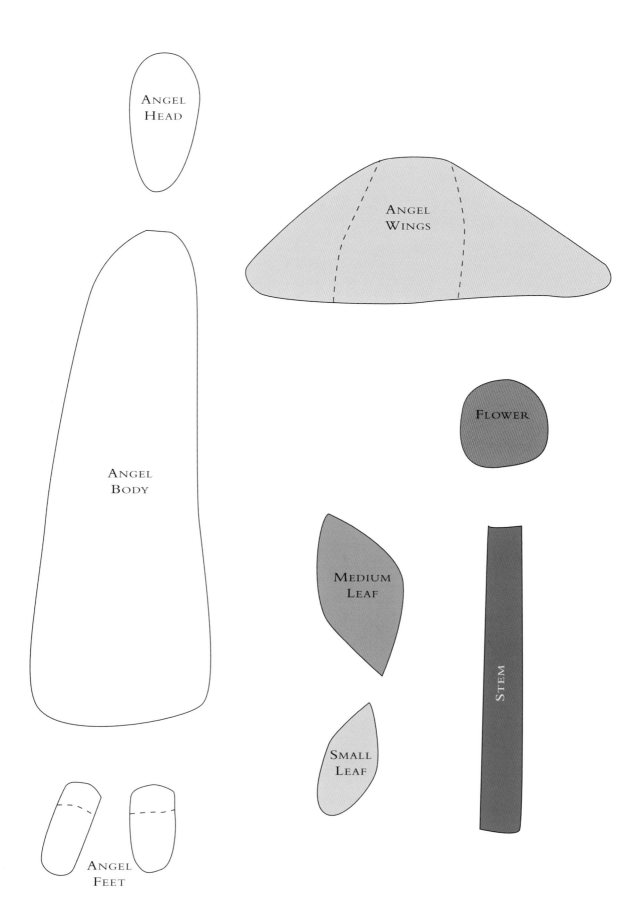

ANGEL
HEAD

ANGEL
WINGS

ANGEL
BODY

FLOWER

MEDIUM
LEAF

STEM

SMALL
LEAF

ANGEL
FEET

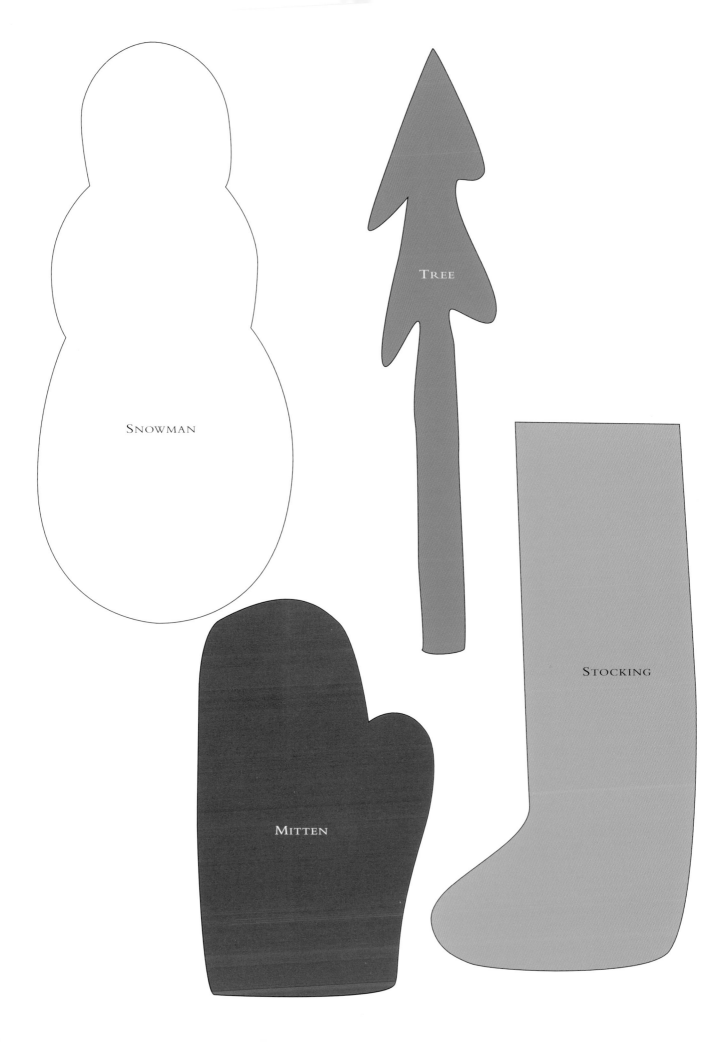

SNOWMAN

TREE

STOCKING

MITTEN

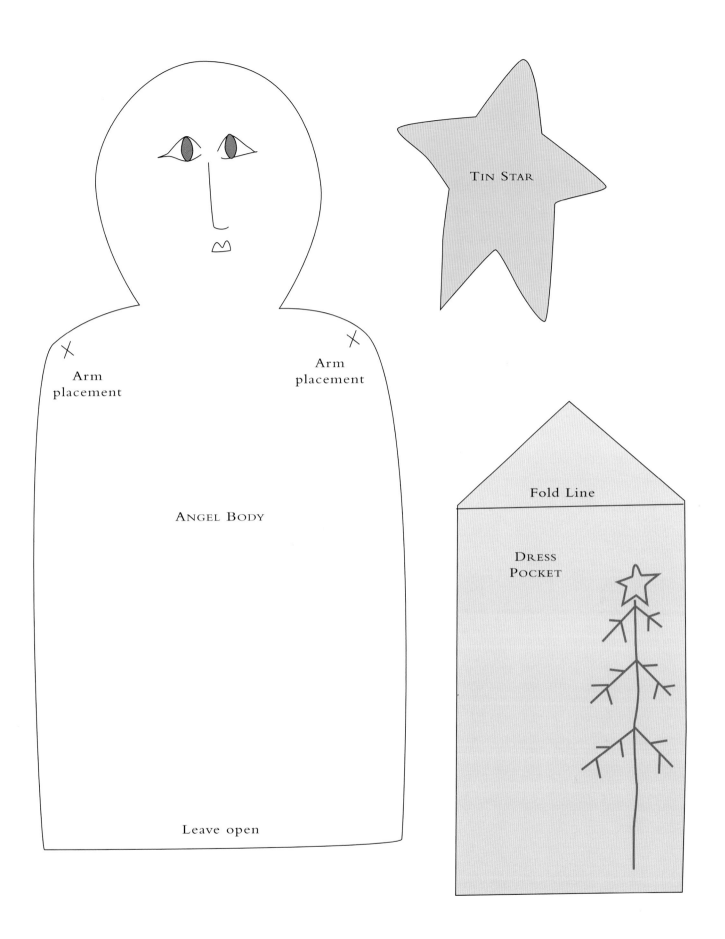

Tin Star

Arm
placement

Arm
placement

Angel Body

Fold Line

Dress
Pocket

Leave open

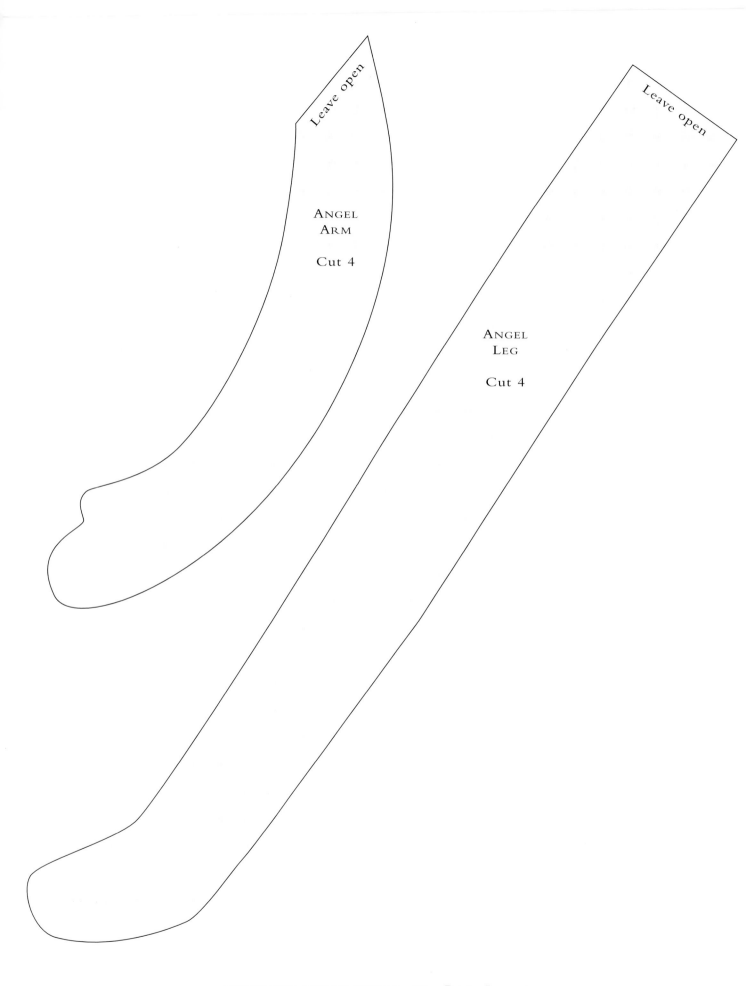

Leave open

ANGEL
ARM

Cut 4

Leave open

ANGEL
LEG

Cut 4

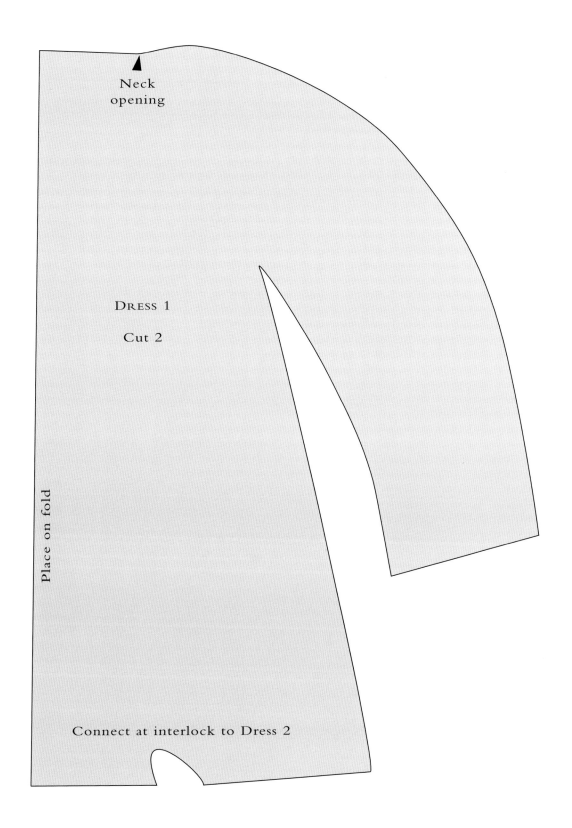

Neck
opening

DRESS 1

Cut 2

Place on fold

Connect at interlock to Dress 2

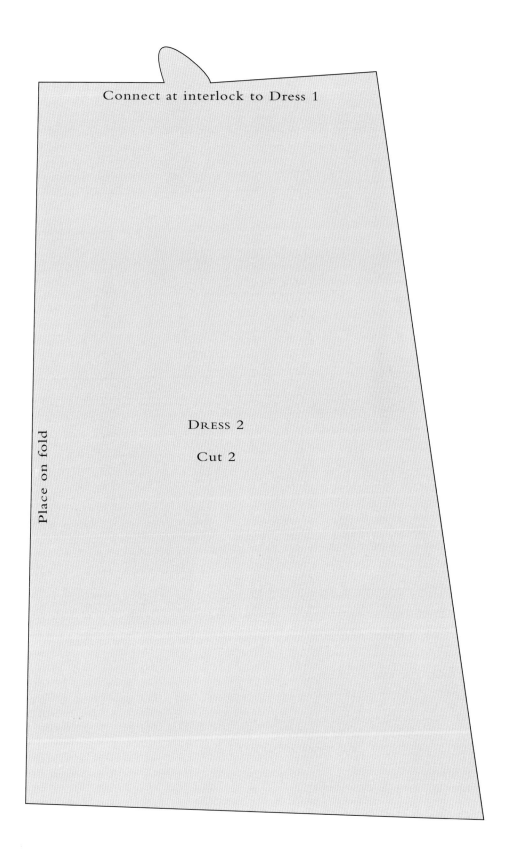

Connect at interlock to Dress 1

Place on fold

Dress 2

Cut 2

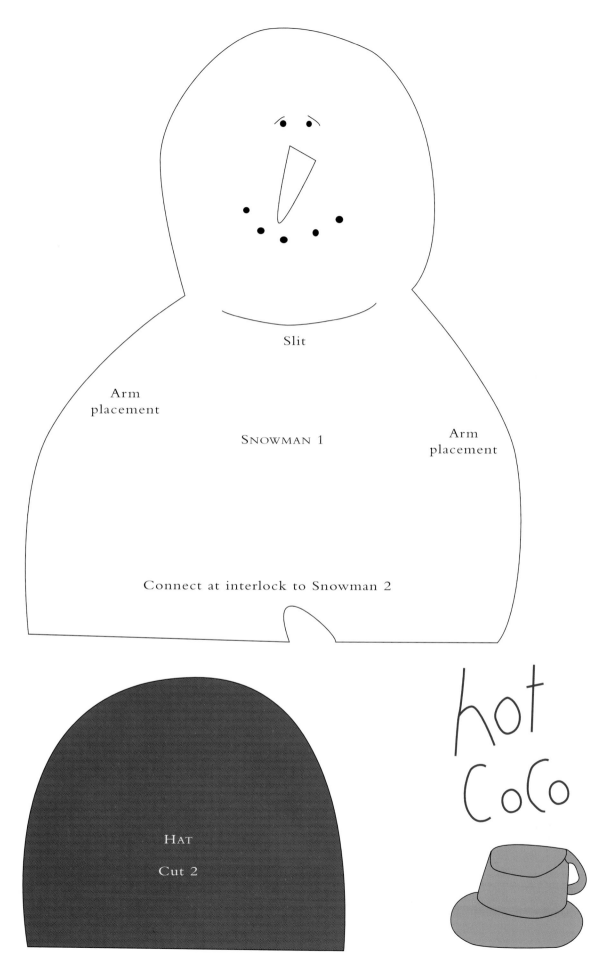

Slit

Arm
placement

SNOWMAN 1

Arm
placement

Connect at interlock to Snowman 2

HAT

Cut 2

hot
CoCo

Connect at interlock to Snowman 1

Snowman

SNOWMAN 2

FLOWER

FLOWER
CENTER

CROW

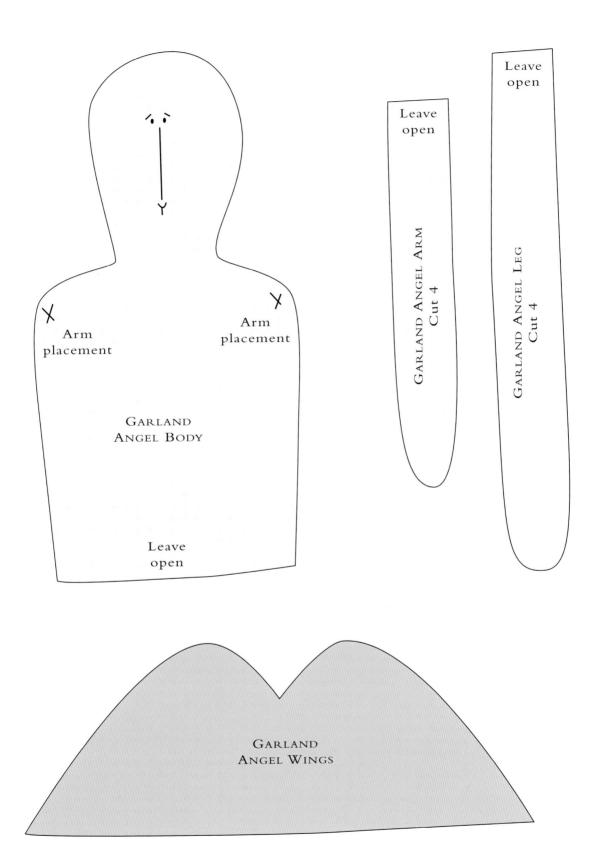

Arm
placement

Arm
placement

GARLAND
ANGEL BODY

Leave
open

Leave
open

GARLAND ANGEL ARM
Cut 4

Leave
open

GARLAND ANGEL LEG
Cut 4

GARLAND
ANGEL WINGS

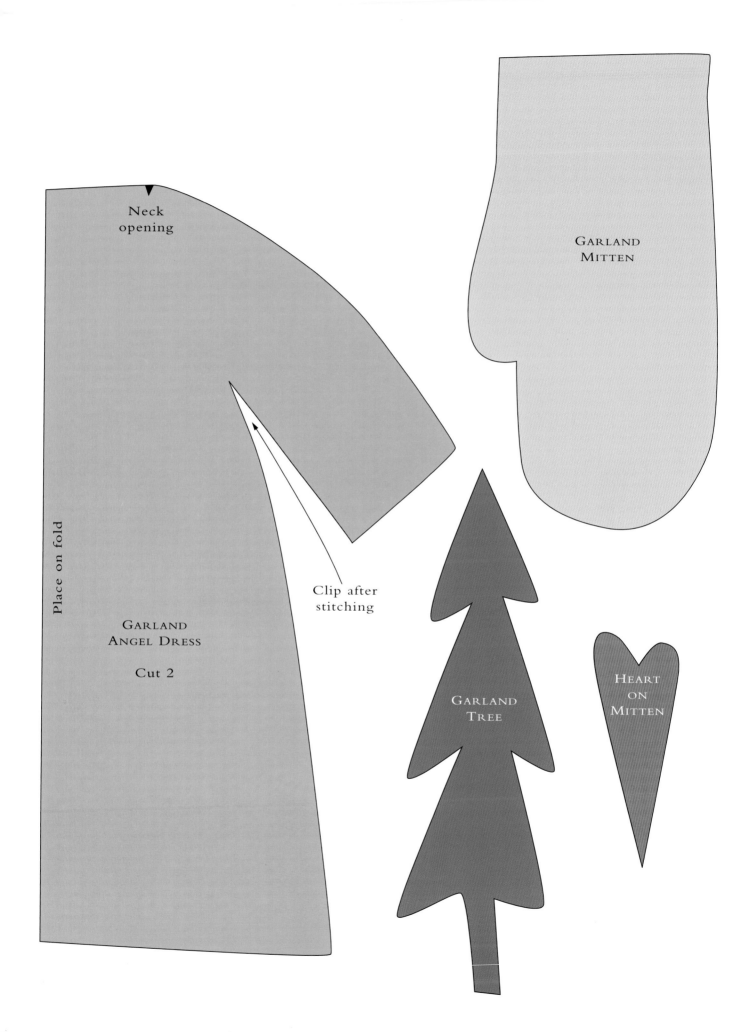

Neck opening

Place on fold

GARLAND
ANGEL DRESS

Cut 2

Clip after
stitching

GARLAND
MITTEN

GARLAND
TREE

HEART
ON
MITTEN

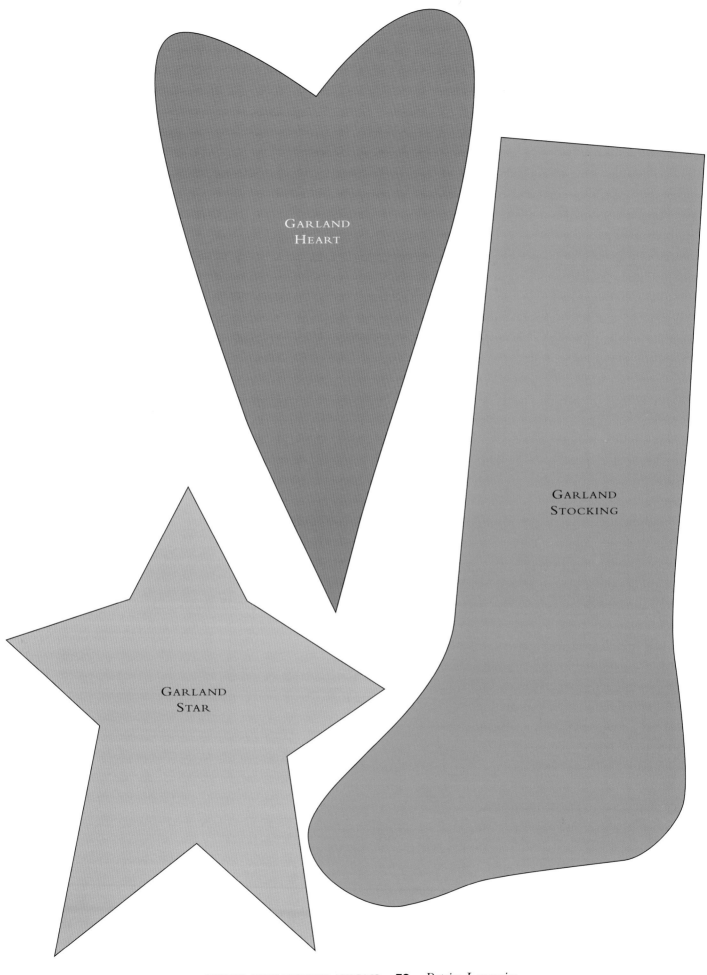

GARLAND
HEART

GARLAND
STOCKING

GARLAND
STAR

McKenna Ryan

CATCHING MEMORIES

Father's Day holds special meaning for McKenna Ryan, whose father passed away when she was still a teenager. He was a man of many talents—a master violinist, a pilot, and a fisherman, among other things—and her memory of him continues to inspire McKenna today. "He was such a creative soul," she says. "And I know he would be so proud if he could see what I'm doing now."

What she's doing now is running a business called Pine Needles, creating and marketing a line of original quilt designs inspired by the Northwoods.

But McKenna inherited more than creativity from her father. She, too, loves fishing and the outdoors, and those two passions inspired her to create this wonderful collection for Father's Day or a special birthday. The wallhanging features a father and his child enjoying a special time together. (McKenna designed the figures in silhouette so that the child could represent either a boy or a girl!) Unique accents such as the three-dimensional fishing line and the real lure add special touches to this fun quilt. Coordinating photo frames and lamp trims bring the outdoors inside, making Dad's den a great place to plan his next fishing trip (or dream about the one that got away!).

MATERIALS

- ⅓ yard each of two medium brown print fabrics for background
- ⅓ yard of light tan print fabric for inner border
- ⅝ yard of green-and-brown leaf print fabric for outer border
- ½ yard of black fabric for appliqués and binding
- Large scraps of assorted green, blue, purple, and dark brown fabrics for appliqués
- 1 yard of fabric for backing
- 29" x 36" piece of batting
- Fusible web
- Clear nylon thread
- Variegated thread
- Black and cream embroidery floss
- One small doll eye
- One fly lure
- White craft glue

Quick-Sew Wallhanging

Finished size 27" x 34"

CUTTING

1. From one medium brown print background fabric, cut a 9" x 25½" rectangle for the sky. From the other background fabric, cut a 7½" x 25½" rectangle for the lake.

2. From the light tan print border fabric, cut two 2¾" x 25½" strips and two 1½" x 20½" strips.

3. From the leaf print fabric, cut four 4" x 27½" strips.

4. From the backing fabric, cut a 29" x 36" rectangle.

5. From the black fabric, cut four 2½" binding strips across the width of the fabric.

6. Refer to the General Instructions on page 6 to trace, apply fusible web to, and cut out the following appliqué pieces from the patterns on pages 78-85: One each of trees A, B (connect both patterns), C, and D, large island and its reflection, grass, boats A and B, child, man and fishing pole, boat reflection, small island and its reflection, medium fish, and bird B. Cut two of bird A.

PIECING AND ASSEMBLY

1. Referring to Diagram A, assemble the top as follows: Sew the two background pieces together to make a 16" x 25½" rectangle. Sew the 2¾"-wide light tan strips to the top and bottom of the rectangle; press the seam allowances toward the strips. Sew the 1½"-wide light tan strips to the sides, press. Sew a 4"-wide leaf print strip to the top and bottom of the rectangle; press. Sew the remaining 4"-wide strips to the sides, and press.

2. Referring to the photograph, and following the directions below, fuse the appliqué pieces to the background, layering as indicated by the dashed lines on the patterns. For best results, position all pieces and check placement before fusing; adjust as needed.

3. Position the small island and its reflection at the seam between the sky and the lake; fuse. Position the four trees, slipping B under A and C under B as marked on the patterns; fuse. Position and fuse the large island, slightly overlapping the bottoms of the trees. Fuse the grass to the lower edge of the island. Position and fuse the island's reflection.

4. Position the two boat pieces and the silhouettes; fuse. Add the reflection.

5. Fuse the medium fish at the lower right and the birds at the upper right.

FINISHING

1. Referring to the General Instructions on page 7, layer the wallhanging.

2. Using clear nylon thread, stitch just

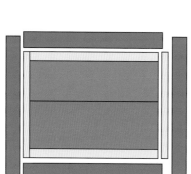

DIAGRAM A

inside the edge of all appliqué pieces. Using variegated rayon thread, machine-quilt a casual wavy pattern in the bottom half of the background and light tan border and freeform cloud shapes in the top half.

3. Use clear nylon thread to quilt a loose meandering pattern in the outer border.

4. Trim the edges of the layers even. Prepare the binding strips and a hanging sleeve as directed in the General Instructions on page 7; pin to the back.

5. Referring to the General Instructions on page 7 for mitered corners, sew the binding in place; fold and whipstitch to the back.

6. To make the child's fishing rod, thread a needle with a 6-inch piece of black floss and knot the end. Bring the floss to the front of the wallhanging at the end of the child's arms. Five inches away, push the needle back through the quilt; pull the floss taut enough so it doesn't sag; knot the floss.

7. To make the child's fishing line, thread a needle with a 7" piece of cream embroidery floss and knot the end. Bring the floss to the front of the wallhanging at the end of the child's rod, and take it through to the back about 4 inches away, leaving a slack line of floss on the front. To shape the line, put a little white craft glue between thumb and forefinger, and run along the length of the floss. Shape as desired, and allow to dry. The line will become slightly stiff and will hold its shape.

8. To make the man's line, thread a needle with a 14" piece of cream embroidery floss and knot the end. Bring it to the front of the wallhanging at the end of the rod, and take it to the back near the fish's mouth. Use a pair of needle-nose pliers to pinch the barb off a lure; stitch the lure in place at the end of the floss, burying the tip inside the batting. Sew a doll's eye to the fish.

DIAGRAM B

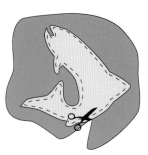

DIAGRAM C

Rod and Reel Photo Frame

8½" x 10" (image size 4" x 6")

MATERIALS

■ Scraps of dark brown, light brown, and black fabric

■ Scraps of felt to match fabrics

■ Fusible web

■ Clear nylon thread

■ Variegated thread

■ Black embroidery floss

■ Fly lure

■ 8½" x 10" wood frame

■ Hot-glue gun and glue sticks

CUTTING

1. Refer to the General Instructions on page 6 to trace, apply fusible web to, and cut out the following appliqué pieces on pages 81 and 85: Medium fish; rod parts A, B, C, and D; and reel.

ASSEMBLY

1. Fuse the medium fish to a slightly larger piece of felt in a matching color. See Diagram B.

2. Using clear nylon thread, stitch just inside the edge of the fish. Using variegated thread, add decorative stitching to accent the fins and tail. Stitch a round eye.

3. Trim the felt along the edge of the pattern piece as shown in Diagram C. Hot-glue the fish to the frame.

4. Fuse the rod parts and the reel to a piece of black felt, overlapping as indicated by the dashed pattern lines. Using clear nylon thread, stitch just inside the edges of the pattern pieces.

5. Trim the felt, and hot-glue the rod and reel to the frame. Fold over ¼" at the end of the rod, and hold in place with a dot of glue. Thread a 14" piece

of black embroidery floss through the loop. Glue one end of the floss under the edge of the reel, and glue the other end near the mouth of the fish.

6. Using needle-nose pliers, pinch the barb off a fly lure. Hot-glue the lure to the frame, covering the end of the floss.

Bear Photo Frame

7½" x 9½" (image size 3" x 5")

MATERIALS

- Scraps of light brown, dark brown, and green fabrics
- Scraps of felt to match fabrics
- Fusible web
- Clear nylon thread
- Variegated thread
- 7½" x 9½" wood frame
- Hot-glue gun and glue sticks

CUTTING

1. Refer to the General Instructions on page 6 to trace, apply fusible web to, and cut out the following appliqué pieces on pages 78-85: Bear, small fish, tree A, and trunk.

ASSEMBLY

1. Peel the paper backing off the fish, and place the fish inside the bear's mouth. Fuse the pieces as a unit to a slightly larger piece of felt. Fuse the tree and trunk to a piece of felt.

2. Using clear nylon thread, stitch just inside the edge of the pattern pieces. Trim the felt close to the pattern pieces; hot-glue to the frame.

Lamp Trims

MATERIALS

- Scraps of green, brown, and black fabrics
- Fusible web
- Scraps of black felt
- Lamp with 10" shade*
- Clear nylon thread
- Variegated thread

Note: The lampshade shown was purchased with the leather lacing already on it. Add lacing to your shade, if desired, using a ¼" single-hole punch and ¹⁄₁₆" leather strips.

CUTTING

1. Refer to the General Instructions on page 6 to trace, apply fusible web to, and cut out the following appliqué pieces on pages 84-85: Large fish, and fly lure pieces A, B, C, D, E, F, and G.

1. To make the lampshade trim, fuse the fish pieces to a slightly larger piece of black felt, overlapping the pieces as indicated by the dashed lines on the fish pattern.

2. Using clear nylon thread, stitch just inside the edges of the appliqué pieces. Fuse the felt to a piece of fusible web. Trim the felt close to the edges of the pattern piece. Carefully fuse the fish to the lampshade.

3. To make the lamp-base trim, layer the lure pieces in order on a slightly larger piece of black felt, overlapping as indicated by the dashed lines on the patterns; fuse.

4. Using clear nylon thread, stitch just inside the edge of the appliqué pieces. Using variegated thread, add decorative stitching as shown in the photograph. Trim away the background felt.

5. Attach the lure to post of the lamp base with a small dot of hot glue or a piece of double-sided foam tape.

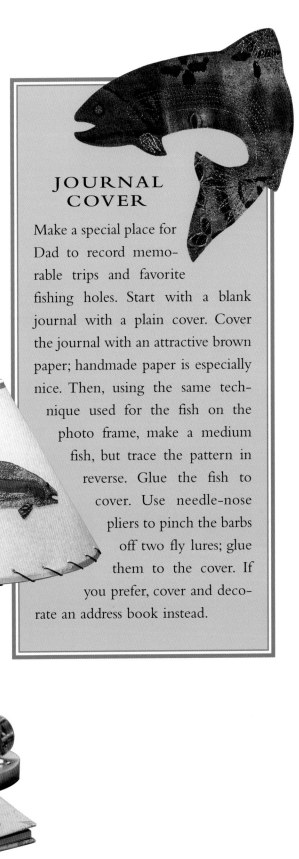

JOURNAL COVER

Make a special place for Dad to record memorable trips and favorite fishing holes. Start with a blank journal with a plain cover. Cover the journal with an attractive brown paper; handmade paper is especially nice. Then, using the same technique used for the fish on the photo frame, make a medium fish, but trace the pattern in reverse. Glue the fish to cover. Use needle-nose pliers to pinch the barbs off two fly lures; glue them to the cover. If you prefer, cover and decorate an address book instead.

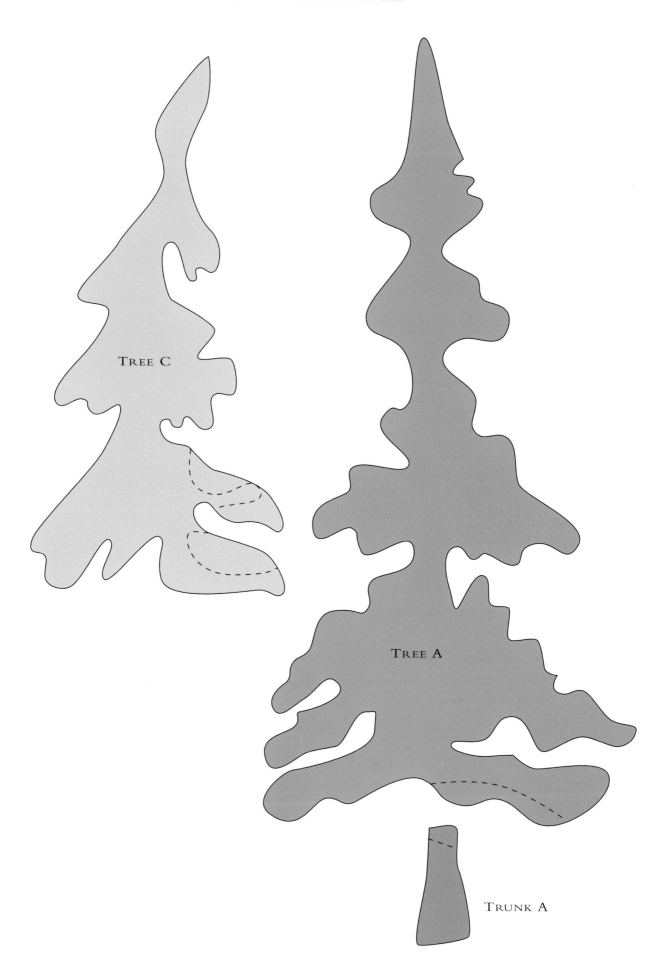

TREE C

TREE A

TRUNK A

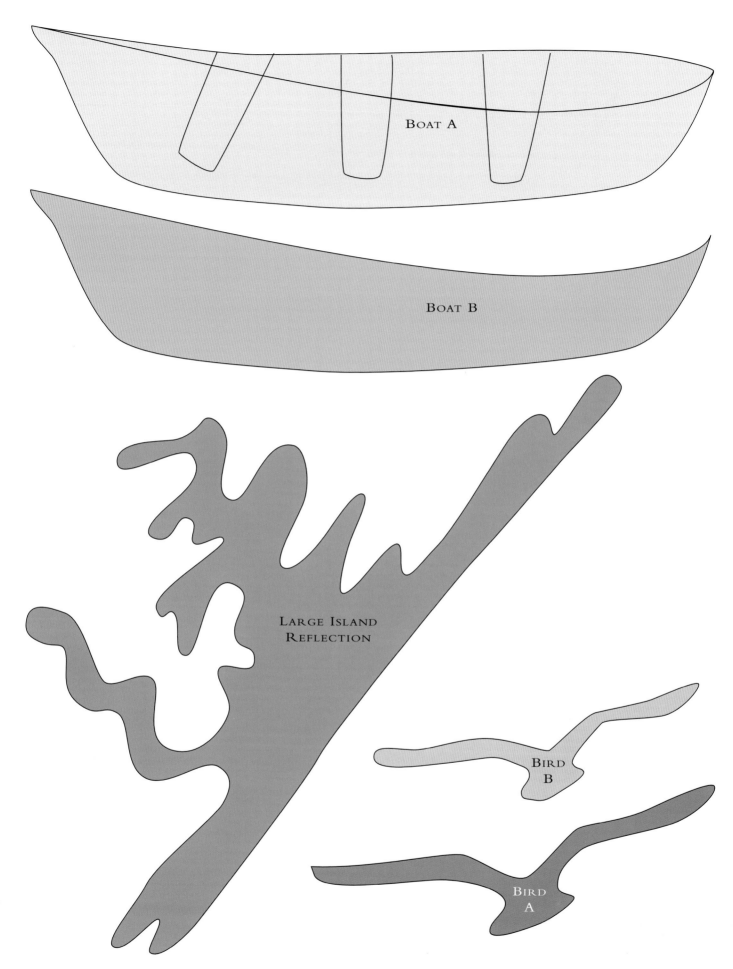

BOAT A

BOAT B

LARGE ISLAND
REFLECTION

BIRD
B

BIRD
A

LARGE ISLAND

TREE D

GRASS

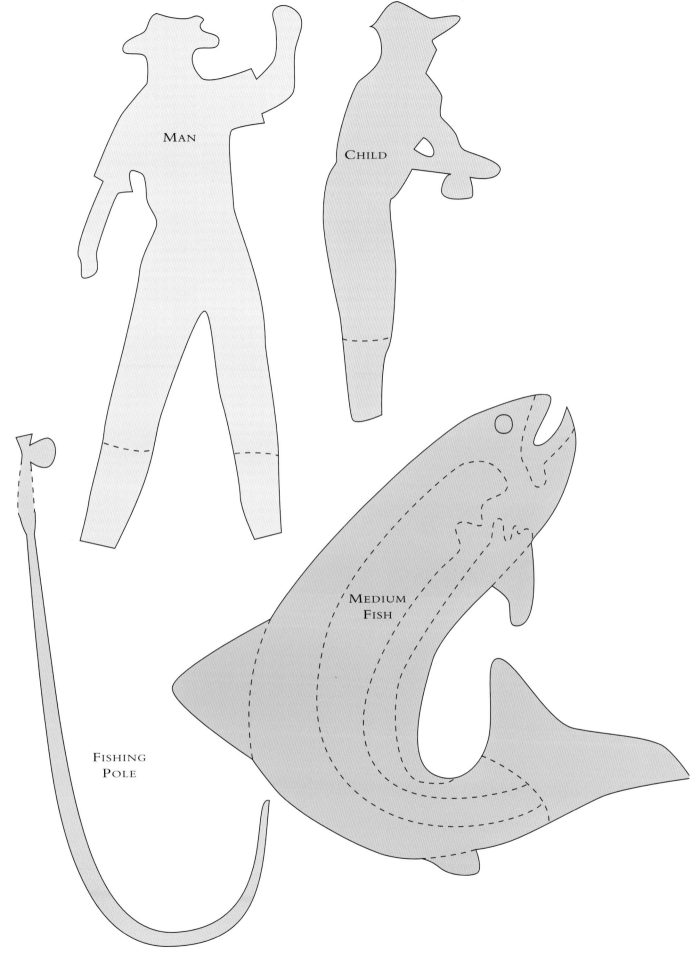

MAN

CHILD

MEDIUM
FISH

FISHING
POLE

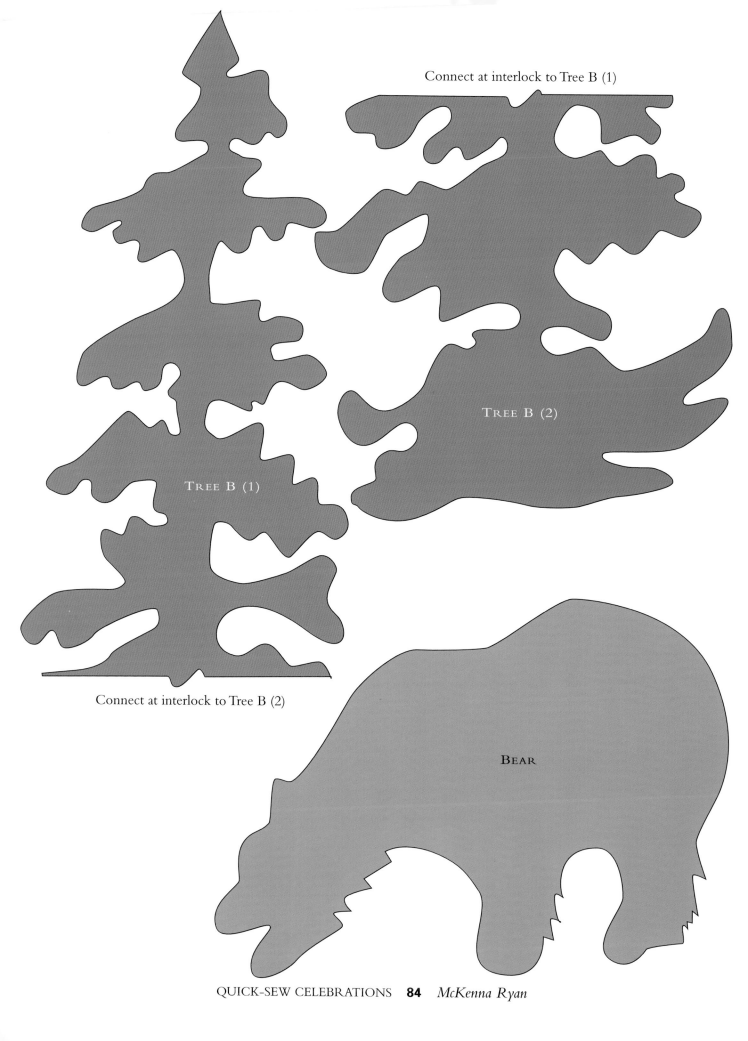

Connect at interlock to Tree B (1)

Tree B (2)

Tree B (1)

Connect at interlock to Tree B (2)

Bear

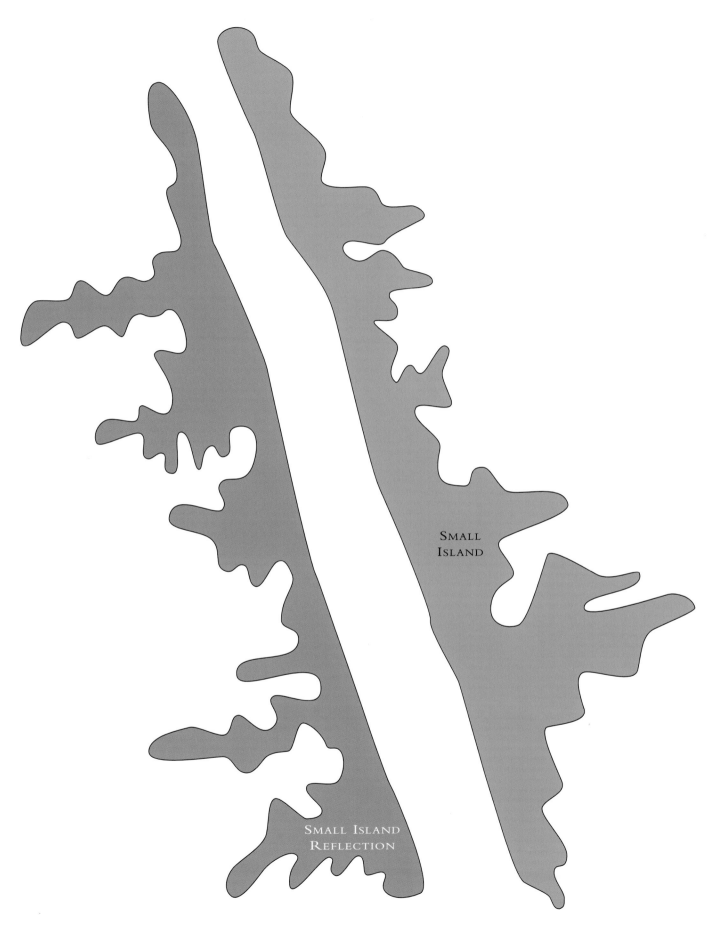

SMALL
ISLAND

SMALL ISLAND
REFLECTION

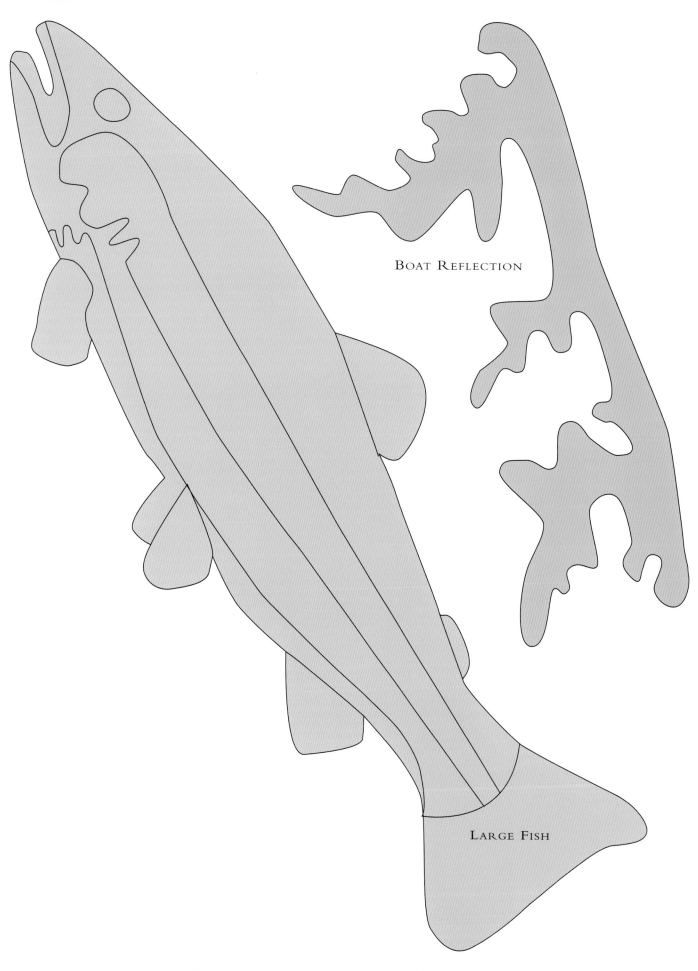

Boat Reflection

Large Fish

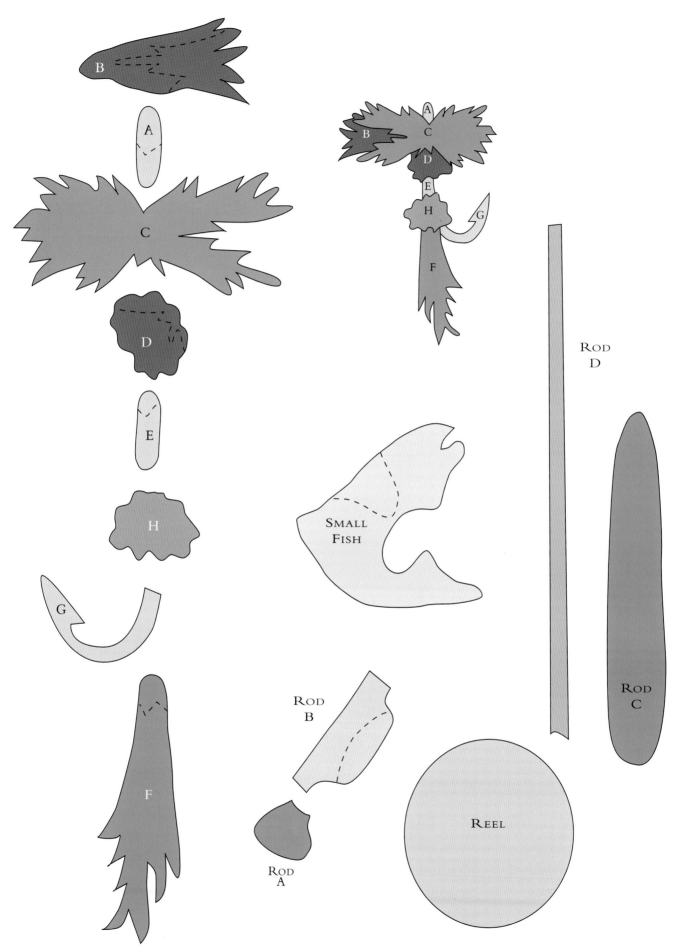

B

A

C

D

E

H

G

F

A
B
C
D
E
H
G
F

SMALL
FISH

ROD
D

ROD
C

ROD
B

ROD
A

REEL

Cheryl Jukich

CELEBRATE— IT'S YOUR DAY!

Memories of magical childhood birthdays inspired Cheryl Jukich to create this festive collection. "In my family, birthdays were second only to Christmas in anticipation," recalls Cheryl. "There were 6 of us kids, and each year we'd wait anxiously as our day approached. It was a special day, allowing such privileges as choice of meal (no liver, thank you!) and amnesty from bickering. The birthday dinner ended with a big sugary confection baked by Mom in secret. Like a fairy godmother, she'd glide into the dining room, candle-bright cake in hand, singing the opening bars of 'Happy Birthday.' Of course, no child's birthday is complete without gifts—and Mom and Dad elevated gift giving to a new art form. They made sure every birthday was a special occasion!"

Cheryl cherishes these memories of birthday magic created by her parents. Create your own special memories with these fun party decorations. The clever wallhanging includes a dry-erase board, so well-wishers can add their greetings. The all-occasion stocking is a great way to present gifts, and the chairback cover creates a special place for the guest of honor.

MATERIALS

- 2 yards of cream solid fabric for banner
- ¾ yard of muslin for lining
- ½ yard each of green and pink solid fabrics for banner and fringe
- ½ yard of pink print fabric for fringe and rod casing
- ⅓ yard of yellow print fabric for window corners and rod casing
- ¼ yard of yellow solid fabric for fringe
- Assorted large scraps for letters and hanging loops
- Fusible web
- Pink and green embroidery floss
- 1⅛ yards of ½" sew-on hook-and-loop tape
- One package of 6mm gold beads
- Five blue porcelain star buttons
- Twenty-four assorted buttons
- 11" x 17" white dry-erase board
- 1" to 1½"-diameter dowel rod, 33" long
- Velcro glue
- Hot-glue gun and glue sticks
- Water soluble marking pen

Quick-Sew Wallhanging

Finished size 24" x 36"

CUTTING

1. From the cream solid fabric, cut two 24" x 35" pieces. From the muslin, cut one 24" square.
2. From the green solid fabric, cut two 3" x 44" strips and two 8½" squares. From the pink solid fabric, cut two 3" x 44" strips and one 8½" square.
3. From the pink print fabric, cut two 4" x 30" rectangles and two 3" x 44" strips.
4. From the yellow print fabric, cut two 4" x 30" rectangles and four 5½" squares.
5. From yellow solid fabric, cut two 3" x 44" strips.
6. From scraps, cut three each 3½" x 7" and 2½" x 7" strips for hanging loops.
7. From the hook-and-loop tape, cut two 11½" and two 8" pieces.
8. Refer to General Instructions on page 6 to trace, apply fusible web to, and cut out the letters using the patterns on pages 98-99.

ASSEMBLING THE BANNER

1. Place one 24" x 35" cream piece right side up on a flat surface. Place the 24" muslin square on top, aligning the top and side edges. Smooth and pin.

2. Remove the black banding from the dry-erase board. Referring to Diagram A for placement, lay the board on the muslin and trace around it with water-soluble pen; remove and set aside.

3. Smooth and pin layers. Stitch on the marked line. Cut out the inside of the rectangle, cutting through both layers and leaving a generous ¼" seam allowance. Pull the muslin to the wrong side of the banner. Match the top and side edges again and machine baste. Using six strands of embroidery floss, prairie-stitch around the opening as shown in photograph. (Prairie-

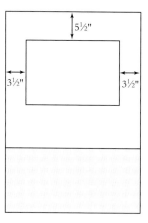

DIAGRAM A

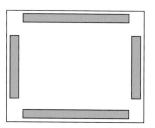

DIAGRAM B

stitching is the name Cheryl coined for the fast running stitches she uses on quilts and wearables. Thread a needle with a single or double length of 6-strand embroidery floss. Knot an end and take large, uneven running stitches through the fabric.)

4. Referring to Diagram B, pin and stitch the prickly side of the hook-and-loop tape around the banner opening on the muslin side, stitching close to the edges of the strips.

5. Fold each 5½" yellow print square in half, right sides together, to form a triangle. Press. Stitch around the triangle, leaving an opening for turning. Turn right side out and press. Stitch opening closed.

6. Lay the banner on a flat surface and arrange the triangles at the corners of the opening as shown in Diagram C. Sew assorted-size buttons at each of the triangle points.

7. Using the photo as a guide, arrange the words across the bottom of the banner. When satisfied with the placement, fuse in place. Stitch around each letter with decorative stitches. Embellish the areas around the opening and the saying with prairie-stitch "squiggles," using the photo for inspiration.

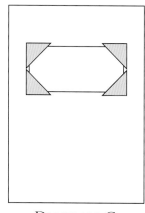

DIAGRAM C

8. To make the banner points, fold each 8½" square in half, right sides together, to form a triangle. Stitch around the triangle, leaving an opening for turning. Turn right side out and press. Place the pink triangle right sides together in the center bottom of the banner as shown in Diagram D. Pin in place. Add the green triangles on each side, leaving a generous ¼" allowance on the sides. Pin, and stitch across using a ¼" seam allowance. Press.

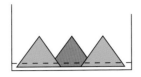

DIAGRAM D

MAKING THE FRINGE

1. Divide the 3" x 44" strips into two stacks, with one strip of each color in each stack. Layer the fabrics wrong side up. Carefully fold each stack in half lengthwise, wrong sides together, and press well. Stitch next to the fold with a scant ¼" seam allowance. See Diagram E.

2. Fringe the strips by cutting through the layers every ½", to within ½" of the fold. Wet the strips thoroughly and squeeze out excess water; place in the dryer with an old towel and dry. Remove while slightly damp, and finger-press.

3. Place the fringe strips on the banner front, matching the fold of each strip with the raw edge on each side of the banner; pin. Stitch using a ¼" seam allowance. Trim away excess fringe at the top and bottom edges of the banner.

DIAGRAM E

ADDING THE BACKING

1. Center each 2½" x 7" strip on top of a 3½" x 7" strip. Fold in half to make a hanging loop. Pin one loop in the center top of the banner, right sides together and raw edges even. Pin the remaining loops 2½" in from each side. Machine baste.

2. Place and pin banner backing right sides together with banner, making sure that fringe and points are out of the seam area. Using a ¼" seam allowance, sew along each side, then across the bottom and the top.

3. Turn the banner right side out through the opening. Press edges well.

FINISHING

1. Using six strands of embroidery floss, begin in the top center and prairie-stitch around the banner edges approximately ½" from the edge. Embellish the ends of the previously stitched "squiggles" with porcelain star buttons, gold beads, and regular colored buttons. Sew a button on the ends of each banner point.

2. To make the dowel rod casing, sew the four 4" x 30" rectangles together along the short sides, making one long strip. Fold the strip in half lengthwise, right sides together, and stitch with a ¼" seam. Turn right side out and press seam area. Place on dowel rod. Fold in one end to cover the exposed dowel, and hot glue. Repeat for the remaining end. Arrange the gathers evenly over the dowel rod.

3. Center the remaining hook-and-loop strips on the top, bottom, and side edges of the front of the board, aligning the long edges of the strips with the edges of the board. Use the Velcro glue to secure in place. When dry, place inside the banner opening. Have family and friends write sentiments on the board with markers.

4. Hang the banner on the dowel rod. If desired, cut leftover fabric into 3" widths and tie around each hanging loop. Cut ends and fluff.

Approximately 8" x 18" or to fit

MATERIALS

- ⅜ yard of cream solid fabric for front
- ⅜ yard of print or solid fabric for lining
- ⅜ yard each or scraps of four solid fabrics and three print fabrics for puffy blocks
- ⅛ yard of muslin for puffy block lining
- ⅛ yard each of two solid fabrics and one print fabric for fringe
- Assorted scraps for letters, face, and queen's dress or king's bowtie
- Polyester batting
- Fusible web
- Embroidery floss
- Twelve round-top shank buttons
- Nine ½" buttons for dress neckline and hands
- Three blue porcelain star buttons
- One banner button
- One ⅝" button cover
- One package of 6mm gold beads
- One package of cotton hair
- Permanent-ink black marking pen
- Hot-glue gun and glue sticks
- 12" length of 18-gauge wire
- 9" length of medium twine

CUTTING

1. Cut three 3½" squares from each of the four solid and three print fabrics for puffy blocks, for a total of twenty-one squares. Cut twenty-one 3½" squares from the muslin. You will cut the remaining pieces for the cover later.

2. Cut one 3" x 40" strip from each of the solid and print fringe fabrics.

3. Cut one 4½" x 8" rectangle from print fabric and one 4½" x 8" rectangle from solid fabric for the queen's dress, or cut a 2" x 4" rectangle for the king's bowtie.

4. Refer to General Instructions on page 6 to trace, apply fusible web to, and cut out the letters for either "Queen" or "King" and "Day", using the patterns on page 100.

ASSEMBLY

1. Using a cloth tape, measure across the back of the chair. Add 2" to this measurement to allow for seam allowances and ease.

2. Place a 3½" solid or print square wrong sides together with a 3½" muslin square. Sew around three sides of the block, leaving the fourth side completely open for stuffing. Start by making twenty-one blocks, and add more if needed.

3. Stuff each block with a small amount of stuffing. Do not overstuff. Stitch the open side closed.

4. Arrange the blocks in a pleasing manner, alternating solids and prints. When satisfied, pin the first three vertical blocks right sides together as shown in Diagram F. Sew together using a ¼" seam. Repeat for each row, then stitch the rows together.

5. Compare the stitched panel with your chair back measurement to determine whether additional blocks are needed. If so, add them now.

6. Sew a round shank button to the center of every other block, pulling the threads tight to make a dent in the block.

7. Cut two pieces of lining fabric and one piece of cream solid the same size as the puffy block unit. Set the cream front piece aside for now.

8. Place one piece of lining fabric right sides together with the puffy block unit. Sew along one long side, as shown in Diagram G. Press seam. Turn right side out and pin-baste along remaining sides. Set unit aside.

9. Place the cover front piece right side up on a flat surface and arrange "Queen" or "King" letters, using the photo as a guide to placement. When satisfied, fuse in place. Repeat for the "Day!" letters. Sew around each letter with small decorative stitches. Using a double length of contrasting embroidery floss, backstitch the words "for the" above the word "Day!".

10. Trace the face template from page 102 onto face fabric and cut out. Place on the cover front under the Queen or King lettering. Keep the face at least 1¾" from the bottom edge of the cover. Stitch around the face with

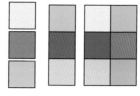

DIAGRAM F

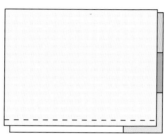

DIAGRAM G

DIAGRAM H

decorative stitches, leaving an opening at the bottom. Stuff face with a small amount of stuffing. Sew the opening closed. Referring to the face template, embroider the face details.

11. To make the hair, cut a 3" piece of cardboard as a form. Wind the cotton hair around the cardboard six times and slide it off. Cut an extra piece of hair and tie it around the hair bundle in the middle. Repeat for three additional bundles. Stitch each hair bundle to the top of the head as shown in Diagram H.

12. Cut a 7" piece of wire, and make a small closed hook at one end. String approximately 31 beads onto the wire. Secure the remaining end with a closed hook, making sure to leave enough room for the beads to move when formed into a crown. Bend the beaded wire into three points. Place the crown ends behind the hair and handstitch firmly in place.

13. Place the 9" piece of twine under the chin and arrange the arms on each side. Stitch in place with a wide zigzag. Sew a ⅝" colored button to the end of each arm.

14. To make the queen's dress, trace the dress template from page 98 onto the solid dress fabric. Cut out and place right side up on the print dress fabric. Sew decorative stitches around the scallops. Fold the raw edges under ¼" on all four sides and press. Turn under again, press, and stitch. Position the dress under the chin, finger-pleating the fabric as you pin in place. Stitch across pleats close to the fabric edge. Handsew a string of buttons to the neck area to cover stitching.

15. To make the king's bow tie, pinch the center of the 2" x 4" rectangle and tie

off with contrasting fabric or twine. Center the bow tie under the chin area and handstitch securely in place.

FINISHING

1. Sprinkle gold beads around the letters and sew on. Add the blue porcelain stars and stitch them on with embroidery floss.

2. Place the second piece of lining fabric right sides together with the appliquéd front. Stitch across the bottom using a ¼" seam allowance. Press. Turn and pin-baste raw edges together.

3. To make the fringe, stack the 3" strips wrong side up, with edges aligned and with the print fabric in the center of the stack. Carefully fold in half lengthwise, wrong sides together, and press well. Stitch through all layers ¼" away from the fold. To form the fringe, cut through the layers every ½", to within ½" of the fold. Thoroughly wet the fringe and gently squeeze dry. Place in dryer with a clean towel and dry. Remove from dryer and finger-press while slightly damp.

4. Fold over one end of the fringe to form a clean edge; press. Machine-baste the fringe to the right side of the appliquéd front, aligning the fold with the raw edge of the front. Turn up the remaining end for a clean finish.

5. Place the front and back right sides together and pin, matching corners and ends. (If you have a ladder-back chair, mark openings for the uprights on the front, and leave these sections unstitched when sewing the front to the back.) Stitch around the three sides using a ¼" seam allowance. Clean-finish with a serger, or zigzag-stitch. Turn right side out and press if needed.

6. With the marking pen, write the king

or queen's name on the banner button. Let dry and then hot glue to the button cover. Slip the button cover over one of the button hands on the front. To hang balloons on the back of the celebration chair, make a hanger loop in the top center of the chair cover seam using a double length of embroidery floss.

All-Occasion Stocking

Approximately 10" x 14"

MATERIALS

- ½ yard or fat quarter of cream solid fabric for front
- ½ yard or fat quarter each of one print and three solid fabrics for fringe and lining
- Assorted scraps for blocks
- Fusible web
- Embroidery floss
- Buttons in assorted colors
- Water-soluble marking pen

CUTTING

1. From the cream solid fabric, cut a 15" x 18" rectangle. From each of the solid and print fringe fabrics, cut one 15" x 18" rectangle.

2. Refer to General Instructions on page 6 to apply fusible web to and cut out ten 2½" squares from the assorted fabric scraps.

ASSEMBLY

1. Trace the stocking pattern from pages 102-103. Place the pattern in the center of the cream fabric and trace

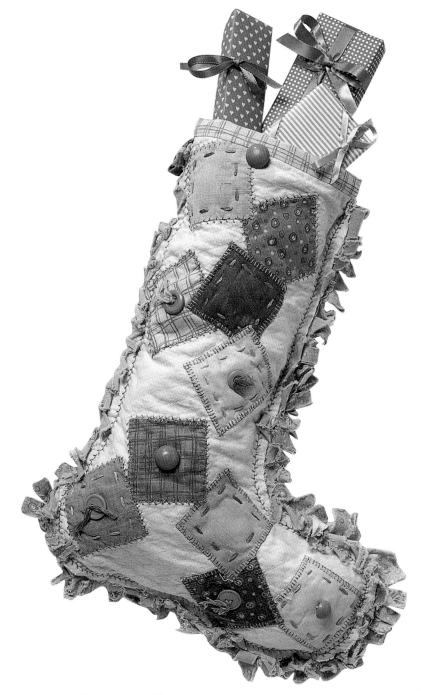

3. The fringe fabrics double as the lining for the stocking so placement is important. Place one 15" x 18" solid-color rectangle wrong side up on a flat surface. Stack the remaining solid and print rectangles on this one, aligning edges and smoothing out wrinkles. Place the stocking in the center of the fabric stack. Pin generously. Begin at the top of the stocking and stitch all around 1/4" from the raw edge using a decorative stitch. Be sure to leave the top open.

4. To make the fringe, cut away the excess fabric from around the stocking, leaving a 1 1/4" border. Now cut through all the fabrics every 1/2", up to the raw edge of the stocking. At the top edge, cut the fringe and lining even with the stocking top, then cut away the first 1/2" of the fringe on each side to make room for the binding.

5. Cut a 2 1/2" square from a scrap of fabric. Press in half with an iron. Open up and press the edges to the center; press in half again. Stitch close to the edge. Place raw ends together to form a hanging loop and baste to the outside of the stocking top as shown in Diagram I.

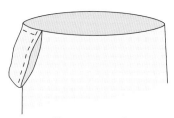

DIAGRAM I

with water-soluble pen; do not cut out yet. Arrange the 2 1/2" squares on the stocking using the photo as a guide. When satisfied with the placement, fuse in place. Machine- or handstitch around each block using decorative stitches.

2. Prairie-stitch along the inside edges of several blocks using a doubled length of 6-strand embroidery floss. Sew buttons the center of the remaining blocks. Cut out the stocking.

6. Measure around the top of the stocking and add 1" to the measurement. Cut a strip of fabric 1 1/2" wide and the length of this measurement for the binding. Pin the binding to the

stocking top, right sides together and raw edges even. Stitch with a ¼" seam allowance, overlapping the ends. Turn under the raw edge to the inside of the stocking and slipstitch.

7. To fluff up the fringe, thoroughly wet the stocking with water and gently squeeze out excess. Put in dryer with a clean towel and dry. Touch up with a warm iron and spray-starch if desired.

8. Fill with gifts and hang on the corner of the birthday boy or girl's bed!

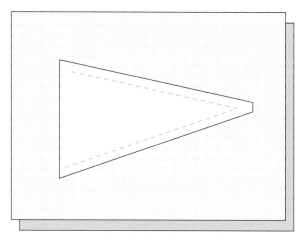

DIAGRAM J

Celebrate! Pennant

MATERIALS

- ½ yard or fat quarter of cream solid fabric for pennant front
- ½ yard or fat quarter each of one print and three solid fabrics for fringe
- Assorted scraps for letters and ties
- Fusible web
- Two 15" lengths of 18-gauge wire
- Three 6mm gold beads
- One blue porcelain star button
- ⅛"-diameter dowel rod, 30" long
- Paint or stain for dowel
- Needle-nose pliers
- Wire cutters
- Hot-glue gun and glue sticks

CUTTING

1. From the cream solid fabric, cut a 12" x 15" rectangle. From each of the solid and print fringe fabrics, cut one 12" x 15" rectangle.

2. From assorted scraps, cut four 1" x 15" strips for pennant ties.

3. Refer to General Instructions on page 6 to trace, apply fusible web to, and cut out the letters, using the patterns on page 101.

ASSEMBLY

1. Using a water-soluble marker, trace the pennant pattern from pages 100-101 onto the cream solid fabric. Mark another line ½" inside the first. Do not cut out the pennant at this time.

2. Remove the backing from the letters and arrange on the pennant front, using the photo as a guide. When satisfied, fuse the letters in place. Machine- or handstitch around each letter if desired, using small decorative stitches such as feather or buttonhole stitches. Now cut out the pennant shape along the outside line.

3. Place one of the solid fringe fabrics wrong side up on a flat surface. Layer the three remaining fringe fabrics on top, aligning edges and smoothing wrinkles. Place the pennant right side

up in the center of the fabric stack. Smooth and pin generously to hold pennant in place. Using decorative or straight stitches, stitch ¼" from the raw edges along the two long sides of the pennant, as shown in Diagram J.

4. Sew a second line of straight stitches ¼" in from the first line of stitches. This forms a casing for the wire.

5. Use needle-nose pliers to form a small closed hook at one end of a piece of wire. Insert the hooked end into the casing, firmly pushing it to the tip of the pennant. Repeat with the second wire. Cut off any excess wire, making sure that the end of the wire is at least ½" in from the edge of the pennant.

6. Align the ends of two 1" x 15" ties, insert between the fabric layers at the side of the pennant near the top, and pin in place. See Diagram K. In the same manner, place the two remaining ties at the bottom of the pennant. Stitch this edge closed using the same straight or decorative stitch used on the other edges.

7. Pin the pennant ties out of the way. Trim away the fringe fabrics leaving a

DIAGRAM K

generous 1¼" border. To make the fringe, begin at one end and cut the fabrics every ½" up to the edge of the pennant.

8. Thoroughly wet the pennant and gently squeeze out excess water. Place in dryer with a clean towel and dry. Remove from the dryer while still damp, and finger-press.

9. As a final touch, sew three to five gold beads around the pennant letters.

10. Sand the dowel rod if necessary. Lightly coat the rod with your choice of stain or acrylic paint. Allow to dry.

11. Thread a small amount of floss through the holes of the star button; trim the ends. Hot glue the button to the top of the pole. Tie the pennant firmly to the pole. The wires in the pennant allow you to wave the pennant in a celebratory breeze!

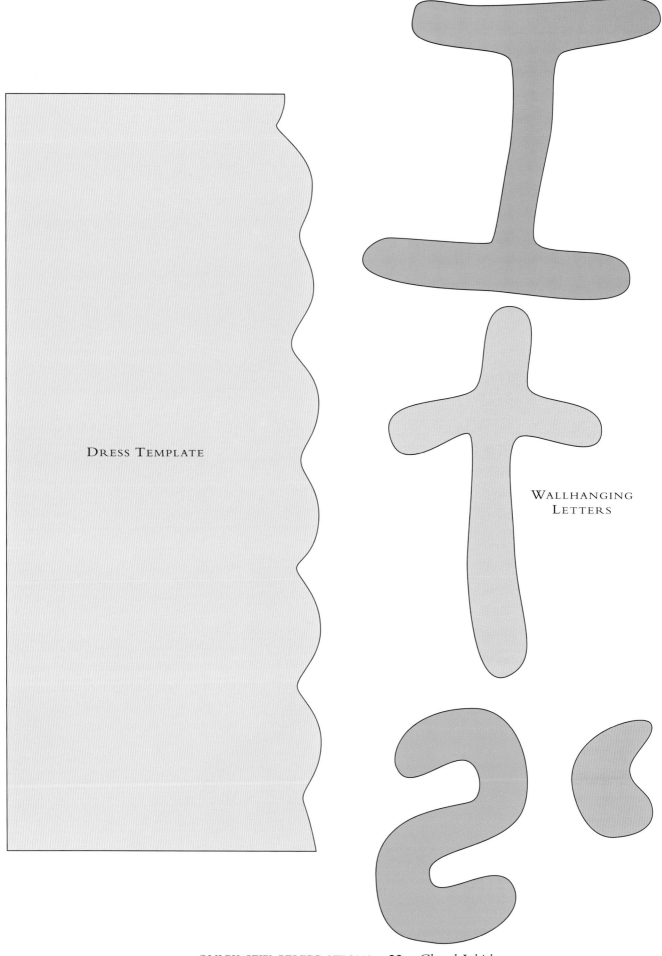

DRESS TEMPLATE

WALLHANGING
LETTERS

Wallhanging
Letters

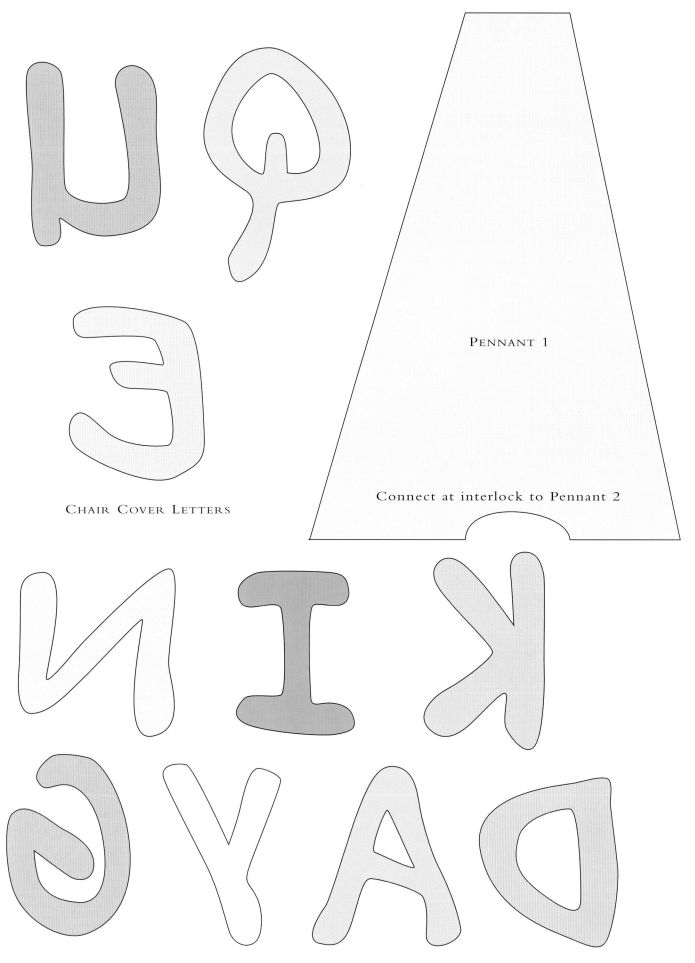

CHAIR COVER LETTERS

PENNANT 1

Connect at interlock to Pennant 2

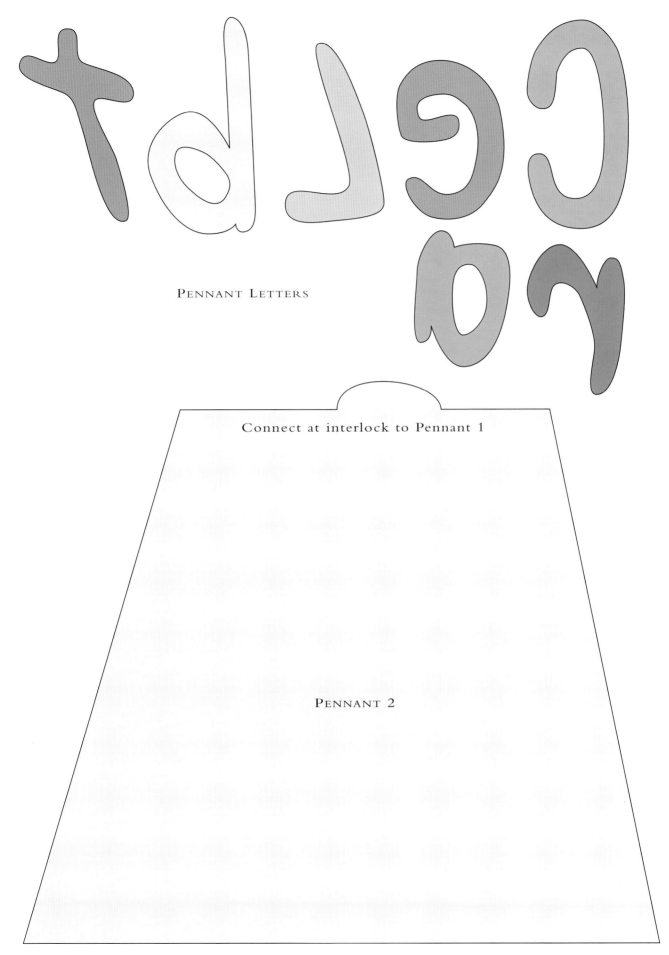

PENNANT LETTERS

Connect at interlock to Pennant 1

PENNANT 2

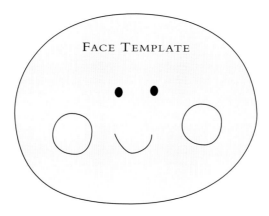

FACE TEMPLATE

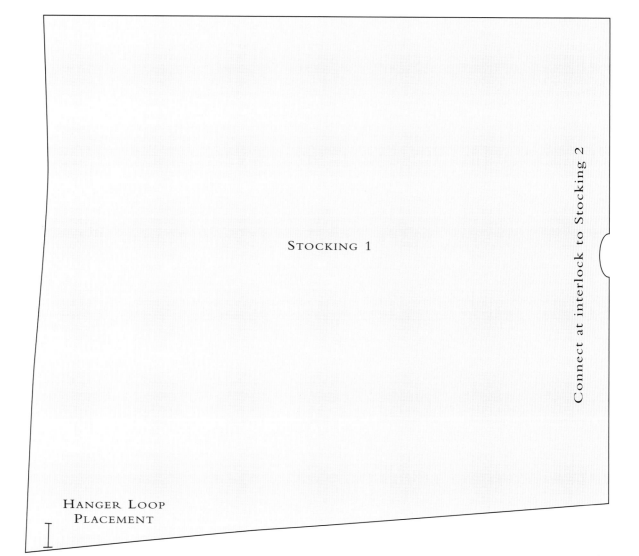

STOCKING 1

Connect at interlock to Stocking 2

HANGER LOOP
PLACEMENT

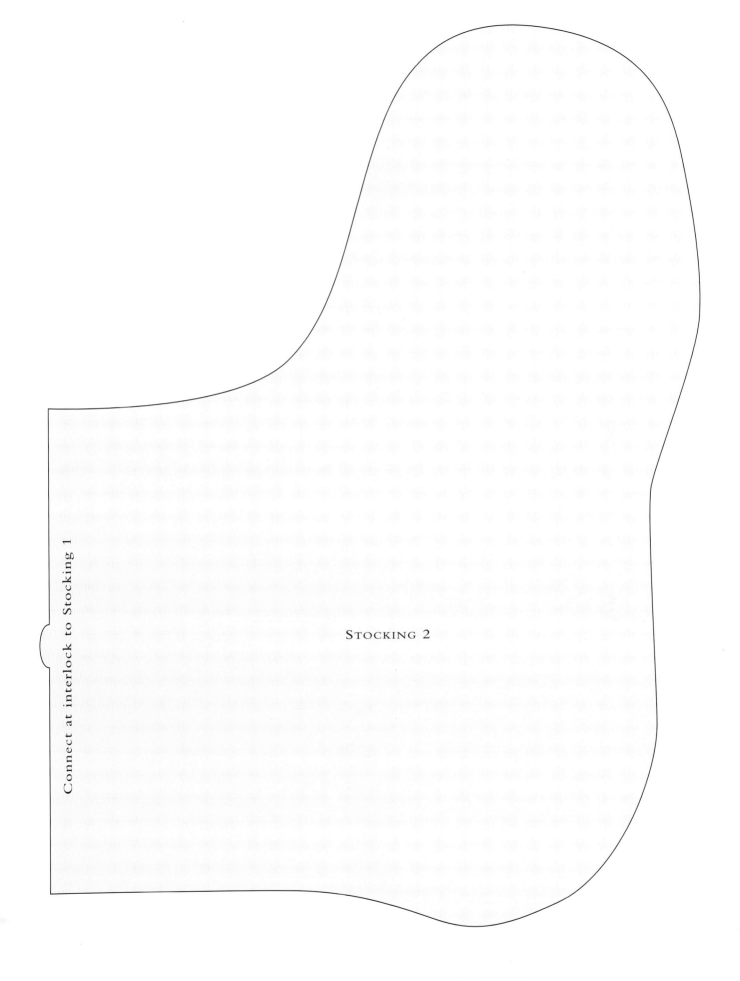

Connect at interlock to Stocking 1

STOCKING 2

Sandy Belt

PUMPKIN PATCH TREATS

With seven children to keep things exciting, every holiday is a major event at Sandy Belt's house and Halloween is no exception. Since they live in a farmhouse out in the country, trick-or-treating has never really been practical. Instead, they've become experts at creating their own fun. Each year, Sandy's husband, Tom, turns their bathroom into a miniature haunted house for the kids to walk through, complete with slimy, scary things to step on and bump into. And the annual trip to the local pumpkin patch is a family tradition, with each child allowed to pick out the biggest pumpkin he or she can carry. A face is designed for each one, then all those pumpkins are carved up and turned into jack-o'-lanterns. "Carving the pumpkins isn't so bad," Sandy says, "it's the pumpkin seed fights that get messy…and it's usually my husband who starts them!" Sandy is pretty good-natured about it all, and says she doesn't really mind "as long as they agree to clean up afterward!"

Bring the spirit of Halloween to your home with these easy projects Sandy designed and made from felt. A couple of quick wallhangings and some cozy pillows can add just the right touch. A whimsical cat pin and a pumpkin mini-purse would make a special Halloween treat for your favorite little girl.

MATERIALS

- ½ yard each of blue felt, cream felt, and blue plaid flannel for background and backing
- Scraps of black, brown, green, orange, yellow, and white felt for appliqués
- Gray, green, and gold embroidery floss
- Black pearl cotton
- 18" x 24" sheet of tracing paper

Finished size 16" x 22"

CUTTING

1. Cut one 18" x 24" rectangle each from the blue felt, cream felt, and blue plaid flannel.
2. Referring to the General Instructions on page 6, trace and cut out the following appliqué pieces: One sun, one bird body, two bird wings, one bird beak, one chicken body, one comb, one wattle, one chicken beak, three chicken spots, one cat body, one cat head, one large pumpkin, one large stem, one leaf, and three flowers.

ASSEMBLY

1. Fold the tracing paper lengthwise in half, and trace the half heart pattern from pages 112-113 onto the paper. Cut out the pattern and unfold the paper. Place the pattern on the blue felt rectangle; trace and cut out the heart. Center the blue heart on the blue plaid rectangle and pin the layers together.
2. Position the appliqués within the heart shape, using the photo as a guide to placement and layering as indicated by the dashed lines on the patterns. Remove the blue hart. Stitch the appliqués in place with black pearl

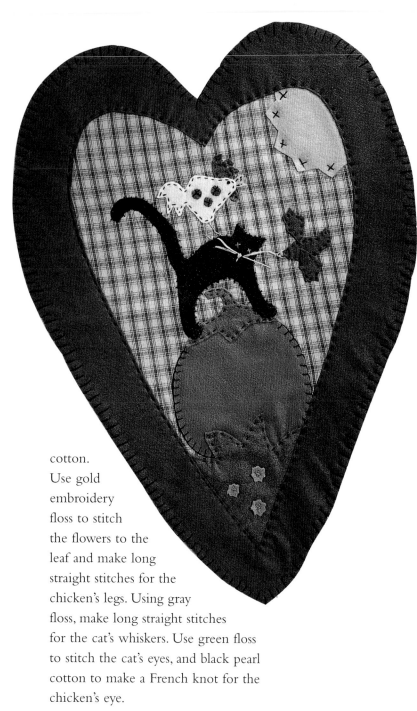

Finished size 12" x 20"

MATERIALS

- ½ yard each of cream felt, black felt, and brown plaid flannel for background and backing
- Scraps of black, blue, gold, green, orange, and white felt for appliqués
- Black and gold pearl cotton
- 12" x 20" sheet of tracing paper

CUTTING

1. Cut one 12" x 20" rectangle each from the cream felt, black felt, and brown plaid flannel.
2. Referring to the General Instructions on page 6, trace and cut out the following appliqué pieces: Scarecrow head, eyes, nose, mouth, hat, crow, shirt, collar, seven shirt patches, pants, two knee patches, and letters to spell the word "Boo."

ASSEMBLY

1. Fold the sheet of tracing paper in half, then in half again. Trace the background pattern from page 115 onto the sheet of paper. Cut out the pattern and unfold the paper. Place the pattern on the cream felt rectangle; trace and cut out the background.
2. Using the photo as a guide to placement, position the appliqués on the cream background. Stitch the pieces in place using black pearl cotton. Use gold pearl cotton and long straight stitches to make the straw

cotton. Use gold embroidery floss to stitch the flowers to the leaf and make long straight stitches for the chicken's legs. Using gray floss, make long straight stitches for the cat's whiskers. Use green floss to stitch the cat's eyes, and black pearl cotton to make a French knot for the chicken's eye.

3. Place the blue plaid rectangle on the cream felt rectangle, aligning the edges, and lay the blue heart on top; pin the layers together. Trim the blue plaid and the cream rectangles even with the outside edge of the heart. Using black pearl cotton, stitch around the inside edge of the heart with a running stitch, sewing through all three layers. Stitch around the outside edge of the wallhanging with a long, irregular blanket stitch.

Finished size 15" square

MATERIALS

- ½ yard of brown plaid flannel for front and back
- 9" x 12" piece of blue felt
- Scraps of orange, black, green, white, brown, and yellow felt
- 1 yard of yellow rickrack
- Gray, green, and yellow embroidery floss
- Black pearl cotton
- Polyester stuffing

CUTTING

1. From the brown plaid flannel, cut two 16" squares. From the blue felt, cut one 8½" x 9¼" rectangle.
2. Referring to the General Instructions on page 6, trace and cut out the following appliqué pieces: Small pumpkin, small stem, cat head, cat arm, cat tail, chicken body, comb, wattle, chicken beak, and three chicken spots.

ASSEMBLY

1. Using the photo as a guide to placement, position the appliqués on the blue felt rectangle, layering as indicated by the dashed lines on the patterns. Stitch the appliqués in place using black pearl cotton. Referring to the pattern as needed, accent the pumpkin with stitching. Use gold floss to make the chicken's legs, gray floss to make the cat's whiskers, and green floss to stitch the cat's eyes. Add a black French knot for the chicken's eye.

hands and feet.

3. Center the cream background on the brown plaid rectangle and pin the layers together. Blanket-stitch around the edges of the background with black pearl cotton.
4. Press under ¼" on all sides of the brown plaid rectangle. Center the rectangle on the black felt rectangle, and pin the layers together. Using a running stitch and gold pearl cotton, stitch around the outside edges of the brown plaid rectangle. Stitch around the outside edge of the cream felt and again just inside the line of blanket stitches. Trim the edges of the black felt with pinking shears.

2. Machine-stitch the yellow rickrack to the edge of the rectangle, sewing very close to the edge of the felt with matching thread.

3. Center the rectangle diagonally on one of the flannel squares and pin in position. Using black pearl cotton, sew the rectangle to the flannel with an irregular straight stitch, taking one stitch between each scallop of the rickrack.

4. Place the stitched front right sides together with the pillow back. Sew with a ½" seam allowance, leaving an opening for turning. Turn the pillow right side out and stuff. Sew the opening closed.

5. Using black pearl cotton, sew running stitches around the outside of the pillow, ½" in from the edge of the pillow, to create a narrow decorative flange.

Pumpkin Patch Accents

MATERIALS

- Scraps of black, green, and orange felt
- Black, green, and orange pearl cotton
- Small amount of polyester stuffing
- 1 yard of ⅛" black satin cord
- ½" button
- Pinback

1. To make the black cat pin, trace and cut out the following pattern pieces from page 117: Two large cat heads, two bow ties, one cat pin stem, and one nose.

2. Using orange pearl cotton, center and stitch the nose to one of the cat heads. Referring to the photo, stitch the mouth and eyes on the face. To add the whiskers, thread a needle with a 4" length of black pearl cotton. Take a single stitch very close to the nose, remove the needle, and tie the thread in a knot to secure. Repeat on the opposite side of the nose.

3. Position the stem on the cat's head, and stitch in place with running stitches, continuing the stitching around the entire edge of the stem.

4. Place the stitched head on the second cat head, aligning the edges. Using running stitches, sew the two layers together about ⅛" in from the edge. Stop stitching about 1" from the starting point, place a small amount of stuffing inside, and complete the line of stitching to close the opening.

5. Layer the two bow tie pieces together and stitch around the outside edges. Sew the button to the center of the tie. Position the tie under the cat's chin and sew it in place, stitching through the holes in the button.

6. To make the pumpkin mini-purse, trace two mini-purse pumpkins, one mini-purse stem, and the face pieces

from page 117. Cut out the shapes, using pinking shears to cut out the mini-purse pumpkins.

7. Using black pearl cotton, blanket-stitch the stem to one of the pumpkin shapes, continuing the line of stitches around the entire edge of the stem. Stitch the face pieces to the pumpkin.

8. Place the stitched pumpkin on the second pumpkin shape. Sew the two layers together with running stitches, starting at the lower edge of the stem on one side and ending at the lower edge of the stem on the opposite side. The purse will be open at the top, behind the stem.

9. Tack the ends of the satin cord just inside the opening on both sides of the mini-purse.

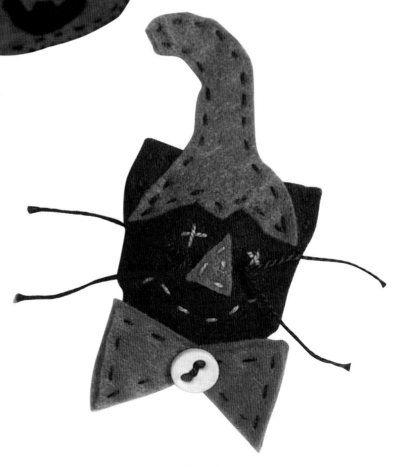

Finished size 12" square

MATERIALS

- ½ yard of brown stripe flannel for background and backing
- Large scraps of black, green, and orange felt for appliqués
- Green and orange pearl cotton
- Polyester stuffing

ASSEMBLY

1. Cut two 13" squares from the brown flannel. Cut one 8½" square from black felt. Trace and cut out one small pumpkin, one stem, and two small leaves from the patterns on page 116.

2. Using the photo as a guide to placement, position the appliqués on the diagonal of the black felt square. Stitch the appliqués in place with green pearl cotton. Accent the pumpkin with stitching as indicated by the dashed lines on the pattern. Create vine tendrils using the pearl cotton and stem stitches.

3. Center the black felt square on one of the brown flannel squares. Using orange pearl cotton, blanket-stitch the edges, and sew running stitches ¼" inside the edges.

4. Place the pillow front right sides together with the back. Stitch with a ½" seam allowance, leaving an opening for turning. Turn right side out through the opening, and stuff. Sew the opening closed.

TRICK OR TREAT BAG

Use the cat appliqué to make a fast and fun trick-or-treat bag. Cut two 9" x 10" rectangles of orange fabric. Appliqué the cat pieces, and add the face details and a bow with embroidery floss or pearl cotton. Turn under a 1" hem on the top edge of both rectangles, and press. Place the rectangles right sides together and sew along the three raw edges with a ½" seam allowance. Thread a needle with a double strand of floss approximately 20" long, and sew long gathering stitches around the top edge of the bag.

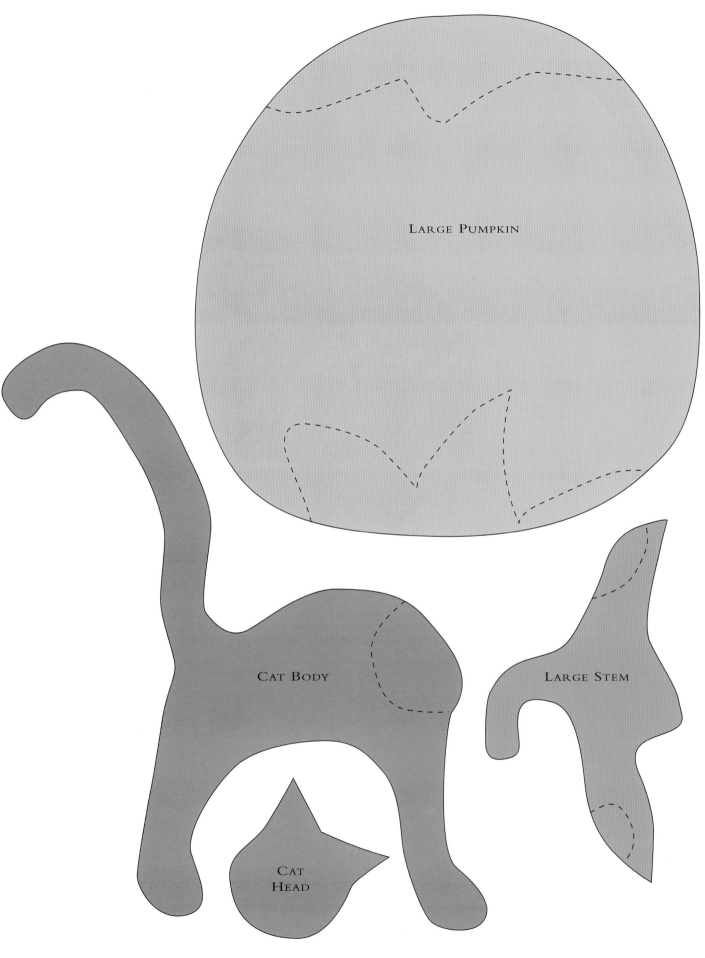

LARGE PUMPKIN

CAT BODY

LARGE STEM

CAT HEAD

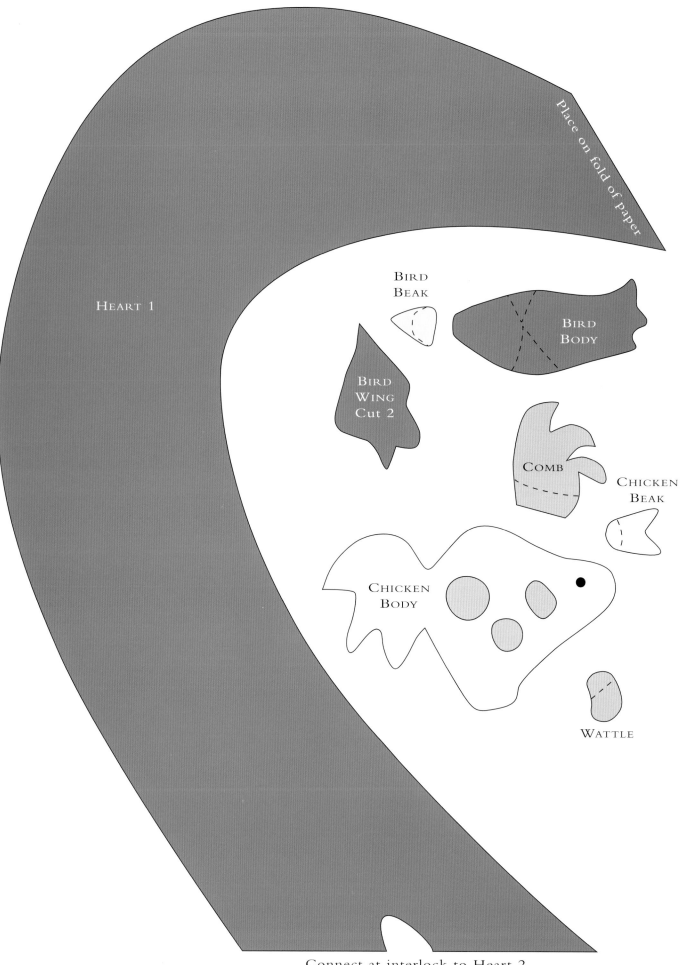

Place on fold of paper

HEART 1

BIRD
BEAK

BIRD
BODY

BIRD
WING
Cut 2

COMB

CHICKEN
BEAK

CHICKEN
BODY

WATTLE

Connect at interlock to Heart 2

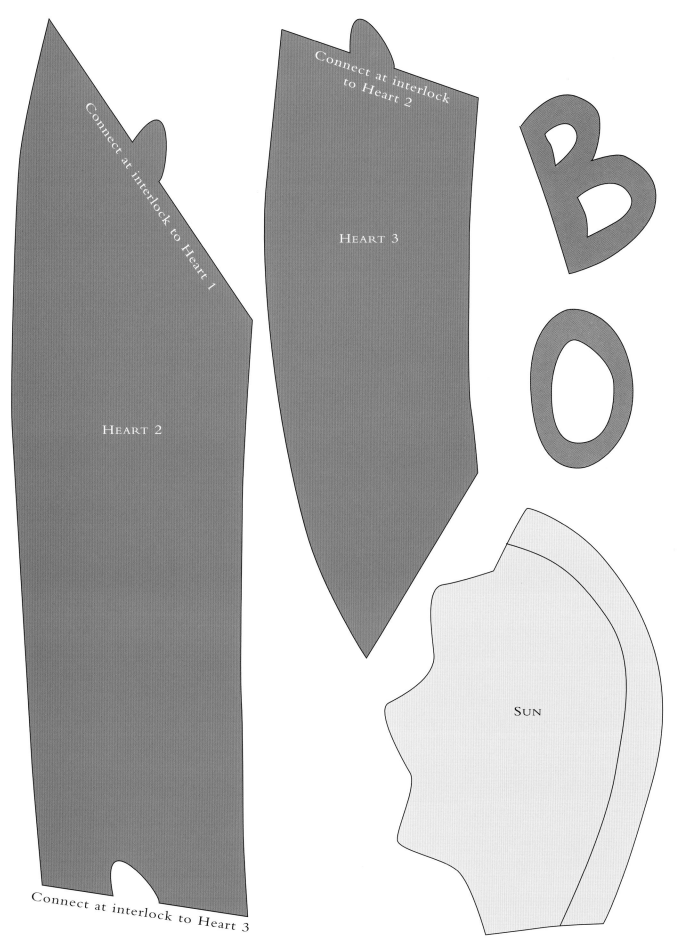

Connect at interlock to Heart 1

Connect at interlock to Heart 2

Heart 3

Heart 2

Connect at interlock to Heart 3

Sun

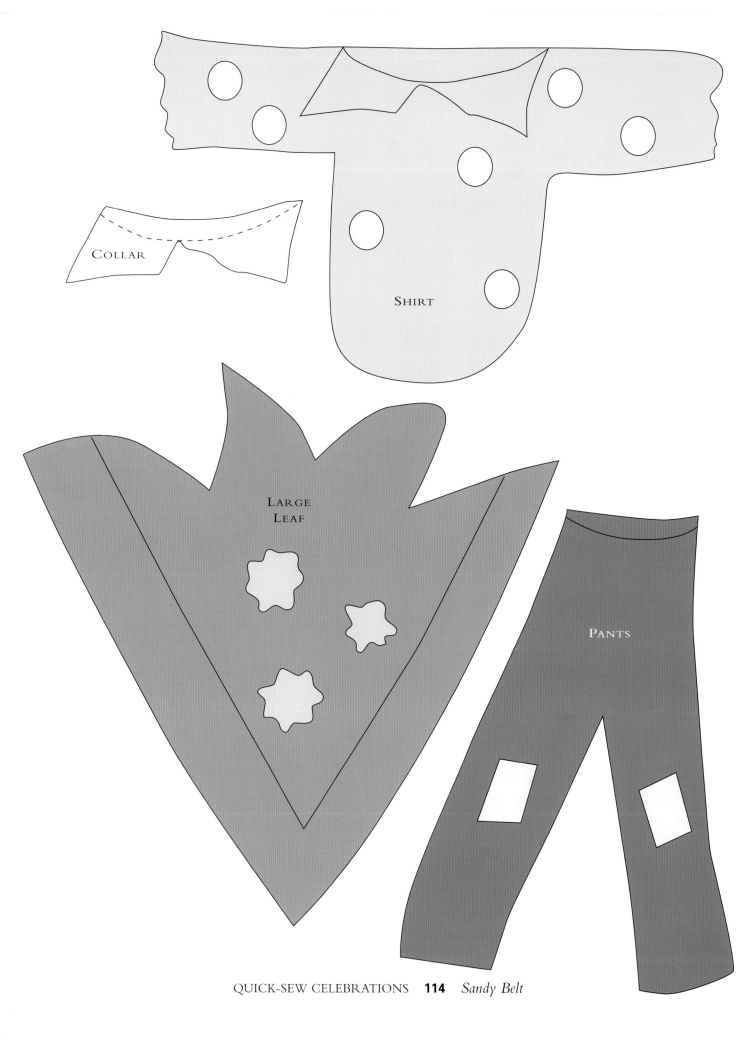

COLLAR

SHIRT

LARGE
LEAF

PANTS

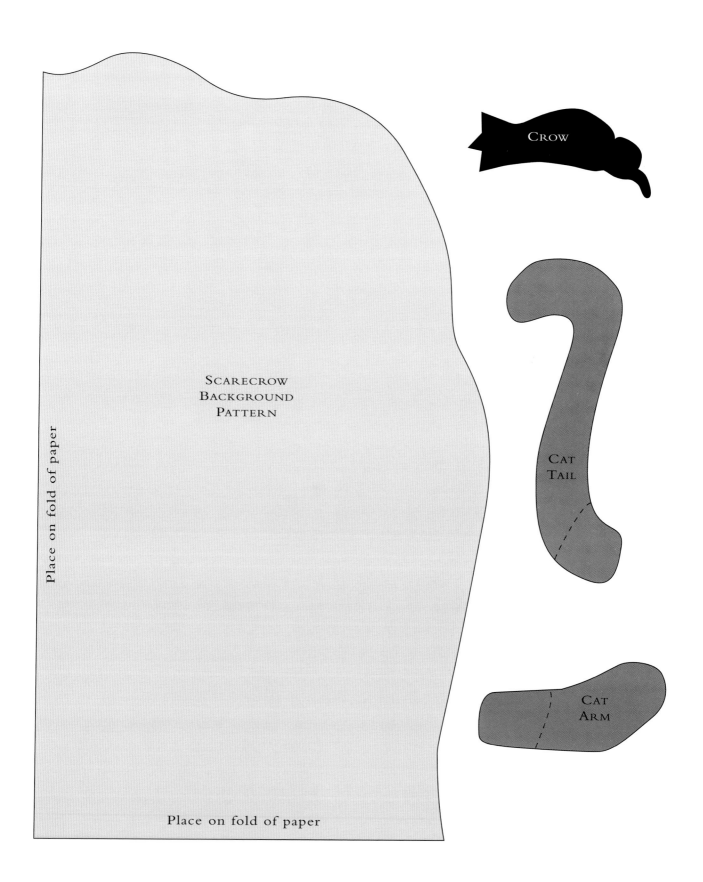

CROW

SCARECROW
BACKGROUND
PATTERN

Place on fold of paper

Place on fold of paper

CAT
TAIL

CAT
ARM

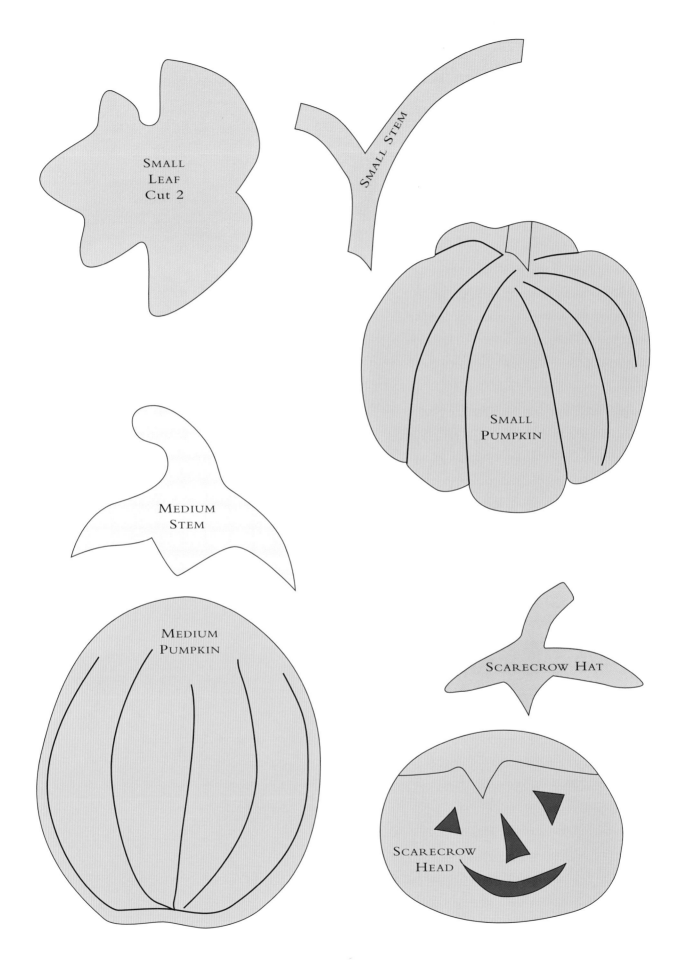

SMALL
LEAF
Cut 2

SMALL STEM

SMALL
PUMPKIN

MEDIUM
STEM

MEDIUM
PUMPKIN

SCARECROW HAT

SCARECROW
HEAD

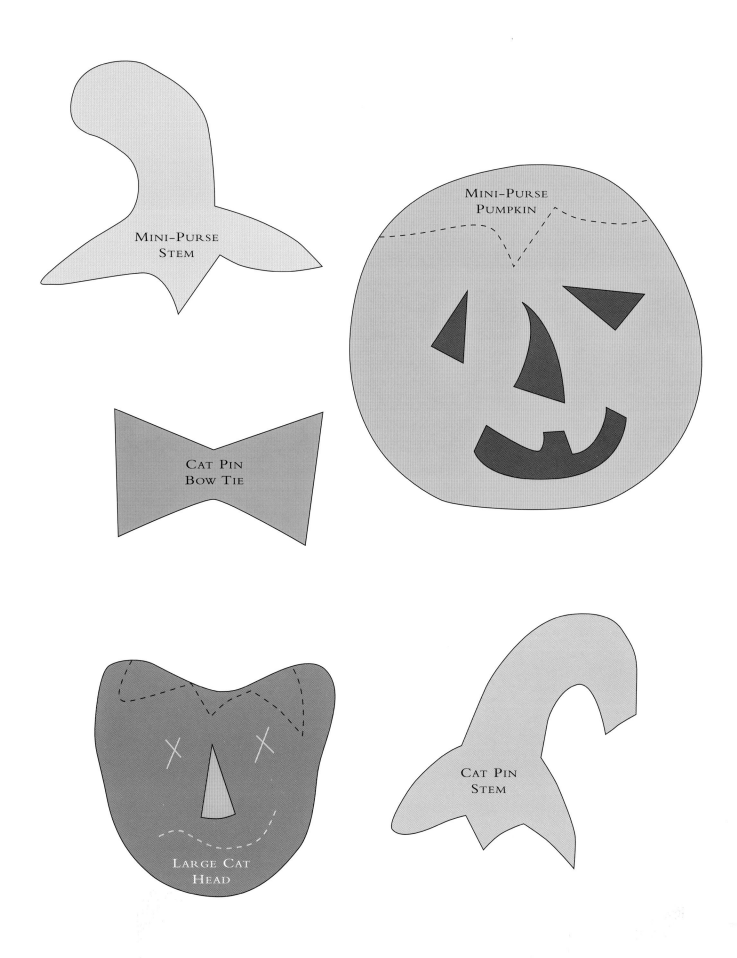

MINI-PURSE
STEM

MINI-PURSE
PUMPKIN

CAT PIN
BOW TIE

LARGE CAT
HEAD

CAT PIN
STEM

Margaret Sindelar

CHRISTMAS WITH A TWIST

When crafts-designer Margaret Sindelar set out to decorate her guest room for the holidays, her goal was to "create a warm and cozy room where someone would feel especially welcome." But Margaret had other, more practical goals, as well. She decided that whatever she designed had to meet certain requirements: It had to be fast and easy, incorporate traditional patterns, and use classic Christmas colors. On top of all that, it had to be reversible so that she could use it throughout the year.

With her checklist in hand, Margaret created this wonderful bedroom ensemble. The simple shapes make construction quick and easy, and the classic colors mean it will never go out of style. The fact that the pieces are reversible means you get two complete looks for the work of one.

Margaret's children are pretty spread-out these days, with a daughter in Denver, a son at the University of Iowa, and another daughter and son-in-law serving in the Peace Corps in Slovakia. She looks forward to the holidays, when they'll all come home to visit. "The only problem is," Margaret says, "everyone's lives are so busy, I'm not sure we'll all be here at the same time. In any event, I have a feeling this room will get lots of use!"

MATERIALS

- 3 yards of cream fabric for blocks
- 2⅝ yards of red fabric for blocks and sashing
- 2⅜ yards of green fabric for blocks and binding
- 2 yards of green print fabric for corner squares and outer border
- ⅝ yard of dark green fabric for inner border
- 6 yards of contrasting fabric for back
- Queen-size batting
- Thirty 1" red buttons
- Thirty 1" buttons to coordinate with backing fabric
- Pearl cotton

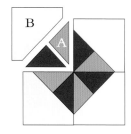

DIAGRAM A

Quick-Sew Quilt

Finished size 82" x 95"

CUTTING

1. From the cream fabric, cut one hundred twenty 5½" squares.
2. From the red fabric, cut sixty 3¾" squares; cut diagonally for two A triangles. Cut seventy-one 3½" x 10½" sashing strips.
3. From the green fabric, cut sixty 3¾" squares; cut diagonally for two A triangles. Cut nine 6" x 44" binding strips.
4. From the green print, cut nine 5½" x 44" strips. Cut forty-two 3½" corner squares.
5. From the dark green fabric, cut eight 1½" x 44" strips.

ASSEMBLY

1. Make a template for B from the pattern on page 126. Place the template on a cream square, align the edges, and trim off the corner. Repeat for all cream squares.
2. Sew a red and a green A triangle together as shown in Diagram A. Sew this unit to a B piece to form a square. Repeat with all remaining red and green triangles and B pieces, making sure the colors are correctly placed each time.
3. Referring to Diagram A, sew four of

the squares together to form a Star Wheel block. Make 30 blocks.

4. Assemble the blocks and sashing strips into rows as shown in Diagram B. Sew the remaining sashing strips and corner squares into alternate rows. Sew the rows together.

5. Sew the 1½"-wide dark green strips end-to-end in pairs. Add the strips to the quilt top, mitering the corners. In the same manner, sew the 5½"-wide green strips together, piecing as needed to achieve the required length. Add them to the quilt top, mitering the corners.

6. Piece the backing fabric. Layer the backing, batting, and quilt top, and baste. Using the pearl cotton, sew a red button to the center of each block, and sew a corresponding button at the same spot on the back of the quilt. Machine-quilt along the edge of the inner border.

7. Trim the backing and batting so that they are ¾" larger than the quilt top on all sides. Prepare the binding strips, referring to the General Instructions for mitered binding on page 7. Pin the binding to the quilt, having the edges even with the batting and backing. Stitch the binding in place with a 1" seam allowance. Bring the folded edges to the back of the quilt and whipstitch in place.

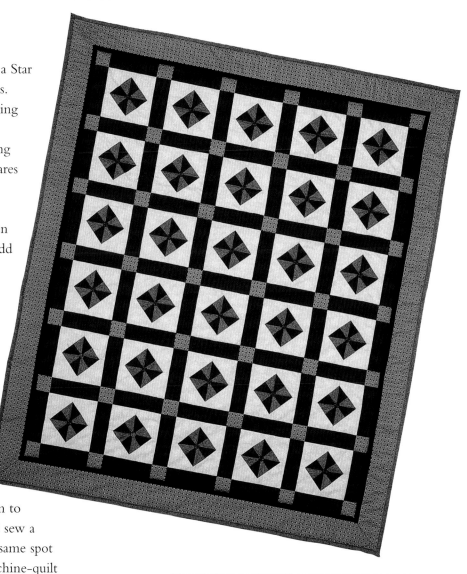

DIAGRAM B

Get two decorating looks at once by making your bedroom ensemble reversible. The items shown in this photo are simply the reverse of those featured on page 119. The back of the Star Wheel quilt is a pretty floral fabric that coordinates with the binding and with the green plaid on the Santa pillow. The bolster pillow is a sumptuous accent that's a snap to make. Simply measure the circumference of the pillow and add several inches for overlap and seam allowances. Measure the width and add about 12". Cut two rectangles of fabric—one to coordinate with each side of the quilt. Place the rectangles right sides together and stitch with a ¼" seam allowance, leaving an opening for turning. Turn right side out, stitch the opening closed, and press. On one short end, add a row of buttonholes, and on the other end, sew a corresponding row of back-to-back buttons. Wrap the rectangle around the pillow, button it on, and tie each end with a tasseled chair tie. The envelope pillow is even easier: Make a two-sided pillowcase that's the width of the pillow and 1½ times its length. Insert the pillow in the case, and fold the excess over as a flap. Add a row of buttons to the flap for a decorative touch.

20" square

MATERIALS

- 1¼ yards of green plaid fabric for ruffle and back

- Fat quarter or large scrap of tan fabric for background

- ⅛ yard each of red and red-and-green print fabrics for patchwork

- Large scraps of red, white-on-white, and flesh color fabrics for appliqués

- Scraps of red, pink, peach, green, and white fabrics for appliqués

- Fusible web

- Fabric stabilizer

- 2 yards of red sew-in piping

- Black and blue embroidery floss

- Red, white, gray, peach, and pink rayon thread

- 14" square pillow form

- Five red beads

- 24 small black bugle beads

- Large red jingle bell

- Powder blush

CUTTING

1. From the green plaid fabric, cut a 14½" square. Cut 7"-wide bias strips, and sew them together end-to-end to make a 120" strip.

2. From the tan fabric, cut a 9½" square.

3. From the red fabric, cut four 3" squares. From the red-and-green print fabric, cut four 3" x 9½" rectangles.

4. Refer to the General Instructions on page 6 to trace, apply fusible web to, and cut out the following appliqué pieces from the scrap fabrics: Santa's hat, hat trim, holly leaves, face, eyebrows, cheeks, mustache, mouth, and beard. Cut out the white part of each eye only; the irises are stitched with floss.

ASSEMBLY

1. Sew a 3" x 9½" rectangle to opposite sides of the tan square. Sew a red square to each end of the two remaining rectangles; sew these to the top and bottom of the pillow top.

2. Center the appliqué pieces on the pillow top. For best results, remove the backing and position all the pieces, checking their placement, before fusing any of them. Fuse. Line the pillow top with stabilizer. Machine-appliqué around all pieces using satin

stitches and matching rayon threads. Satin-stitch the eyes with blue floss. With black floss, add French knot pupils and straight-stitch eyelashes. Sew on red beads for holly berries and black bugle beads to decorate the hat trim.

3. Pin the piping to the right side of the pillow top, aligning the raw edges. Stitch with a ¼" seam allowance.

4. To make the ruffle, fold the 120" strip in half lengthwise, wrong sides together, and press. Sew a long gathering stitch ¼" from the raw edge. Divide the ruffle into quarters and mark. Place the ruffle on the pillow top, right sides together, raw edges even, and quarter marks pinned at the midpoint of each side. Pull the gathering thread so the ruffle fits the pillow top. Stitch the ruffle in place on top of the piping.

5. Place the pillow front and back right sides together with the ruffle inside, out of the seam area. Stitch with a ¼" seam allowance, leaving an opening for turning. Trim the corners, and turn right side out. Insert the pillow form. Stitch the opening closed. Stitch the jingle bell to the hat and add powder blush to cheeks and nose.

Star Wheel Tree Garland

Approximately 48"

MATERIALS

- Scraps of red, green, tan, and red-and-green print fabrics
- 14" x 16" sheet each of red and green card stock paper
- Fusible web
- The following beads: sixteen 18 x 21mm moss oval; sixteen 14 x 8.5mm moss cushion; thirteen 18 x 21mm red clay oval; eight 18 x 11mm gold cushion; seven 6mm gold round; seven 25mm sunburst
- Fifteen ½" gold sleigh bells
- 2 yards of red cotton craft string
- Red and gold embroidery floss
- Pinking shears
- Tapestry needle

ASSEMBLY

1. Referring to the General Instructions on page 6, apply fusible web to and cut out sixteen 1½" red fabric squares and sixteen 1½" green fabric squares. Cut each square in half diagonally. Trim the edges with pinking shears.

2. Arrange the triangles into the Star Wheel design on a piece of green paper as shown in Diagram C, leaving a slight space between the pieces. Fuse the triangles to the paper. Cut out the green paper square with pinking shears, cutting ⅛" outside the design.

3. Fuse the green square to a piece of red paper. Using pinking shears, cut out the red paper, cutting ⅛" outside the green paper. Repeat to make three more Star Wheel blocks.

4. To make the trees, trace the outline of the tree pattern from page 129 onto red paper. Trace, apply fusible web to, and cut out nine green triangles,

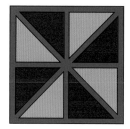

DIAGRAM C

18 red-and-green print triangles, and three tan trunks. Trim the pieces with pinking shears. Arrange them on the red paper, leaving a slight space between the pieces; fuse. With pinking shears, cut out along the traced lines.

5. Fuse the red tree onto green paper. Using pinking shears, cut out ⅛" from the design. Make two more trees.

6. Make a knot approximately 12" from one end of the craft string. Using the photo as a guide, string the beads in the following order: red clay oval, moss oval, moss cushion, gold cushion, moss cushion, moss oval, red clay oval. Leave a space for a Star Wheel block, then repeat the sequence twice, then leave another space. Continue in this manner until all the beads have been strung. Knot the string, leaving approximately 12" free at the end.

7. Thread the tapestry needle with gold floss. Sew a sunburst bead onto the center of a Star Wheel block, securing it with a gold bead. Tie the block onto the garland with red floss.

STAR WHEEL STOCKING

Use the Star Wheel block to make a patchwork front for your favorite stocking pattern. Simply make enough complete blocks to cover the stocking pattern, plus seam allowances. Sew the blocks together as shown in the diagram. Pin the stocking pattern to the patchwork and cut out around the pattern. (The stocking shown was made extra long so that the top could be turned down as a cuff.) Cut a back and two lining pieces from contrasting fabric, and assemble the stocking.

Embellish the stocking as desired. The one shown has red sew-in piping around the edges, and a pretty gold bead at the center of each block.

8. Using gold floss, stitch five gold sleigh bells to each tree. Add a sunburst and bead at the top. Tie the tree to a red clay bead on the garland. Add two trees and three Star Wheel blocks to complete the garland.

Triangle Tree Table Topper

24" diameter

MATERIALS

- 1¼ yards of red fabric for sashing, back, and binding
- ⅜ yard of red-and-green print fabric for patchwork
- ¼ yard of green fabric for patchwork
- ⅛ yard or large scrap of tan fabric for patchwork
- 26" square of thin batting
- Six 1" gold star buttons
- Ten each red, green, and gold ¼" sleigh bells
- Twenty-four 2½" gold tassels

CUTTING

1. From red fabric, cut a 26" square and four 1½" x 44" strips. Cut six E and six E reverse pieces using the pattern on page 127. Cut enough 1½"-wide bias strips to make 80" of binding.
2. From the red-and-green print fabric, cut 36 C triangles.
3. From the green fabric, cut 18 C triangles.
4. From the tan fabric, cut six D pieces.

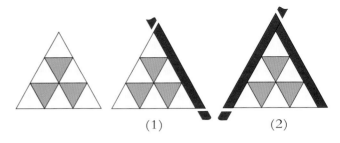

(1)   (2)

DIAGRAM D

ASSEMBLY

1. Referring to the photo, sew the triangles together in rows, then sew the rows together to form the larger triangle.
2. Place a 1½" x 44" red strip face down on the right-hand side of the pieced triangle, aligning the raw edges. Stitch with a ¼" seam allowance, and press the strip open. Trim the top and bottom even with the triangle, as shown in Diagram D(1). In the same manner, place the strip on the left side of the triangle. Stitch, press, and trim the excess as shown in Diagram D(2).

3. Sew the E and E reverse pieces to opposite sides of the tan D trunk. Stitch the trunk section to the tree as shown in Diagram E. Repeat to make five more triangle trees.

4. Sew the triangle trees together in two sets of three, then join the halves to complete the quilt top. Layer the backing, batting, and quilt top, and baste. Machine quilt as desired. Finish the outside edge with a 1/4" bias binding, preparing the strips as directed on page 7 in the General Instructions.

5. Sew five sleigh bells to each tree and add a star button at the top. Add two tassels to the outside edge at each tree trunk and sashing seam.

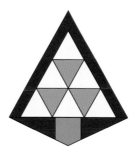

DIAGRAM E

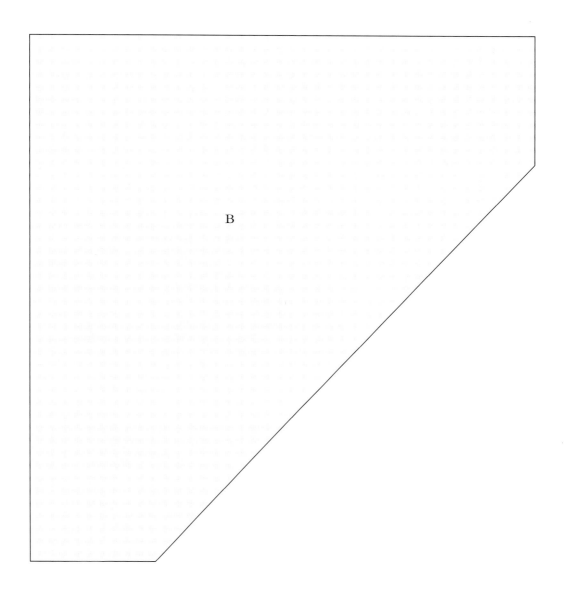

B

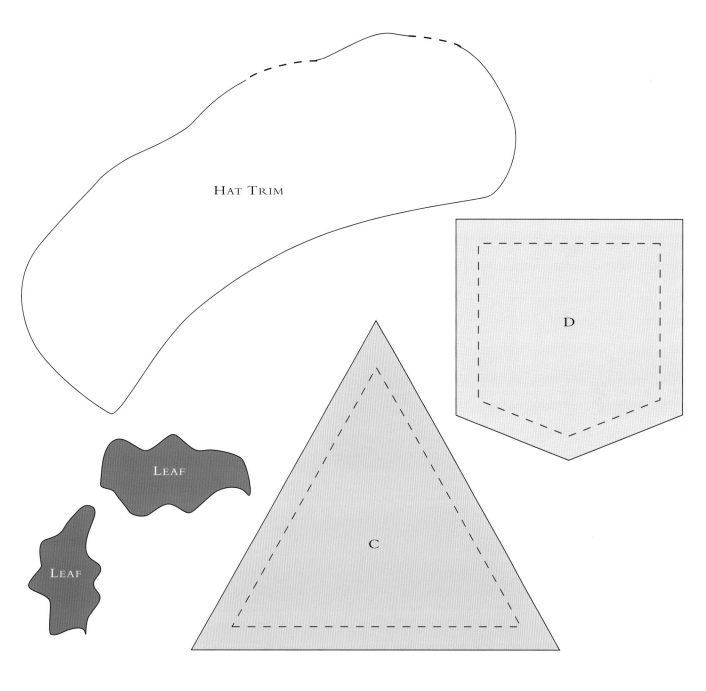

HAT TRIM

LEAF

LEAF

C

D

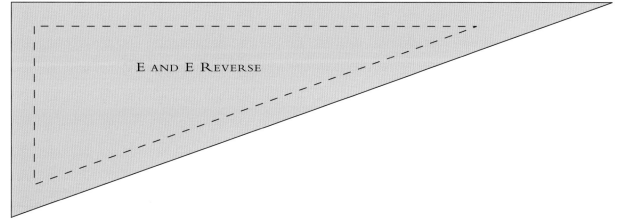

E and E Reverse

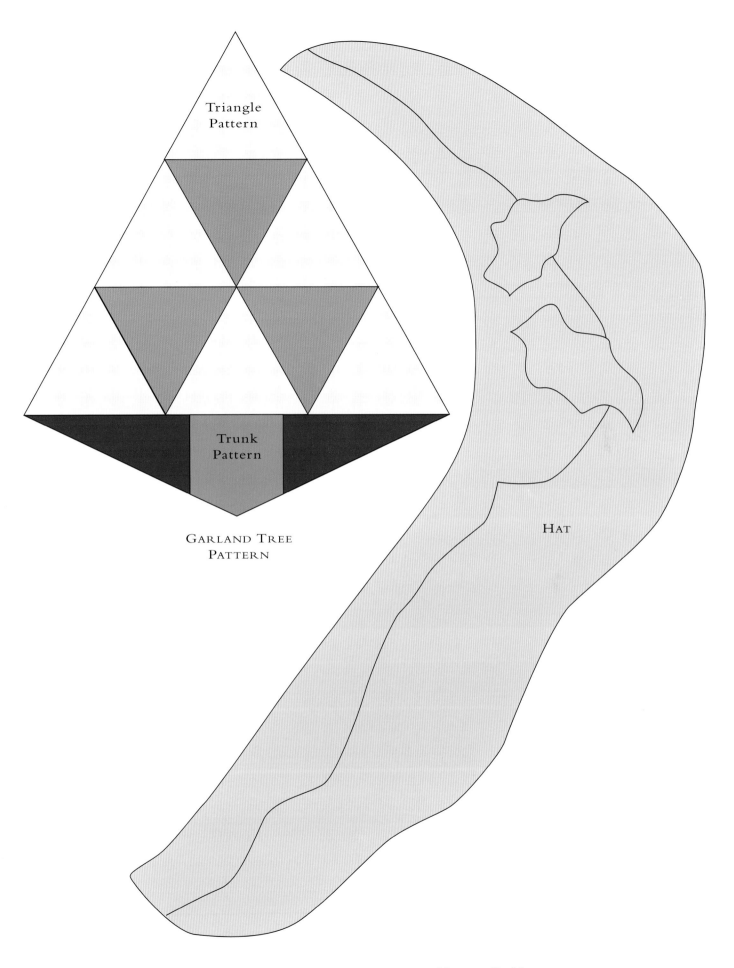

Triangle
Pattern

Trunk
Pattern

GARLAND TREE
PATTERN

HAT

Suellen Wassem

WILDFLOWER WEDDING

I t was a happy coinci-dence that Suellen's son and future daughter-in-law, Heath and Becky, were planning their wed-ding just as she was designing this collection. Their plans provided not only inspiration but the color scheme and theme, as well. The colors co-ordinate with the bridesmaids' navy blue dresses. And the wildflowers are Suellen's way of fulfilling the bride's wish: It seems Becky wants wildflowers at her wedding, but cannot have them because of her sister's allergies. Suellen's solution was to work the wildflowers into the collection. The wildflower motif may also help to remind the wedding guests of the sea-son. An early spring wedding is planned but, Suellen says, "Since the wedding is in Rochester, New York, I'm afraid it might be spring only in our imaginations!"

Suellen's charming collec-tion of keepsakes makes a perfect wedding gift. Guests can record their names and sentiments in the guest book or on the wallhanging itself. An album provides ample room for photos and mementos, and the keepsake box is a special place to store small treasures.

MATERIALS

- 3½ yards of navy print fabric for borders, backing, and binding
- ⅞ yard of cream solid for piecing
- ¼ yard each of the follow-ing fabrics for piecing and appliqués: two different red prints, red mini check, red homespun, tan homespun, blue plaid, blue print, green homespun, and black print
- Scraps of 20 to 30 medium and dark print and plaid fabrics for piecing
- 50" square of batting
- Navy and light gold embroidery floss
- Navy Pigma .05 pen
- Fusible web

Quick-Sew Wallhanging

Finished size 46" square

CUTTING

1. From navy print fabric, cut the following borders: two each 5½" x 46½", 5½" x 36½", 2½" x 24½", 2½" x 20½", 1½" x 14½" and 1½" x 12½". Cut five 2½" x 44" strips for the binding.

2. From cream solid fabric, cut one 12½" square center block, four 5½" corner squares, and forty 3⅞" squares, cut diagonally for 80 triangles.

3. From one red print, tan homespun, blue plaid, and blue print fabrics, cut four 3⅞" squares each. Cut the squares diagonally.

4. From medium and dark scraps, cut two 3⅞" squares of each fabric for a total of 40 squares; cut the squares diagonally.

5. Refer to the General Instructions on page 6 to trace, apply fusible web to, and cut out the following appliqué shapes: One large heart, one medium heart, six corner flowers plus two cen-ter pieces for each flower, six extra large flowers plus a center for each,

14 large leaves, and four vine pieces (two and two reversed). For the vines, trace the patterns onto white paper, joining the pieces. Trace two vines from the front and two from the back of the paper to make right and left vines.

ASSEMBLY

1. Stitch two 1½" x 12½" navy borders to opposite sides of the center square. Add the two 1½" x 14½" borders to the top and bottom.

2. Place the square on the diagonal. Write the words "To have and to hold from this day forward" along the bottom edges of the cream block, using a navy Pigma pen. You may want to pencil in the words first, then darken the lines with the pen. Write the names of the bride and groom along the top edges. Embellish the writing as desired.

3. Center the two hearts on the cream block, and fuse in place. Blanket-stitch around the hearts using four strands of navy floss. Outline-stitch "Love" in the medium heart. With the Pigma pen, write the wedding date on both sides of the large heart.

4. Piece the four corner units as shown in Diagram A, and sew them to the center square. Layer and fuse a corner flower, black center, and tan homespun center in each corner block.

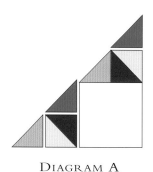

DIAGRAM A

Using floss, blanket-stitch around each appliqué piece.

5. Stitch a 2½" x 20½" border strip to the top and bottom of the center block, then add the 2½" x 24½" border strips to the sides.

6. Piece 80 bias-square units from the cream solid and medium and dark print and plaid fabrics. Sew the squares into four rows of eight squares each, and four rows of twelve squares each. Sew the rows together in pairs. Sew the shorter rows to the top and bottom of the center block, then sew the longer rows to the sides.

7. Add the 5½" x 36½" border strips to the top and bottom of the quilt top, then add the 5½" x 46½" border strips to the sides.

8. Referring to the photo, position and fuse the flowers, vines, and leaves on the borders. Blanket-stitch around all appliqué pieces using four strands of floss. Outline-stitch the stamens.

FINISHING

1. Press the completed top and take it to the wedding for the guests to sign, or mark quilting lines as desired. Refer to the General Instructions on page 7 to layer the wallhanging.

2. Quilt as desired. Trim the edges of the layers even. Prepare the binding strips and a hanging sleeve as directed on page 7. Sew the binding in place using a ¼" seam allowance; turn to the back and whipstitch in place.

10½" x 11⅝"

MATERIALS

- ½ yard of cream solid fabric for cover
- ⅓ yard of navy print fabric for cording
- ⅛ yard each or scraps of red print, red homespun, blue plaid, and green homespun fabrics for appliqués
- Fusible web
- ½ yard of thin fleece
- 2 yards of ¹⁄₁₆" cording
- Navy and green embroidery floss
- Navy Pigma .05 pen
- Plain 10½" x 11⅝" photo album or three-ring binder
- Large sheet of plain paper

ASSEMBLY AND APPLIQUÉ

1. Open the album flat on a large sheet of paper; trace around the outside edges. Add a scant ¼" on all sides to allow for ease, plus an additional ½" seam allowance on the long sides and 1" on the short sides. Cut out the pattern.

2. Using the paper pattern, cut one layer of cream fabric and one piece of thin fleece. From the remaining cream fabric, cut two facing pieces the same height as the pattern but about 2"

shorter in width than the inside cover.

3. With the album open, measure along the top edge, down the front, and along the bottom edge. Cut the cording to this length, plus an extra inch or two. Cut enough 1½"-wide navy bias strips to cover the cording. Sew the strips together end to end to make one long strip. Using matching thread, cover the cording with the bias strip.

4. Using a ½" seam allowance, baste the cording to the right side of the cream fabric cover, aligning the raw edges. Begin at the back top corner, work along the top edge, around the front, and finally along the bottom edge. See Diagram B. Trim excess cording. Clip the seam allowance at the corners.

DIAGRAM B

5. Using a black permanent marker, write the words "Our Wedding Memories" and the couple's names on the pattern. Refer to the General Instructions on page 6 to trace, apply fusible web to, and cut out the following appliqué pieces: One large flower and flower center, two medium flowers and flower centers, three medium leaves, two small hearts, and two medium vines (one and one reversed).

6. Pin the cream fabric onto the paper pattern. Trace the lettering using the navy Pigma pen, embellishing the

writing as desired. Use a light box under the paper pattern if necessary. Position and fuse the appliqué shapes. If necessary, trim the horizontal vine slightly to fit the space.

7. Remove the paper pattern, and place the thin layer of fleece under the cream fabric. Stitch in place following the basting on the cording. Cut away the fleece from the seam allowances. Blanket-stitch the appliqués using three strands of floss.

8. Stitch a ¼" hem in one long side of each facing piece. Pin one facing piece to the right side of the cover, aligning the raw edges. Stitch in place, again following the previous stitching beside the cording. Trim the corners close to the stitching. Turn right side out and press.

9. Insert the album into the stitched end of the cover and check the fit; remove. Turn the cover inside out, pin the other facing piece in place, and baste. Turn right side out and slip the cover on the book again to check the fit. You may need to take a narrower or wider seam allowance. When pleased with the fit, stitch, and then trim the corners. Turn right side out and press. Insert the album into the cover.

Guest Book

5½" x 7½"

MATERIALS

- ⅓ yard of cream solid fabric for cover
- ¼ yard of navy print fabric for cording
- Scraps of red print, and red and green homespun fabrics for appliqués
- ¾ yard of ¹⁄₁₆" cording
- Scraps of fusible web
- ¼ yard of thin fleece
- Navy, green, and yellow embroidery floss
- ⅓ yard of ½"-wide satin ribbon
- One brass heart charm
- Navy Pigma .05 pen
- One large sheet of plain paper
- Plain 5½" x 7½" guest book

1. Follow the instructions for the Wedding Album, Steps 1 through 4, to create a paper pattern; cut the fabric and fleece, and add covered cording.

2. Using a black permanent marker, write the words "Guests of" and the couple's names onto the paper pattern. Refer to the General Instructions on page 6 to trace, apply fusible web to, and cut out the following appliqué pieces: Three small flowers, three small leaves, two small hearts, and two small vines (one and one reversed).

3. Pin the cream fabric onto the paper pattern. Trace the lettering using the navy Pigma pen. Use a light box under the pattern if necessary. Position and fuse the appliqué shapes. If necessary, trim the vertical vine to fit the space.

4. Remove the paper pattern, and place the thin layer of fleece under the cream fabric; stitch in place following the basted cording line. Cut away the fleece from the seam allowances. Blanket-stitch the appliqués using three strands of floss.

5. Stitch a ½" hem in one short side of each facing piece. Pin one piece to the right side of the cover, aligning the raw edges. Stitch in place, again following the stitching line on the cording. Trim the corners close to the stitching. Turn right side out and press.

6. Insert the book into the stitched end of the cover and check for fit; remove. Turn the cover inside out, pin the other facing piece in place, and baste. Turn right side out and slip the cover on the book to check for fit; you may need to take a narrower or wider seam allowance. When you are pleased with the fit, stitch, and then trim the corners and turn right side out. Press. Insert the book into the completed cover.

7. Tack the ribbon to the inside top edge of the cover. Drape the ribbon over the book and determine the amount you want to extend from the bottom edge. Cut the ribbon and tie a knot at the end. Tack a brass heart at the knot.

Picture Frame

10" x 12"

MATERIALS

- ½ yard of navy fabric
- ¼ yard of red print fabric
- Scraps of red prints, cream plaid, and green homespun fabrics
- 10" x 12" piece of batting
- Scraps of fusible web
- Light gold embroidery floss
- 2 yards of ¹⁄₁₆" cording
- Three pieces of mat board, two 10" x 12" and one 4" x 9"
- Hot-glue gun and glue sticks or white fabric glue
- X-Acto knife or utility knife
- Spray adhesive

1. Find the center of one large mat board as shown in Diagram C, and mark lines with a pencil. Cut out a 3" x 5" paper pattern for the frame opening (larger if desired). Fold the paper in half both ways and crease. Open up, and align the creases on the paper pattern with the lines on the mat. Trace around the paper. Cut out the opening on the traced lines.

2. Lay the mat board on the batting, trace around the inside of the opening, and cut on the traced lines.

3. Apply spray adhesive to the front of the mat board. Center the mat on the batting, adhesive side down, and press.

4. Cut two 12" x 14" pieces from navy fabric. Center the mat board on the wrong side of one piece, leaving 1" of fabric showing on all sides; trace the opening; remove. Cut ½" inside the traced lines, and clip the fabric almost to the corners.

5. Refer to the General Directions on page 6 to trace, apply fusible web to, and cut out one large flower and flower center, three medium leaves, and two small hearts. Position and fuse the appliqué pieces to the fabric, using the photograph on page 135 as a guide to placement. Blanket-stitch around the appliqués using three strands of floss. Press the stitched fabric front.

6. Center the mat board, batting-side down, on the wrong side of the stitched fabric. Bring the fabric in the opening toward the back; glue the top and bottom edges in place first, then the sides. Fold the outside edges to the back and glue.

7. Cut enough 1½"-wide red bias strips to cover 72" of cording. Stitch the

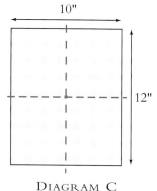

10"

12"

DIAGRAM C

strips together end to end to make one long strip. Using matching thread, cover the cording with the bias strip.

8. Cut two 3½" and two 5½" pieces of covered cording. Glue the 3½" pieces to the inside top and bottom of the picture opening and the 5½" strips to the sides. Let dry.

9. Glue the remaining cording along the outside edges, beginning at the center bottom edge, clipping the seam allowance at the corners and overlapping the ends.

10. For the frame back, cover the remaining large mat board in the same manner as the front, omitting the opening. Cut one 9½" x 11½" piece of navy fabric, and glue to the remaining (inside) surface of the frame back.

11. Place the frame front on the back and glue the sides and bottom together, leaving the top open to insert a photo.

12. Referring to Diagram D, make an easel from the 4" x 9" mat board. Mark the shape on the board as shown, and mark a score line 1" down from the top so that the easel can bend. Cut out the shape, and score the board along the line, being careful not to cut all the way through the mat. Cover with navy fabric and glue the edges. Fold on the score line. Center the easel on the frame back, aligning the bottom edge with the bottom of the frame. Glue the top, above the fold, to the frame back. Insert the picture from the top of the frame.

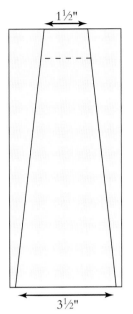

1½"

3½"

DIAGRAM D

10" x 7" x 5"

MATERIALS

- ¾ yard each of navy print and red homespun fabrics for box and box lining
- ¼ yard of red print fabric for box lid and cording
- Scraps of red print, cream solid, and tan homespun fabrics for box lid
- ½ yard of fusible fleece
- Scrap of fusible web
- Navy embroidery floss
- ½ yard of ⅛"-wide red satin ribbon
- Navy quilting thread
- ¾ yard of 1/16" cording
- 15" x 20" piece of cardboard
- Navy Pigma .05 pen
- 3 brass heart charms in various sizes
- Fabric glue

CUTTING

1. From the navy print fabric, cut two 6½" x 1½" strips and two 3½" x 1½" strips for the patchwork top.

2. From the red homespun fabric, cut two 6½" x 1½" and two 3½" x 1½" strips, and two 2" squares cut diagonally.

3. From the cream solid fabric, cut one 3½" x 6½" rectangle. From the tan homespun, cut two 2" squares and cut these diagonally.

4. Refer to the General Instructions on

page 6 to trace, apply fusible web to, and cut the memory box heart pattern on page 142 from a scrap of red print.

5. From the fusible fleece, cut four 7" x 10" pieces for the tops and bottoms, four 5" x 10" pieces for the front and back, and four 5" x 7" sides. You will cut the corresponding fabric pieces later.

6. From the cardboard, cut two 6½" x 9½" pieces for the top and bottom, two 4½" x 9½" pieces for the front and back, and two 4½" x 6½" pieces for the sides.

ASSEMBLY

1. To piece the patchwork top, place the 1½" red and navy strips right sides together in pairs, and sew with a ½" seam allowance. Sew the red and tan homespun triangles together into squares. Sew the squares to the ends of the 6½" strips, referring to the photo as needed for correct color placement. Sew the 3½" strips to the short sides of the cream rectangle. Join the three rows as shown in Diagram F.

2. Using a black marker, trace the heart from page 142 and write the words

DIAGRAM F

"Two souls in one" and "Two hearts into one heart" onto white paper. Pin the patchwork top onto the paper with the cream fabric over the lettering. Place the heart appliqué in position and fuse. Trace the lettering using the navy Pigma pen, embellishing your writing as desired. Remove the paper pattern. Blanket-stitch around the heart using two strands of navy floss. Press the top.

3. Following the manufacturer's directions, adhere the fusible fleece pieces to the wrong side of the navy print and red homespun fabrics, allowing 1" to 2" between the pieces. On the patchwork top, you will have only ½" seam allowance on all edges. Cut out the pieces, adding a ½" fabric margin on all edges.

4. Pin a navy and a red 5" x 7" side piece right sides together; machine-stitch together along one long and two short edges, sewing right next to the fleece edges. Turn right side out. Baste the unstitched edge closed. Repeat for the other side piece, and the front and back pieces. Sew all four sides of the bottom piece, leaving an opening for turning; turn right side out and sew the opening closed. Set aside the top.

5. Pin a 5" x 7" side piece to the bottom piece, navy sides together, matching the closed edges. Using navy quilting thread, whipstitch the pieces together, catching all layers. Repeat with the remaining side and front and back pieces. Now stitch the 5" sides together to form the box. Turn the box right side (navy side) out.

6. Remove the basting stitches from the top edges of all four sides and slip the cardboard pieces between the fabric layers. Turn the seam allowances in and blind-stitch the top edges closed.

7. Cut enough 1½"-wide red bias strips to cover 27" of cording. Sew the strips together end to end to make one long strip. Using matching thread, cover the cording with the bias strip.

8. Using a ½" seam allowance, baste the cording to the wrong side of the patchwork top, starting at the back corner on a 7" side, working across the front and along the other side; tuck in the raw ends.

9. Cut three 9" pieces of ribbon. Thread a brass heart charm onto each piece and tie a knot at the end of each ribbon. Tie all three ribbons together at the opposite end, letting the hearts hang at various lengths. Center and pin the knotted end of the ribbons to the wrong side of the patchwork top.

10. Pin the patchwork top and the lid lining wrong sides together, and blind-stitch the corded edges, allowing the ribbons to dangle away from the lid.

11. Slip a 6½" x 9½" cardboard between the patchwork top and the red lining. Baste the back edge, then place this edge of the lid along the back of the box, right sides together. Pin and then whipstitch in place.

12. Cut an 8" x 11" piece of the lining fabric to cover the 6½" x 9½" bottom cardboard piece. Bring the cut edges to the back of the cardboard and glue in place. Set this covered piece into the bottom of the box.

BALL JAR SCRUNCHY

Here's a clever way to turn a simple canning jar into a charming vase—add a scrunchy! Cut a 3¼" x 16" strip of navy fabric. Hem the short ends, then fold the strip lengthwise, right sides together, and stitch with a ¼" seam allowance. Turn right side out and press. Insert a 1¼" x 12" piece of elastic into the tube, bring the ends together and stitch. Pull the fabric ends together and blindstitch. Trace, apply fusible web to, and cut out assorted flowers and matching centers. Fuse each flower to the wrong side of a matching flower, inserting the end of a piece of wire about 7" long between the layers before fusing. Fuse a flower center in place. Tie a narrow strip of green homespun around each wire below the flower. Gather the stems as you would a bouquet, wrap them together with another wire, and cut the ends even. Whipstitch to the inside of the scrunchy. Cut a ½" x 16" strip of green homespun and tie into a bow. Hot glue the bow at the top edge of the scrunchy, just below the flower stems. Place the scrunchy around a 12½" diameter Ball jar and fill the jar with your favorite wildflowers.

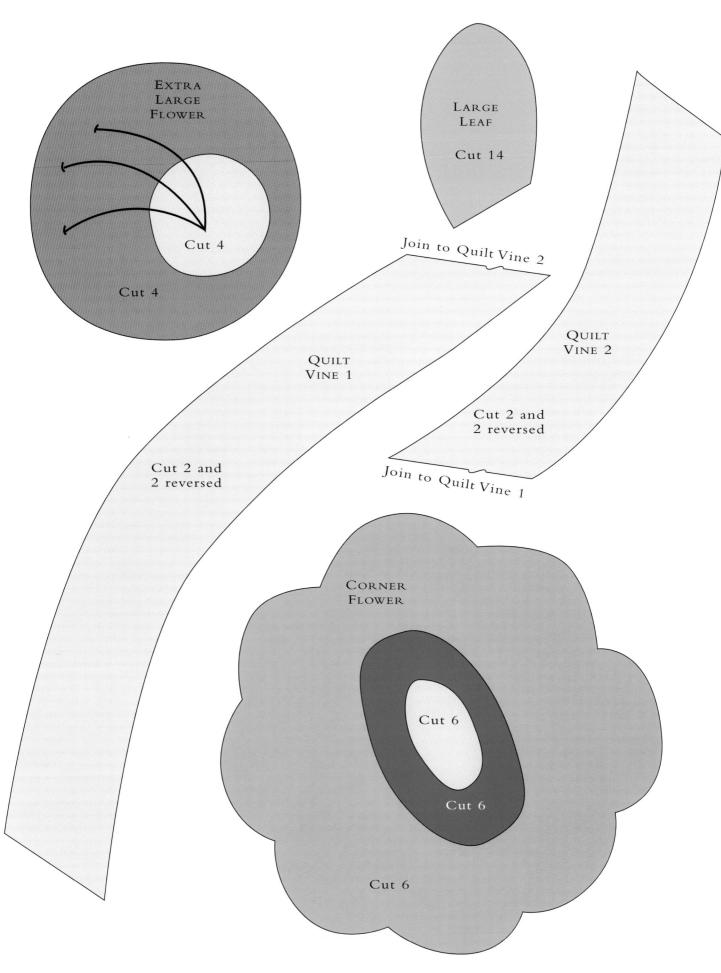

EXTRA LARGE FLOWER

Cut 4

Cut 4

LARGE LEAF

Cut 14

Join to Quilt Vine 2

QUILT VINE 1

QUILT VINE 2

Cut 2 and 2 reversed

Cut 2 and 2 reversed

Join to Quilt Vine 1

CORNER FLOWER

Cut 6

Cut 6

Cut 6

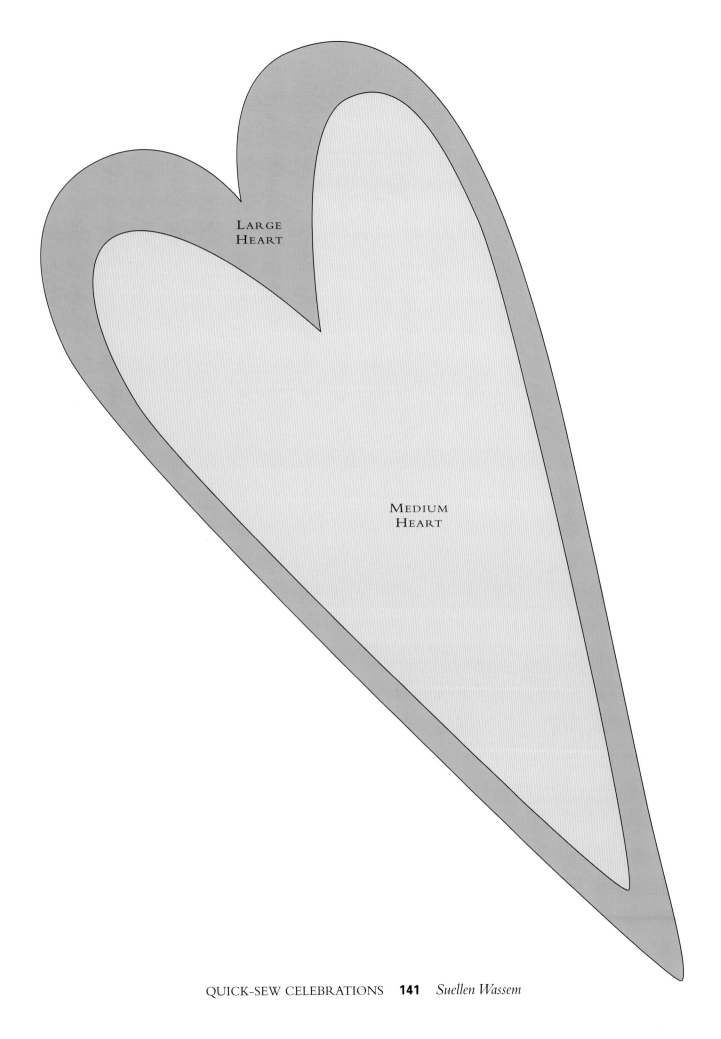

LARGE
HEART

MEDIUM
HEART

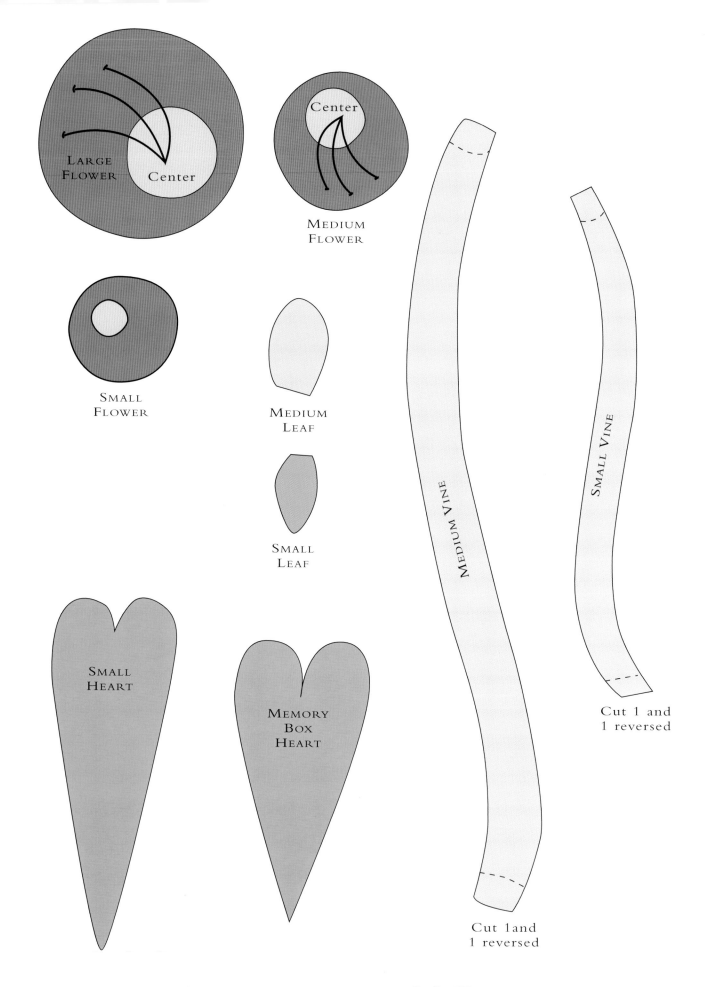

LARGE
FLOWER

Center

Center

MEDIUM
FLOWER

SMALL
FLOWER

MEDIUM
LEAF

SMALL
LEAF

SMALL
HEART

MEMORY
BOX
HEART

MEDIUM VINE

SMALL VINE

Cut 1 and
1 reversed

Cut 1 and
1 reversed

SOURCES

SALLY KORTE AND ALICE STREBEL—*Friendship in Bloom*
In addition to designing unique clothing, quilts, and crafts, Sally and Alice enjoy traveling and teaching, sharing their creativity with others. For more information about their classes, or for a catalog of their patterns, including an extensive line of rug-hooking kits and supplies, send $3 to: Kindred Spirits, 115 Colonial Lane, Dayton, OH 45429; 937/435-7758.

KRIS KERRIGAN—*A Busy Hen's Kitchen*
The projects in this collection feature fabrics from Pieces of my Heart, P.O. Box 112, 1215 E. Elm St., Afton, IA 50511; 515/295-5672. Kris' Button Weeds line includes quick-sew patterns for a variety of home accents, including kitchen sets, appliance covers, and wallhangings. For a catalog, send $2 to: Button Weeds, 1275 Pheasant Avenue, Afton, IA 50830; 515/347-8831.

JANET CARIJA BRANDT—*From Heart to Home*
Janet used hand-dyed cottons from Country House Cottons (319/425-4384) and wool flannel from King's Road Imports (800/433-1546). Other products featured include Fashion Craft™ markers from Sakura of America (510/475-8880), and embroidery floss from The DMC Corp. (201/589-0606). The footstool is from Rubbermaid, Inc. (330/264-6464). For information about Janet's books, contact her at: 2136 Silver Lane Drive, Indianapolis, IN 46203; 317/352-0059.

LYNETTE JENSEN—*Autumn Rose*
The Thimbleberries fabrics featured in Lynette's projects are from the Winter Cottage, Paint Box, and Garden Gate collections, designed by Lynette Jensen for RJR Fashion Fabrics (310/217-9800). The pillow form is from Morning Glory Products (800/234-9105). For a catalog of patterns and books, send $2 to: Thimbleberries, 7 North Main, Department LB, Hutchinson, MN 55350; 320/587-3944.

PATRICE LONGMIRE—*Make a Christmas Wish*
Some of Patrice's projects use Warm & Natural batting from Warm Products, Inc. (800/234-WARM). The projects in this collection are just a sampling of Patrice's extensive line of quilt, craft, and doll designs. For a catalog of her patterns and books, send $2 to: Patrice & Company, 152 East 11th Avenue, Escondido, CA 92025; 619/743-7528.

MCKENNA RYAN—*Catching Memories*
McKenna's designs are inspired by her love of nature and the outdoors, and often feature fish and animal motifs. The Pine Needles line includes patterns, packaged in McKenna's distinctive brown paper bag with raffia ties, plus decorative resin-cast finials and quilt hangers. For a catalog, send $2 to: Pine Needles, P.O. Box 2379, Big Fork, MT 59911; 406/837-0423.

CHERYL JUKICH—*Celebrate—It's Your Day!*
The projects in Cheryl's collection are just a sampling of the many wonderful products coming from the design tables of the Threadbare Pattern Company. The fabrics featured in Cheryl's collection are from Pieces of my Heart, P.O. Box 112, 1215 E. Elm St., Afton, IA 50511; 515/295-5672. Cheryl's extensive line includes an interchangeable embellished vest series and the Quik-Quilt™ collection, which features a technique for turning a humble sweatshirt ino a quilted garment using no batting or lining. For more information about Threadbare Patterns or to order the specialty porcelain buttons featured in the chapter, contact: Threadbare Pattern Company, Department QSQ2, P.O. Box 1484, Havelock, NC 28532; 800/4-Pattern (800/472-8837).

SANDY BELT—*Pumpkin Patch Treats*
The projects in Sandy's collection feature felt from Kunin Felt (603/929-6100), flannel from Moda Fabrics (800/468-4209), and pearl cotton and embroidery floss from The DMC Corp. (201/589-0606). For information about Sandy's book *Folk Art Felt,* or her designs and one-of-a-kind dolls, contact: Town Folk Designs, 6612 U.S. 41 South, Marquette, MI 49855; 906-249-1898.

MARGARET SINDELAR—*Christmas with a Twist*
Margaret used fabrics from the "Roommates" collection, designed by Nancy J. Martin for Clothworks, a division of Fasco/Fabric Sales Co., Inc. (206/762-7886). Other products featured in Margaret's collection include buttons from JHB International (303/751-8100), beads from The Beadery Craft Products (401/539-2432), and trims and tassels from St. Louis Trimming, Inc. (314/771-8388) and Prym Dritz (864/576-5050). The pillow form and batting are from Morning Glory Products (800/234-9105). Margaret used the Viking #1+ Sewing Machine (800/446-2333) for the machine-appliqué. She can be contacted at: Cottonwood Classics, 4813 Cody Drive, West Des Moines, IA 50265; 515/225-8409.

SUELLEN WASSEM—*Wildflower Wedding*
For a catalog of Suellen's project books and patterns, send $2 to: Pieceful Heart Designs, 2715 East Tara Trail, Beavercreek, OH 45434-6256; 937/320-9003.

PROJECT INDEX

MOCHA CHIFFON CAKE

Tia Maria is a coffee-flavoured liqueur.

The imported tube pan we used in this recipe is available from specialty cook ware shops. It measures 21cm across the base and has a 4 litre fluid capacity. The mixture needs to cling to the tube pan so it is important not to grease it. To remove cake from the tube pan, run a spatula around the side of the pan, shake and tap well and the cake will come out easily. Cake can be cooked in a 20cm baba pan; it will take about 1½ hours in a moderately slow oven.

1 cup plain flour
1 cup self-raising flour
1½ cups castor sugar
100g dark chocolate, chopped
2 tablespoons dry instant coffee
¼ cup Tia Maria
½ cup water
½ cup oil
7 eggs, separated
COFFEE ICING
2 cups icing sugar
15g butter
3 teaspoons dry instant coffee
2 tablespoons water
COFFEE LIQUEUR CREAM
300ml carton thickened cream
2 tablespoons Tia Maria

Sift flours and sugar into a large bowl. Combine chocolate, coffee, Tia Maria, water and oil in double saucepan, stir constantly over hot water until smooth. Remove from heat, quickly stir in lightly beaten egg yolks, pour into centre of sifted flour mixture, stir until smooth.

Beat egg whites in large bowl with electric mixer until soft peaks form. Fold a third of the egg whites lightly into cake mixture. Pour cake mixture into remaining whites, fold ingredients together lightly. Pour cake mixture into an ungreased tube pan. Bake in moderately slow oven for about 1¼ hours. Cake should feel firm to the touch and have a slightly sugary crust. Remove from oven, immediately invert tube pan; so the cake is suspended. Cake will not fall out of the pan, leave undisturbed until completely cold. Cover cold cake with icing, serve with cream.

Coffee Icing: Sift icing sugar into small heatproof bowl, stir in butter and combined coffee and water. Stir over hot water until icing is spreadable.

Coffee Liqueur Cream: Beat cream and liqueur until soft peaks form.

Keeping time: 2 days.

ABOVE: Mocha Chiffon Cake.
RIGHT: back: Fudgy Chocolate Cake; front: Frosted Chocolate Yoghurt Cake.

Laminate (Metalli, 874) above from Abet Laminati; china above is Aragon by Kosta Boda; cutlery above is Gold Line by Kosta Boda; background marble is from Metro Marble; plates at right are Marble Buffet by Villeroy & Boch.

FUDGY CHOCOLATE CAKE

185g butter
1/3 cup cocoa
1¼ cups castor sugar
3 eggs, separated
1¼ cups self-raising flour
2/3 cup plain flour
¾ cup water

Grease 2 deep 20cm round cake pans, line bases with paper; grease paper. Cream butter, sifted cocoa and sugar in small bowl with electric mixer until light and fluffy, beat in egg yolks. Transfer mixture to large bowl, fold in sifted flours and water. Beat egg whites in small bowl until soft peaks form, fold lightly into chocolate mixture. Pour into prepared pans, bake in moderately slow oven for about 1¼ hours. Turn on to wire rack to cool. Join cakes with whipped cream and dust with icing sugar if desired.

Keeping time: 2 days.

FROSTED CHOCOLATE YOGHURT CAKE

100g dark chocolate, chopped
½ cup water
185g butter
1 teaspoon vanilla essence
1½ cups brown sugar, firmly packed
3 eggs
½ cup plain yoghurt
2¼ cups self-raising flour
FROSTING
250g dark chocolate
½ cup sour cream
1 cup icing sugar

Grease 2 deep 20cm round cake pans, line bases with paper; grease paper. Melt chocolate and water over hot water; cool. Cream butter, essence and sugar in small bowl with electric mixer until light and fluffy, beat in eggs one at a time, beat until combined. Transfer mixture to large bowl, stir in the chocolate mixture and yoghurt, then sifted flour in 2 lots. Spread into prepared pans. Bake in moderate oven for about 40 minutes. Turn on to wire rack to cool.

Split cold cakes in half, join with ¾ of the frosting. Spread top with remaining frosting. Spread side with whipped cream and toasted almonds.

Frosting: Melt chocolate in heatproof bowl over hot water; stir in sour cream, gradually stir in sifted icing sugar. Refrigerate until frosting is thick.

Keeping time: 2 days.

CHOC-ORANGE MARBLE CAKE

60g dark chocolate, chopped
125g butter
2 teaspoons vanilla essence
1⅓ cups castor sugar
2 eggs
2 cups self-raising flour
¾ cup milk
1 tablespoon grated orange rind
CHOCOLATE FUDGE FROSTING
125g dark chocolate
125g butter
3½ cups icing sugar
¼ cup milk
1 teaspoon vanilla essence

Grease 2 deep 19cm square cake pans, line with paper; grease paper.

Melt chocolate over hot water; cool to room temperature.

Cream butter, essence and sugar in small bowl with electric mixer until light and fluffy. Add eggs one at a time, beating well after each addition. Transfer to large bowl; fold in sifted flour and milk in 2 lots.

Divide mixture into 2 bowls, stir chocolate into 1 bowl and orange rind into the other. Drop spoonfuls of chocolate mixture into the corners and centre of each cake pan. Spoon the orange mixture into the spaces. Swirl knife through mixture once or twice. Bake in moderate oven for about 35 minutes. Stand 5 minutes, before turning on to wire rack to cool. Join cold cakes with about ¼ of the frosting. Spread top and sides of cake with remaining frosting.

Chocolate Fudge Frosting: Melt chocolate over hot water; cool to room temperature. Beat butter in small bowl with electric mixer until light and fluffy. Gradually beat in half the sifted icing sugar. Beat in chocolate, milk and essence, then remaining icing sugar; beat until frosting is spreadable.

Keeping time: 3 days.

LEFT: back: Choc-Orange Marble Cake; front: Chocolate Ripple Cake (recipe over page).

Plates are Sienna and Medici by Villeroy & Boch.

CHOCOLATE RIPPLE CAKE

185g butter
1¼ cups castor sugar
3 eggs
1½ cups plain flour
½ cup self-raising flour
2 tablespoons milk
2 tablespoons cocoa
¼ cup milk, extra
Grease a 20cm baba pan.

Cream butter and sugar in small bowl with electric mixer until light and fluffy. Beat in eggs one at a time, beat until combined. Transfer mixture to large bowl. Stir in half the sifted flours and half the milk, then stir in remaining flours and milk. Blend cocoa with extra milk, stir until smooth with 2 tablespoons of the cake mixture. Fold chocolate mixture lightly through cake mixture to give rippled effect. Spoon into prepared pan, smooth top slightly. Bake in moderate oven for about 40 minutes. Turn on to wire rack to cool. Dust with icing sugar before serving.
Keeping time: 2 days.

CHOCOLATE ZUCCHINI LOAF

90g butter
1 teaspoon grated orange rind
1 cup castor sugar
2 eggs
1¼ cups self-raising flour
¼ cup cocoa
½ teaspoon ground cinnamon
¼ cup milk
1 cup grated zucchini
½ cup chopped pecan nuts
ORANGE FROSTING
30g soft butter
1 teaspoon grated orange rind
2 cups icing sugar
2 tablespoons orange juice
Grease a 15cm x 25cm loaf pan, line base with paper; grease paper.

Cream butter, rind and sugar in small bowl with electric mixer until light and fluffy. Add eggs one at a time, beating well after each addition. Transfer to large bowl. Stir in sifted dry ingredients, milk, zucchini and pecans. Spread into prepared pan. Bake in moderate oven for about 45 minutes. Stand 3 minutes before turning on to wire rack to cool. Spread cold cake with frosting.
Orange Frosting: Beat butter and rind in small bowl with wooden spoon until smooth, gradually beat in sifted icing sugar and juice; beat until spreadable.
Keeping time: 2 days.

ABOVE: clockwise from front left: Chocolate Zucchini Loaf; Peanut Butter Choc Cake; Fluffy Chocolate Cake.

Dresser, blue china, wooden board, round plate, tea towel all from Appley Hoare Antiques, Sydney; rectangular plate is Val D'Or by Royal Doulton.

PEANUT BUTTER CHOC CAKE

125g dark chocolate, chopped
125g unsalted butter
2 teaspoons vanilla essence
1½ cups castor sugar
4 eggs, separated
¼ cup smooth peanut butter
1 cup self-raising flour
¾ cup plain flour
1 cup milk
PEANUT BUTTER CREAM
90g butter
90g packaged cream cheese
1½ cups icing sugar
½ cup smooth peanut butter
2 tablespoons honey

Grease a deep 23cm round cake pan, line base with paper; grease paper.

Melt chocolate over hot water, cool to room temperature.

Cream butter, essence and sugar in small bowl with electric mixer until light and fluffy. Beat in egg yolks one at a time, then beat in chocolate and peanut butter. Transfer mixture to large bowl. Stir in half the sifted flours and milk, then remaining flours and milk.

Beat egg whites in small bowl until soft peaks from, fold half into mixture, then fold in remaining half. Pour into prepared pan. Bake in moderately slow oven for about 1½ hours. Stand 5 minutes before turning on to wire rack.

Split cold cake in half, join with half the peanut butter cream, spread top of cake with remaining cream.
Peanut Butter Cream: Cream butter and cream cheese in small bowl with electric mixer until light and fluffy, beat in half the sifted icing sugar with half the combined peanut butter and honey, then beat in remaining icing sugar and peanut butter mixture.
Keeping time: 2 days.

FLUFFY CHOCOLATE CAKE

125g butter
2 tablespoons cocoa
½ cup milk
2 eggs
¾ cup castor sugar
1 cup self-raising flour
RICH CHOCOLATE ICING
2 tablespoons cream
2 tablespoons cocoa
2 tablespoons brown sugar
1 cup icing sugar

Combine butter, sifted cocoa and milk in saucepan, stir over low heat without boiling until butter is melted; cool to room temperature.

Grease a deep 20cm round cake pan, line base with paper; grease paper well.

Beat eggs in small bowl with electric mixer until thick and creamy, gradually beat in sugar, beating until dissolved between each addition. Transfer to large bowl. Fold in half the sifted flour and half the cocoa mixture, then remaining flour and cocoa mixture. Pour into prepared pan. Bake in moderate oven for about 40 minutes. Stand 5 minutes before turning on to wire rack to cool. Spread cold cake with icing. Decorate with cream, fruit and chocolate curls if desired.

Rich Chocolate Icing: Combine cream, sifted cocoa and brown sugar in saucepan, stir over low heat without boiling until a smooth, thin paste is formed. Remove from heat, gradually stir in sifted icing sugar.

Keeping time: 2 days.

CHOC-MALLOW CAKE

125g butter
1 teaspoon vanilla essence
½ cup castor sugar
1 egg
2 tablespoons golden syrup
2½ cups self-raising flour
1¼ cups milk
2 tablespoons cocoa
¼ cup milk, extra
100g packet white marshmallows
100g dark chocolate, chopped
30g butter, extra

Lightly grease a deep 20cm round springform pan.

Cream butter, essence, sugar, egg and syrup in small bowl with electric mixer until light and fluffy. Transfer to a large bowl, stir in half the sifted flour with half the milk, then stir in remaining flour and milk. Place half the mixture into separate bowl; stir in blended sifted cocoa and extra milk. Drop alternate spoonfuls of mixture into prepared pan, run knife through the mixture to give marbled effect. Bake in moderate oven for about 45 minutes. Remove cake from oven, place a layer of marshmallows evenly on top of cake, return to oven for about a further 5 minutes or until marshmallows are beginning to melt. Cool 5 minutes, remove side of pan, drizzle with combined melted chocolate and extra butter.

Keeping time: 3 days.

CHOCOLATE PEPPERMINT CREAM CAKE

60g dark chocolate, chopped
¼ cup water
125g butter
¾ cup castor sugar
⅓ cup brown sugar
2 eggs
⅓ cup milk
1¼ cups self-raising flour
2 tablespoons cocoa
½ teaspoon bicarbonate of soda
PEPPERMINT CREAM
125g butter
4 cups (500g) icing sugar
1 tablespoon milk
½ teaspoon peppermint essence
CHOCOLATE ICING
1½ cups icing sugar
2 tablespoons cocoa
1 teaspoon butter
¼ cup hot water

Grease a 23cm square slab pan, line base with paper; grease paper.

Melt chocolate and water in heatproof bowl over hot water, cool to room temperature.

Combine all ingredients in large bowl, beat on low speed with electric mixer until ingredients are combined. Increase speed to medium, beat for about 3 minutes or until mixture is changed in colour and smooth. Pour into prepared pan, bake in moderate oven for about 40 minutes. Stand 5 minutes before turning on to wire rack to cool. Spread cold cake with peppermint cream, refrigerate 1 hour. Spread icing over cream, refrigerate until set.

Peppermint Cream: Cream butter in small bowl with electric mixer until light and fluffy, gradually beat in sifted icing sugar, then milk and essence.

Chocolate Icing: Sift icing sugar and cocoa into bowl, stir in combined butter and water, beat until smooth.

Keeping time: 3 days.

MOCHA WALNUT CAKE

1 cup castor sugar
125g dark chocolate, chopped
1 teaspoon dry instant coffee
2 tablespoons water
125g unsalted butter
6 eggs, separated
250g (1½ cups) finely chopped walnuts
2 tablespoons plain flour
½ cup chopped walnuts, extra
MOCHA FROSTING
60g dark chocolate, chopped
90g unsalted butter
1¼ cups icing sugar
1 teaspoon dry instant coffee
2 teaspoons hot water

Grease 2 deep 20cm round cake pans, line bases with paper; grease paper.

Combine sugar, chocolate, coffee and water in saucepan, stir over low heat without boiling until mixture is smooth; cool.

Beat butter in small bowl with electric mixer until creamy, beat in egg yolks. Transfer to large bowl, stir in chocolate mixture, walnuts and sifted flour. Beat egg whites in medium bowl until soft peaks form, fold into cake mixture in 2 lots, pour into prepared pans. Bake in moderate oven for about 35 minutes. Stand 10 minutes before turning on to wire rack to cool.

Mocha Frosting: Melt chocolate in heatproof bowl over hot water; cool. Beat butter in small bowl with electric mixer until creamy, gradually beat in sifted icing sugar, chocolate and combined coffee and water.

Keeping time: 4 days.

BRANDIED APRICOT CAKE

125g dark chocolate, chopped
½ cup water
125g butter
1 cup brown sugar, firmly packed
2 eggs
½ cup sour cream
1⅓ cups plain flour
⅓ cup self-raising flour
½ cup apricot jam
2 tablespoons brandy
300ml carton thickened cream
CHOCOLATE ICING
90g dark chocolate, chopped
15g butter, extra

Grease a deep 20cm round cake pan, line base with paper; grease paper.

Melt chocolate and water over hot water; cool.

Cream butter and sugar in small bowl with electric mixer until light and fluffy. Beat in eggs one at a time, beat until combined. Transfer mixture to large bowl, stir in chocolate mixture, sour cream and sifted flours in 2 lots. Spread into prepared pan. Bake in moderately slow oven for about 1 hour. Stand 5 minutes before turning on to wire rack to cool.

Split cold cake into 4 layers. Combine jam and brandy. Beat cream in small bowl until soft peaks form. Join layers together with jam mixture and cream. Spread cake with icing, refrigerate until set.

Chocolate Icing: Melt chocolate and butter over hot water, cool.

Keeping time: 2 days.

LEFT: back: Chocolate Peppermint Cream Cake; front: Choc-Mallow Cake (recipes previous page).
BELOW: back: Brandied Apricot Cake; front: Mocha Walnut Cake.

Dresser, cake stand at left from Appley Hoare Antiques; china and spoon at left is Val D'Or by Royal Albert; marble below from Metro Marble; plates below are Contrast de Per Spook by Limoges from Studio Haus.

RICH BLACK FOREST CAKE

250g butter
1 tablespoon dry instant coffee
1½ cups hot water
200g dark chocolate, chopped
2 cups castor sugar
1½ cups self-raising flour
1 cup plain flour
¼ cup cocoa
2 eggs
2 teaspoons vanilla essence
2 x 300ml cartons thickened cream
2 x 425g cans cherries, drained
¼ cup kirsch

RIGHT: Apricot Chocolate Chip Cake.
BELOW: Rich Black Forest Cake.

Table and chair at right from The Welsh Pine Shop; china at right from The Old Ark Antique Market; cake slice at right from Royal Copenhagen; doily at right from Linen and Lace, Balmain, NSW; marble below from Metro Marble; cake slice below from Studio Haus.

Grease a deep 23cm round cake pan, line base and sides with paper; grease paper well.

Melt butter in saucepan, stir in combined coffee and hot water, then chocolate and sugar; stir over low heat without boiling until smooth. Transfer to large bowl, cool to warm. Beat mixture on low speed with electric mixer; gradually beat in sifted dry ingredients in 3 lots. Beat in eggs one at a time, then essence. Pour into prepared pan. Bake in slow oven for about 1¾ hours. Stand 5 minutes before turning on to wire rack to cool.

Beat cream until firm peaks form. Trim the top of the cake to make it flat. Split cake into 3 even layers. Place one layer on to serving plate, brush with ⅓ of the kirsch, top with a layer of cream and half the halved cherries. Repeat layering twice more, brush top of cake with remaining kirsch. Cover cake with remaining cream, decorate with cherries and chocolate curls if desired.

Keeping time: 3 days.

APRICOT CHOCOLATE CHIP CAKE

1 cup chopped dried apricots
1 cup apricot nectar
125g butter
⅔ cup raw sugar
2 eggs, separated
1½ cups coconut
1½ cups self-raising flour
½ cup Choc Bits

Grease a deep 20cm round cake pan, line base with paper, grease paper.

Combine apricots and nectar in bowl, stand 1 hour.

Cream butter and sugar in small bowl with electric mixer until light and fluffy, beat in egg yolks one at a time, beat until combined. Transfer mixture to large bowl, stir in coconut, then half the sifted flour and half the apricot mixture. Stir in remaining flour and apricots, then Choc Bits.

Beat egg whites in small bowl until soft peaks form, fold into mixture, spread into prepared pan.

Bake in moderate oven for about 1¼ hours. Stand 5 minutes before turning on to wire rack to cool. Dust with sifted icing sugar if desired.

Keeping time: 3 days.

Processor

Processor cakes are ideal for people who want to speed up the normal mixing process. These recipes have been carefully formulated for the processor; they do not need the aeration created by an electric mixer.

It is important the butter be at room temperature (not melted or cold unless specified). Eggs and milk should also be at room temperature for best results. We didn't sift dry ingredients for these recipes, since aeration is unimportant. The time to process these mixtures will vary depending on the type and size of your processor. It is better to process in short stages and scrape the bowl down several times during processing. Simply process the mixtures until they are evenly combined; cake mixtures will change slightly in colour when they are ready.

We used the metal mixing blade for all these recipes.

PROCESSOR CAKE MIX

The dry part of this cake mix can be made, stored in an airtight container and kept in the refrigerator for up to 3 months. It can be reconstituted immediately it is taken from the refrigerator, it will take a little longer to mix than if it were at room temperature.

1½ cups self-raising flour
¾ cup castor sugar
2 tablespoons skim milk powder
125g butter

Combine flour, sugar and milk powder in processor, add chopped cold butter, process for about 20 seconds or until butter is evenly distributed through dry ingredients.

To make cake: Place cake mix into small bowl of electric mixer, add 2 eggs, 1 teaspoon vanilla essence and ½ cup water, beat on low speed until ingredients are combined. Increase speed to medium, beat for about 3 minutes or until mixture is smooth and changed in colour. Spread mixture into prepared pan.

The cake mix can be cooked in a variety of cake pans. We have included a list of alternatives with approximate cooking times. All pans need to be greased, the base lined with paper, then the paper greased. All the cakes are cooked in a moderate oven. Patty cakes are the only exception, if you prefer them "peaked" increase the temperature to moderately hot.

RIGHT: back: Frosted Chocolate Cake (recipe over page); front: Quick Honey Gingerbread.
BELOW: from left: Lemon Ginger Cake; Coffee and Walnut Cake; Chocolate Fleck Cake; Fairy Cakes.

Tiles from Fred Pazotti Pty Ltd, Sydney; plates at right are Minton by Royal Doulton; plates below are Taitu from Lifestyle Imports, Sydney.

VARIATIONS

CHOCOLATE FLECK CAKE: Stir 60g grated dark chocolate into the beaten cake mixture. Spread cold cake with topping.

Chocolate Topping: Melt 100g chopped dark chocolate with 90g butter; stir until smooth. Cool until chocolate is set enough to spread on to cakes. Refrigerate to speed setting if weather is hot.

LEMON GINGER CAKE: Stir 2 teaspoons grated lemon rind and ¼ cup finely chopped glace ginger into beaten cake mixture.

COFFEE AND WALNUT CAKE: Dissolve 1 tablespoon dry instant coffee in the specified ½ cup water. Heat to dissolve if necessary; cool before using. Stir ½ cup finely chopped walnuts into beaten cake mixture. Top cold cake with frosting.

Mocha Frosting: Dissolve 1 teaspoon cocoa and 1 teaspoon dry instant coffee in 1 tablespoon boiling water. Beat 60g butter in small bowl with electric mixer until creamy, beat in 1½ cups sifted icing sugar and coffee mixture.

FAIRY CAKES: It is best to cook patty cakes used for fairy cakes in a moderate oven to keep them as flat-topped as possible. When the cakes are cold, cut out a circle from the top, cutting down to a depth of about 2cm.

Place a small amount of jam in the cavity, top with whipped cream, replace tops, dust with sifted icing sugar.

These variations can also be used for the Basic Butter Cake in the Butter section — page 89.

Keeping time: 2 days.

CAKE PANS AND COOKING TIMES

20cm baba pan
40 minutes

20cm ring pan
40 minutes

14cm x 21cm loaf pan
1 hour

2 x 8cm x 26cm bar pans
35 minutes

deep 20cm round cake pan
50 minutes

24 patty pans
15 minutes

QUICK HONEY GINGERBREAD

1 cup plain flour
½ cup self-raising flour
½ teaspoon bicarbonate of soda
3 teaspoons ground ginger
½ teaspoon ground nutmeg
½ cup brown sugar
½ cup honey
½ cup water
125g butter

Grease a 19cm x 29cm lamington pan, line base with paper; grease paper.

Combine flours, soda, spices and sugar in processor, process a few seconds until combined. Combine honey, water and butter in saucepan, stir over low heat until butter is melted, add to processor, process until mixture is smooth. Pour into prepared pan, bake in moderate oven for about 35 minutes. Stand 2 minutes before turning on to wire rack to cool. Dust with sifted icing sugar before serving.

Keeping time: 3 days.

CARROT AND PRUNE CAKE

You will need to grate about 3 carrots for this recipe. Use the grating blade of the processor if desired.

¾ cup self-raising flour
¾ cup plain flour
1 tablespoon mixed spice
½ teaspoon bicarbonate of soda
¾ cup pitted prunes
½ cup pecan nuts
½ cup sultanas
3 eggs
1 cup brown sugar, firmly packed
300g carton sour cream
¼ cup oil
2 cups grated carrots

Grease a 19cm square cake pan, line base with paper; grease paper.

Combine flours, spice and soda in processor, process a few seconds to combine. Transfer mixture to a large bowl, leaving a tablespoonful of mixture in the processor. Add prunes and pecans to processor, process until coarsely chopped; stir into flour mixture with sultanas.

Combine eggs, sugar, sour cream and oil in processor, process until combined, stir into flour mixture with carrots. Pour into prepared pan. Bake in moderately slow oven for about 1¼ hours. Stand 10 minutes before turning on to wire rack to cool.

Keeping time: 5 days.

APPLE CHOCOLATE CAKE

We used Granny Smith apples.

185g butter
1¼ cups castor sugar
3 eggs
⅓ cup cocoa
¼ teaspoon bicarbonate of soda
⅓ cup water
2 apples, peeled, quartered
2 cups self-raising flour
CHOCOLATE ICING
1 cup icing sugar
1 tablespoon cocoa
1 teaspoon soft butter
1 tablespoon milk, approximately

Grease a 23cm square slab pan, line base with paper; grease paper.

Combine butter, sugar, eggs, blended cocoa, soda and water, apple and flour in processor, process until mixture is smooth. Pour into prepared pan. Bake in moderate oven for about 1 hour. Stand 5 minutes before turning on to wire rack to cool. Spread cold cake with icing.

Chocolate Icing: Sift icing sugar and cocoa into small heatproof bowl, stir in butter and enough milk to make a stiff paste. Stir over hot water until icing is spreadable.

Keeping time: 3 days.

FROSTED CHOCOLATE CAKE

125g butter
½ cup castor sugar
2 eggs
1½ cups self-raising flour
2 tablespoons cornflour
2 tablespoons cocoa
¾ cup milk
CHOCOLATE FROSTING
90g butter
1½ cups icing sugar
1 tablespoon cocoa
2 tablespoons milk, approximately

ABOVE: back: Carrot and Prune Cake; front: Apple Chocolate Cake.

Front plate is Taitu from Lifestyle Imports.

Grease a 20cm ring pan, line base with paper; grease paper.

Combine butter, sugar and eggs in processor, process for a few seconds until combined. Add dry ingredients and milk, process until mixture is smooth and changed in colour. Spread into prepared pan. Bake in moderate oven for about 35 minutes. Stand 2 minutes before turning on to wire rack to cool. Spread cold cake with frosting; decorate with walnut halves.

Chocolate Frosting: Beat butter in small bowl with electric mixer until creamy. Gradually add sifted icing sugar and cocoa and milk, beat until frosting is spreadable.

Keeping time: 2 days.

Sponges

Featherlight sponges and rolls are often considered the yardstick by which "light-handed" cooks are measured. With our Best Ever Sponge and the wonderfully luscious rolls in this section, you will soon fit into this category.

ABOVE: back, from left: Chocolate Sponge, Citrus Sponge; front, from left: Hazelnut Sponge (recipes over page), Best Ever Sponge.

Plates are Fifth Avenue by Noritake.

BEST EVER SPONGE

This is our favourite never-fail sponge recipe; it does not contain liquid or butter, which makes it ideal for Swiss rolls. It is simple to adapt to many flavours and will work as a cake or a roll.

2 EGG SPONGE
2 eggs
⅓ cup castor sugar
2 tablespoons cornflour
2 tablespoons plain flour
2 tablespoons self-raising flour
3 EGG SPONGE
3 eggs
½ cup castor sugar
¼ cup cornflour
¼ cup plain flour
¼ cup self-raising flour
4 EGG SPONGE
4 eggs
⅔ cup castor sugar
⅓ cup cornflour
⅓ cup plain flour
⅓ cup self-raising flour

Have eggs at room temperature. Beat whole eggs in small bowl with electric mixer until thick and creamy (the small bowl is necessary to give maximum volume to eggs); beating time on a moderately high speed should be about 7 minutes. Add sugar, about 1 tablespoon at a time, beating after each addition until sugar is dissolved.

While eggs and sugar are beating, prepare pans by greasing evenly (see list of pan sizes over page); and sift dry ingredients together 3 times, to aerate and mix the flours.

When sugar is dissolved, transfer mixture to larger basin; this makes it easier to fold the dry ingredients through the egg mixture (it is not necessary to transfer the 2 egg mixture to a larger basin). Sift the flours over the egg mixture, use a spatula to lightly fold the flours through; heavy handling at this stage will give a flat, tough sponge. Spread mixture evenly into pan, bake in moderate oven for cooking time specified over page. When cooked, sponge will have shrunk very slightly from side of pan and top of sponge will feel springy when touched gently with fingertips. Turn sponge immediately on to wire rack to cool, then reverse sponge so that wire rack does not mark the top.

We have listed the quantities of this recipe needed for different cake pans and their cooking times, over page. They are all baked in a moderate oven.

CAKE PANS AND COOKING TIMES

2 egg: Deep 20cm round cake pan or recess pan about 20 minutes. We prefer to use a deep pan rather than a sandwich pan as the sponge will be less crusty on top because the high sides protect the top during cooking.

3 egg: 2 deep 17cm cake or sandwich pans about 15 minutes, or 25cm x 30cm Swiss roll pan about 12 minutes.

4 egg: 2 deep 20cm round cake pans about 20 minutes, or deep 23cm round cake pan about 40 minutes.

VARIATIONS:

CITRUS: Beat in 2 teaspoons of your favourite grated citrus rind with the sugar. Try lemon, mandarin, lime, orange or grapefruit.

NUT: Fold in ¼ cup of any type of ground nuts with the flours.

CHOCOLATE: Fold in 60g grated dark chocolate with the flours.
Fill and ice sponges as desired.
Keeping time: 2 days.

SPONGE ROLLS

Use the 3 egg mixture given on previous page.

Grease the Swiss roll pan evenly and line with either baking or greaseproof paper, bringing the paper up the 2 short sides of the pan. Grease greaseproof paper again lightly. It is not necessary to grease baking paper.

While the roll is baking get everything ready so that when it is cooked it can be handled quickly.

Cover a wire rack with baking or greaseproof paper. Sprinkle the paper lightly and evenly with about 2 tablespoons castor sugar; this prevents the roll sticking to the paper.

It is important not to overcook Swiss rolls, or they will be dry and will crack when rolled. Feel the top of the cake to check for "springiness", then quickly turn cake on to sugared paper.

Quickly cut all the crisp crusts from the roll. A finely serrated knife is ideal.

Roll the cake with the paper from either side of the sponge. Stand 2 minutes, unroll, cool to room temperature. Spread with warmed jam then roll again. This method of cooling the unrolled sponge minimised cracking.
Keeping time: 1 day.

ABOVE: Honey Roll with Washed Mock Cream.
RIGHT: Grated Chocolate Roll.

China above is Haworth by Royal Doulton; china at right is Coraline by New Chelsea from Goodmans Antiques, Sydney.

HONEY ROLL WITH WASHED MOCK CREAM

This delicious cake tastes like the commercially made variety. The old fashioned mock cream can be beaten with a wooden spoon instead of an electric mixer if time and energy permit. Roll can be made and stored in an airtight container a day before serving.

60g butter
¾ cup golden syrup
¾ cup plain flour
½ cup self-raising flour
2 teaspoons ground ginger
1 teaspoon ground cinnamon
¾ teaspoon ground nutmeg
¼ teaspoon ground cloves
2 eggs, lightly beaten
1 teaspoon bicarbonate of soda
¼ cup boiling water
½ cup coconut
WASHED MOCK CREAM
125g butter
1 teaspoon vanilla essence
½ cup castor sugar

Grease a 25cm x 30cm Swiss roll pan, line base with paper; grease paper.

Beat butter in small bowl with electric mixer until smooth and creamy, gradually beat in golden syrup. Stir in sifted flours and spices, then eggs. Quickly stir in combined soda and water. Spread mixture evenly into prepared pan. Bake in moderate oven for about 18 minutes, stand cake a few minutes. Cover a wire rack with paper, sprinkle with coconut, turn cake on to paper, roll up loosely. Stand a few minutes, unroll, cool to room temperature. Spread mock cream over cake, roll up.

Washed Mock Cream: Cream butter, essence and sugar in small bowl with electric mixer until light and fluffy. Remove bowl from electric mixer, cover mixture with cold water, swirl around bowl 1 minute, pour off water. Return bowl to electric mixer, beat mixture well. Repeat washing and beating for about 6 times or until mixture is white in colour and sugar dissolved.

Keeping time: 2 days.

GRATED CHOCOLATE ROLL

4 eggs, separated
½ cup castor sugar
2 tablespoons hot water
60g dark chocolate, grated
½ cup self-raising flour
2 tablespoons castor sugar, extra
VANILLA CREAM
¾ cup thickened cream
2 teaspoons icing sugar
1 teaspoon vanilla essence

Grease a 25cm x 30cm Swiss roll pan, line base and sides with paper; grease paper well.

Beat egg yolks and sugar in small bowl with electric mixer for about 5 minutes or until thick and creamy. Transfer mixture to large bowl, fold in hot water and chocolate, then fold in sifted flour. Beat egg whites in small bowl with electric mixer or rotary beater until soft peaks form, fold into mixture, pour into prepared pan. Bake in moderate oven for about 12 minutes.

Turn immediately on to paper which has been sprinkled with extra sugar. Trim crisp edges from sides of cake, roll up in paper from the long side. Stand 2 minutes, unroll, cool. Spread with vanilla cream, roll up. Serve topped with extra whipped cream and chocolate curls if desired.

Vanilla Cream: Beat cream, icing sugar and essence in small bowl with electric mixer or rotary beater until soft peaks form.

Keeping time: 2 days.

JAM ROLL

This is delicious served warm with cream either as a cake or a dessert.

3 eggs
½ cup castor sugar
¾ cup self-raising flour
2 tablespoons boiling water
⅓ cup jam
2 tablespoons castor sugar, extra

Grease a 25cm x 30cm Swiss roll pan, line base and sides with paper, grease paper well.

Beat eggs in small bowl with electric mixer for about 3 minutes or until thick and creamy. Gradually add sugar, beat until dissolved between each addition. Transfer mixture to large bowl, fold in sifted flour and water. Spread mixture into prepared pan, bake in moderate oven for about 10 minutes. Warm jam gently in saucepan over low heat. Turn cake immediately on to paper, sprinkled with extra sugar. Trim edges from sides of cake. Spread hot cake evenly with hot jam, roll up from the short side using paper as a guide.

Keeping time: 1 day.

RIGHT: back: Coffee Liqueur Roll; front: Hazelnut Coffee Roll.
BELOW: Jam Roll.

Table at right from The Welsh Pine Shop, Sydney; china at right and below is Myott from Olde Wares Shop, Glebe, NSW.

HAZELNUT COFFEE ROLL

Kahlua is a coffee-flavoured liqueur

4 eggs
¾ cup castor sugar
¼ cup self-raising flour
1 tablespoon plain flour
⅓ cup packaged ground hazelnuts
2 tablespoons warm water
¼ teaspoon bicarbonate of soda
30g dark chocolate, melted
2 tablespoons castor sugar, extra
COFFEE CREAM
2 teaspoons dry instant coffee
1 teaspoon water
300ml carton thickened cream
1 tablespoon Kahlua
1 tablespoon icing sugar

Grease a 25cm x 30cm Swiss roll pan, line base and sides with paper, grease paper well.

Combine eggs and sugar in medium bowl, beat with electric mixer for about 10 minutes or until sugar is dissolved and mixture is thick and creamy. Fold in sifted flours and ground hazelnuts. Stir water and soda into chocolate, fold into flour mixture. Pour into prepared pan, bake in moderate oven for about 12 minutes.

Turn immediately on to paper sprinkled with extra sugar. Trim crisp edges from cake, roll up in paper from the long side, stand 2 minutes, unroll, cool. Spread with half the coffee cream, roll up, cover and decorate with remaining cream. Top with chocolate-dipped hazelnuts if desired.

Coffee Cream: Dissolve coffee in water. Combine with remaining ingredients in small bowl, beat until firm peaks form.

Keeping time: 2 days.

COFFEE LIQUEUR ROLL

Tia Maria is a coffee-flavoured liqueur

5 eggs
¾ cup castor sugar
1 cup self-raising flour
90g butter, melted
1 tablespoon dry instant coffee
1 tablespoon hot water
1 tablespoon cocoa
1 tablespoon castor sugar, extra
LIQUEUR CREAM
2 teaspoons dry instant coffee
1 tablespoon hot water
1 tablespoon Tia Maria
300ml carton thickened cream

Grease a 25cm x 30cm Swiss roll pan, line base and sides with paper; grease paper well.

Beat eggs in medium bowl with electric mixer for about 3 minutes or until thick and creamy. Gradually beat in sugar, about a tablespoon at a time, beat until dissolved. Fold in sifted flour, then combined butter, coffee and water. Spread mixture into prepared pan. Bake in moderately hot oven for about 15 minutes. Turn immediately on to paper sprinkled with combined sifted cocoa and extra sugar. Trim edges from cake. Roll up in paper from the long side, stand 2 minutes, unroll, cool. Spread with liqueur cream, roll up.

Liqueur Cream: Dissolve coffee in water, cool. Combine coffee mixture, Tia Maria and cream in small bowl, beat with electric mixer or rotary beater until soft peaks form.

Keeping time: 1 day.

Syrup

Syrup cakes are delightfully moist and wickedly sweet. They keep well in an airtight container if the weather is cool, or in the refrigerator if it's hot. When cake is removed from the tin on to a wire rack, turn the cake right way up, then stand it, on its rack, over a tray to catch any excess syrup that may drip. This applies to most cakes in this section; follow individual recipes. Serve these cakes plain or as a dessert with whipped cream.

RIGHT: Macaroon Syrup Cake.
BELOW: back: Pumpkin Citrus Syrup Cake; front: Lime Syrup Buttermilk Cake.

Plates below from Studio Haus. Plates at right from Dansab.

PUMPKIN CITRUS SYRUP CAKE

You will need to cook 350g pumpkin for 1 cup mashed pumpkin.

250g butter
2 tablespoons grated orange rind
2 tablespoons grated lemon rind
1 cup castor sugar
3 eggs, separated
2 cups self-raising flour
1 cup mashed pumpkin
SYRUP
2 tablespoons lemon juice
2 tablespoons orange juice
¾ cup sugar

Grease a deep 23cm round cake pan, line base with paper; grease paper.

Cream butter, rinds and sugar in small bowl with electric mixer until light and fluffy, add egg yolks; beat until combined. Transfer to large bowl. Stir in half the sifted flour with half the cold pumpkin, then stir in remaining flour and pumpkin.

Beat egg whites in small bowl until soft peaks form, fold through cake mixture. Spread mixture into prepared pan. Bake in moderate oven for about 1 hour, pour hot syrup over hot cake. Stand 10 minutes, before turning on to wire rack to cool.

Syrup: Combine all ingredients in saucepan. Stir constantly over heat without boiling until sugar is dissolved. Bring to boil, reduce heat, simmer 2 minutes without stirring.

Keeping time: 4 days.

LIME SYRUP BUTTERMILK CAKE

Buttermilk makes a deliciously light cake; if unavailable use skim milk. Lime rind and juice give this cake a fresh flavour, but any citrus rind and juice of your choice can be used.

250g butter
1 tablespoon grated lime rind
1 cup castor sugar
3 eggs, separated
2 cups self-raising flour
1 cup buttermilk
LIME SYRUP
⅓ cup lime juice
¾ cup sugar
¼ cup water

Grease and lightly flour a 20cm baba pan; shake out excess flour.

Cream butter, rind and sugar in small bowl with electric mixer until light and fluffy, beat in egg yolks one at a time, beat until combined. Transfer mixture to large bowl, stir in half the sifted flour and half the buttermilk, then stir in remaining flour and buttermilk. Beat egg whites in small bowl until soft peaks form, fold lightly into mixture in 2 batches.

Spread mixture into prepared pan. Bake in moderate oven for about 1 hour. Stand 5 minutes before turning on to wire rack. Pour hot lime syrup evenly over hot cake.

Lime Syrup: Combine lime juice, sugar and water in saucepan, stir over heat until sugar is dissolved, bring to the boil; remove from heat.

Keeping time: 2 days.

MACAROON SYRUP CAKE

125g butter
1 cup castor sugar
4 eggs
2 cups coconut
1 cup self-raising flour
LEMON SYRUP
1 cup sugar
⅔ cup water
6 strips lemon rind

Grease a 20cm ring pan, line base with paper; grease paper.

Cream butter and sugar in small bowl with electric mixer until light and fluffy, beat in eggs one at a time, beat until combined. Transfer mixture to large bowl, stir in coconut, then sifted flour. Spread mixture into prepared pan. Bake in moderately slow oven for about 45 minutes. Pour hot syrup over hot cake; cool in pan. Decorate with toasted, flaked coconut if desired.

Lemon Syrup: Combine all ingredients in saucepan, stir over heat without boiling until sugar is dissolved, bring to the boil, reduce heat, simmer uncovered without stirring for 3 minutes; strain syrup.

Keeping time: 4 days.

ALMOND ORANGE HALVA CAKE

Semolina is a cereal made from wheat. It can be bought from some supermarkets and health food stores. The semolina and almonds replace flour in this recipe.

125g butter
2 teaspoons grated orange rind
½ cup castor sugar
2 eggs
1 teaspoon baking powder
1 cup semolina
1 cup packaged ground almonds
3 tablespoons orange juice
SYRUP
1 cup orange juice
½ cup castor sugar
1 tablespoon brandy

Grease a deep 20cm round cake pan.

Cream butter, rind and sugar in small bowl with electric mixer until light and fluffy; beat in eggs one at a time, beat until combined. Transfer mixture to large bowl, stir in half the dry ingredients with half the orange juice, then stir in remaining dry ingredients and orange juice.

Pour mixture into prepared pan, bake in moderate oven for about 40 minutes. Turn cake on to wire rack, place over tray, brush with half the hot syrup, return to oven (on wire rack), bake further 5 minutes, remove from oven, brush with remaining hot syrup. Serve warm or cold.

Syrup: Combine orange juice and sugar in saucepan, stir constantly over heat without boiling until sugar is dissolved, bring to the boil, reduce heat, simmer uncovered without stirring for 5 minutes; stir in brandy.

Keeping time: 3 days.

WHOLE-ORANGE SYRUP CAKE

We used a medium-sized seedless navel orange for this recipe.

1 orange
125g butter
½ cup castor sugar
2 eggs
1½ cups wholemeal self-raising flour
½ teaspoon bicarbonate of soda
½ cup buttermilk
ORANGE BUTTER SYRUP
½ cup sugar
¼ cup orange juice
60g butter

Grease a 15cm x 25cm loaf pan.

Squeeze the juice from the orange, reserve juice for syrup. Process or blend remaining skin and pulp finely.

Cream butter and sugar in small bowl with electric mixer until light and fluffy, beat in eggs one at a time, beat until combined. Transfer mixture to large bowl, stir in half the sifted flour and soda with half the buttermilk, then stir in remaining dry ingredients, buttermilk and orange pulp.

Pour mixture into prepared pan,

bake in moderate oven for about 45 minutes. Stand cake 5 minutes before turning on to wire rack, pour hot syrup evenly over hot cake.

Orange Butter Syrup: Combine sugar, orange juice and butter in saucepan, stir constantly over heat without boiling until sugar is dissolved and butter melted; bring to the boil, remove syrup from heat.

Keeping time: 3 days.

CINNAMON AND WALNUT SYRUP CAKE

This cake looks best if it is served upside down.

3 eggs
¾ cup castor sugar
¾ cup self-raising flour
3 teaspoons ground cinnamon
185g butter, melted
¾ cup chopped walnuts
SYRUP
1 cup sugar
¾ cup water

Grease a 23cm square slab pan.

Beat eggs in a small bowl with electric mixer until thick and creamy, gradually add sugar, beat until dissolved between each addition. Beat in sifted flour and cinnamon in several batches, beat in butter, stir in walnuts.

Pour mixture into prepared pan, bake in moderate oven for about 30 minutes. Stand 5 minutes, turn on to wire rack, leave upside down. Place tray under rack. Pour hot syrup over hot cake. Serve cake warm or cold.

Syrup: Combine sugar and water in saucepan, stir constantly over heat without boiling until sugar is dissolved, bring to the boil, reduce heat, simmer uncovered 5 minutes.

Keeping time: 3 days.

LEFT: in descending order: Almond Orange Halva Cake; Whole-Orange Syrup Cake; Cinnamon and Walnut Syrup Cake.

Tiles from Fred Pazotti Pty Ltd, Sydney; Plates are Copco, cups are Bodum from Vasa Agencies, Sydney.

Quick-Mix

Quick-mix cakes are always popular. Remember to have all the ingredients at room temperature. Beat the ingredients with an electric mixer on a low speed until combined; then increase the speed to medium and continue to beat until the mixture is smooth and changed to a paler colour. Keep scraping the mixture down from the side of the bowl for even mixing.

The recipes in this section are not meant to be made in a food processor; they require the aeration created by an electric mixer.

MOIST ORANGE CAKE

155g butter
2 teaspoons grated orange rind
⅔ cup castor sugar
3 eggs
1¼ cups self-raising flour
¼ cup milk
ORANGE ICING
1 cup icing sugar
1 teaspoon soft butter
1 tablespoon orange juice,
   approximately
1 tablespoon coconut

Grease a deep 20cm round cake pan, line base with paper; grease paper.

Combine all ingredients in large bowl, beat on low speed with electric mixer until ingredients are combined. Increase speed to medium, beat for about 3 minutes or until mixture is changed in colour and smooth. Spread into prepared pan. Bake in moderate oven for about 45 minutes. Stand 2 minutes before turning on to wire rack to cool. Spread cold cake with icing, sprinkle with coconut.

Orange Icing: Sift icing sugar into small heatproof bowl, stir in butter and enough juice to make a stiff paste. Stir over hot water until icing is spreadable.

Keeping time: 2 days.

HONEY-ICED COFFEE CAKE

3 teaspoons dry instant coffee
1 tablespoon hot water
125g butter
2 teaspoons vanilla essence
¾ cup brown sugar, firmly packed
2 eggs
1 cup self-raising flour
¼ cup custard powder
⅓ cup milk
HONEY ICING
30g butter
1 teaspoon dry instant coffee
1 tablespoon hot water
1 teaspoon honey
1 teaspoon vanilla essence
1 cup icing sugar, approximately

Grease a 20cm ring pan, line base with paper; grease paper.

Dissolve coffee in water, combine in large bowl with butter, essence, sugar, eggs, sifted flour and custard powder and milk. Beat on low speed with electric mixer until ingredients are combined, increase speed to medium, beat for about 3 minutes or until mixture is smooth and changed in colour.

Spread mixture into prepared pan. Bake in moderate oven for about 40 minutes. Stand 5 minutes, before turning on to wire rack to cool. Spread cold cake with icing.

Honey Icing: Melt butter in saucepan remove from heat, stir in combined coffee and water, honey, essence and half the sifted icing sugar. Gradually stir in enough remaining icing sugar to mix to a spreadable consistency.

Keeping time: 3 days.

CHOCOLATE FUDGE CAKE

250g dark chocolate, chopped
125g butter
⅔ cup castor sugar
⅔ cup self-raising flour
4 eggs, lightly beaten

Grease a 19cm x 29cm lamington pan, line base with paper, grease paper.

Melt chocolate and butter over hot water, cool. Combine all ingredients in medium bowl, beat on low speed with electric mixer until ingredients are combined. Increase speed to medium, beat for about 3 minutes or until mixture is changed in colour and smooth.

Pour mixture into prepared pan, bake in moderate oven for about 30 minutes. Stand 5 minutes before turning on to wire rack to cool. Serve dusted with sifted icing sugar.

Keeping time: 3 days.

RIGHT: in descending order: Honey-Iced Coffee Cake; Moist Orange Cake; Chocolate Fudge Cake.

Tiles from Fred Pazotti Pty Ltd, Sydney; plates are Copco, cup and saucer is Bodum, knife and tray all from Vasa Agencies, Sydney.

VANILLA BUTTER CAKE

125g butter
¾ cup milk
3 eggs
1 tablespoon vanilla essence
1 cup castor sugar
1½ cups self-raising flour

Grease a deep 19cm square cake pan, line base with paper; grease paper.

Combine butter and milk in saucepan, stir constantly over heat until butter is melted. Remove from heat; cool to room temperature.

Beat eggs and essence in small bowl with electric mixer until thick and creamy; gradually add sugar, beat until dissolved between each addition.

Transfer mixture to large bowl, stir in half the sifted flour and half the butter mixture, then remaining flour and butter mixture. Pour into prepared pan. Bake in moderate oven for about 45 minutes. Stand 2 minutes before turning on to wire rack to cool. When cold, dust with sifted icing sugar.

Keeping time: 1 week.

RICH CHOCOLATE CAKE

185g butter
2 teaspoons vanilla essence
1¾ cups castor sugar
3 eggs
2 cups self-raising flour
⅔ cup cocoa
1 cup water
CHOCOLATE ICING
90g dark chocolate, chopped
30g butter
1 cup icing sugar
2 tablespoons hot water,
   approximately

Grease a deep 23cm round cake pan, line base with paper; grease paper.

Combine butter, essence, sugar, eggs, sifted flour and cocoa and water in large bowl, beat on low speed with electric mixer until ingredients are combined. Increase speed to medium, beat for about 3 minutes or until mixture is smooth and changed in colour. Spread into prepared pan.

Bake in moderate oven for about 1½ hours. Stand 5 minutes before turning on to wire rack to cool. Spread cold cake with icing.

Chocolate Icing: Melt chocolate and butter in bowl over hot water, gradually stir in sifted icing sugar, then stir in enough hot water to mix to a spreadable consistency.

Keeping time: 3 days.

FROSTED CHOC-ORANGE CAKE

125g butter
1 tablespoon grated orange rind
3 eggs
1¾ cups self-raising flour
1⅓ cups castor sugar
½ cup cocoa
½ teaspoon bicarbonate of soda
½ cup orange juice
¼ cup water
CHOC-ORANGE FROSTING
60g butter
1 tablespoon grated orange rind
1½ cups icing sugar
2 tablespoons milk
1 tablespoon cocoa

Grease a deep 19cm square cake pan, line base with paper; grease paper.

Combine all ingredients in large bowl, beat on low speed with electric mixer until ingredients are combined. Increase speed to medium, beat for about 3 minutes or until mixture is changed in colour and smooth. Pour into prepared pan, bake in moderate oven for about 1 hour. Stand 5 minutes before turning on to wire rack to cool. Top cold cake with frosting.

Choc-Orange Frosting: Beat butter and rind in small bowl with electric mixer until light and fluffy, gradually beat in sifted icing sugar and milk. Divide frosting in half, stir sifted cocoa into one half, mix well. Top cake with spoonfuls of orange and chocolate icing, swirl icing with knife to give a marbled effect.

Keeping time: 2 days.

ONE-BOWL SULTANA LOAF

125g butter, melted
750g sultanas
½ cup brown sugar
2 tablespoons marmalade
2 eggs, lightly beaten
¼ cup sweet sherry
¾ cup plain flour
¼ cup self-raising flour

Grease a 15cm x 25cm loaf pan, line base with paper, grease paper.

Combine all ingredients in large bowl, beat with wooden spoon until ingredients are combined. Spread into prepared pan, decorate top with blanched almonds if desired. Bake in slow oven for about 1½ hours. Cover with foil, cool in pan.

Keeping time: 2 weeks.

LEFT: back: Vanilla Butter Cake; front: Rich Chocolate Cake (recipes previous page).
BELOW LEFT: Frosted Choc-Orange Cake.
BELOW: back: Orange Date Cake with Orange Frosting; front: One-Bowl Sultana Loaf.

ORANGE DATE CAKE WITH ORANGE FROSTING

125g butter
2 teaspoons grated orange rind
¾ cup castor sugar
2 eggs
1 cup self-raising flour
½ cup plain flour
⅓ cup orange juice
1 cup chopped dates
ORANGE FROSTING
60g butter
1 teaspoon grated orange rind
1½ cups icing sugar
2 tablespoons orange juice, approximately

Kitchen from Liv-Better (Aust) Pty Ltd; plates are Copco, coffee cups, pot and tray are Bodum from Vasa Agencies.

Grease a 20cm ring pan, line base with paper; grease paper.

Combine butter, rind, sugar, eggs, sifted flours and orange juice in small bowl of electric mixer, beat on lowest speed until ingredients are combined. Increase speed to medium, beat 2 minutes or until mixture changes in colour and is smooth. Stir in dates; spread mixture into prepared pan. Bake in moderate oven for about 40 minutes. Stand 2 minutes, before turning on to wire rack to cool. Top cold cake with frosting, decorate with shredded orange rind if desired.

Orange Frosting: Beat butter and rind in small bowl with electric mixer until creamy. Gradually add sifted icing sugar and orange juice, beat until frosting is spreadable.

Keeping time: 2 days.

Vegetable

Cakes based on a vegetable are always moist and hearty. They usually improve in flavour and texture a day or two after cooking. If the weather is humid, store them in the refrigerator.

If the recipe requires a mashed vegetable, make sure it is well drained after boiling or steaming, and it is not mashed with butter or any liquid; this upsets the balance of ingredients. Make sure the vegetable is at room temperature before mixing it with other ingredients.

PUMPKIN CHOC-ORANGE CAKE

You will need 250g raw pumpkin for this recipe.

125g butter
2 teaspoons grated orange rind
½ cup castor sugar
1 egg
1 tablespoon golden syrup
¾ cup cold mashed pumpkin
1¼ cups self-raising flour
½ teaspoon bicarbonate of soda
2 tablespoons cocoa
1 tablespoon custard powder
¼ cup orange juice
CHOCOLATE ICING
1 cup icing sugar
1 tablespoon cocoa
1 teaspoon butter
1 tablespoon milk

Grease a 14cm x 21cm loaf pan, line base with paper; grease paper.

Cream butter, rind and sugar in small bowl with electric mixer only until combined. Beat in egg and golden syrup, transfer to large bowl. Stir in pumpkin, then half the sifted dry ingredients and half the orange juice. Stir in remaining dry ingredients and orange juice. Pour mixture into prepared pan. Bake in moderate oven for about 1 hour, stand 5 minutes before turning on to wire rack to cool. Spread cold cake with icing.

Chocolate Icing: Sift icing sugar and cocoa into small heatproof bowl, stir in butter and enough milk to make a stiff paste. Stir over hot water until icing is spreadable.

Keeping time: 3 days.

PUMPKIN CINNAMON AND WHOLEMEAL BREAD

185g butter, melted
½ cup honey
1 egg, lightly beaten
3 cups (375g) finely grated raw pumpkin
¾ cup raw sugar
3 cups wholemeal self-raising flour
1 tablespoon ground cinnamon

Grease a 15cm x 25cm loaf pan, line base and sides with paper; grease paper well.

Combine butter, honey and egg in large bowl, stir in pumpkin, sugar, flour and cinnamon. Pour into prepared pan, bake in moderate oven for about 50 minutes. Stand 5 minutes before turning on to wire rack to cool. Serve with butter if desired.

Keeping time: 3 days.

PUMPKIN DATE CAKE

You will need to cook 200g pumpkin for this recipe.

250g butter
1 tablespoon grated orange rind
¾ cup castor sugar
2 eggs
1 cup chopped dates
½ cup coconut
½ cup cold mashed pumpkin
2 cups self-raising flour
½ cup milk

Grease a deep 19cm square cake pan, line base with paper; grease paper.

Cream butter, rind and sugar in small bowl with electric mixer until light and fluffy; beat in eggs one at a time, beat until combined. Transfer mixture to large bowl, stir in dates, coconut and pumpkin. Stir in half the sifted flour and half the milk, then stir in remaining flour and milk. Spread into prepared pan. Bake in moderately slow oven for about 1¼ hours. Stand 5 minutes before turning on to wire rack to cool. Dust with sifted icing sugar.

Keeping time: 3 days.

RIGHT: back: Pumpkin Date Cake; centre: Pumpkin Choc-Orange Cake; front: Pumpkin Cinnamon and Wholemeal Bread.

China is Basket by Villeroy & Boch.

POTATO CHOCOLATE CAKE

You will need 185g raw potato (about 2) for this recipe.

125g butter
⅔ cup castor sugar
2 eggs
½ cup cold mashed potato
1¼ cups self-raising flour
⅓ cup cocoa
⅓ cup milk
CHOCOLATE FROSTING
90g butter
1½ cups icing sugar
2 tablespoons cocoa
2 tablespoons milk, approximately

Grease a 20cm ring pan, line base with paper; grease paper.

Cream butter and sugar in small bowl with electric mixer until light and fluffy, beat in eggs, one at a time; beat until combined. Stir in potato with half the sifted flour and cocoa and half the milk, then stir in remaining flour, cocoa and milk. Spread mixture into prepared pan. Bake in moderate oven for about 40 minutes. Stand 5 minutes before turning on to wire rack to cool. Spread cold cake with frosting.

Chocolate Frosting: Beat butter in small bowl with electric mixer until creamy. Gradually beat in sifted icing sugar and cocoa and milk, beat until frosting is spreadable.

Keeping time: 2 days.

POTATO GINGER CAKE

185g butter
⅓ cup brown sugar
2 eggs
⅓ cup golden syrup
¾ cup self-raising flour
⅓ cup plain flour
2 teaspoons ground ginger
1 teaspoon ground cinnamon
½ cup grated raw potato
LEMON ICING
1½ cups icing sugar
1 teaspoon butter
1 tablespoon lemon juice, approximately

Grease a 14cm x 21cm loaf pan, line base with paper; grease paper.

Cream butter and sugar in small bowl with electric mixer until light and fluffy, beat in eggs one at a time, beat until combined, gradually beat in golden syrup. Transfer mixture to large bowl, stir in sifted dry ingredients and potato. Pour into prepared pan, bake in moderate oven for about 1¼ hours. Stand 10 minutes before turning on to wire rack to cool. Spread cold cake with icing.

Lemon Icing: Sift icing sugar into small heatproof bowl, stir in butter and enough lemon juice to make a stiff paste, stir over hot water until icing is spreadable.

Keeping time: 3 days.

ABOVE: Zucchini Walnut Loaf.
LEFT: from left: Potato Chocolate Cake;
Potato Ginger Cake.

Kitchen from Bosch Liv-Better (Aust) Pty
Ltd; china is Basket by Villeroy & Boch.
Cane basket from Swatow Imports.

ZUCCHINI WALNUT LOAF

3 eggs
1½ cups brown sugar, firmly packed
1 cup oil
1½ cups (about 3 medium) finely
    grated zucchini
1 cup chopped walnuts
1½ cups self-raising flour
1½ cups plain flour

Grease a 15cm x 25cm loaf pan, line base and sides with paper, grease paper well.

Beat eggs, sugar and oil in large bowl with electric mixer until combined. Stir in zucchini and walnuts, then sifted flours in 2 lots. Spread into prepared pan. Bake in moderate oven for about 1¼ hours. Stand 5 minutes before turning on to wire rack to cool. Serve with butter if desired.

Keeping time: 3 days.

Carrot

Here are 7 different carrot cakes; one made with a light salad oil and topped with the traditional cream cheese frosting and 6 other varieties using butter. Grate the carrots on a medium-sized grater (unless otherwise specified).

SOUR CREAM CARROT CAKE

You will need to finely grate about 2 large carrots for this recipe.

¾ cup self-raising flour
½ cup plain flour
½ teaspoon bicarbonate of soda
1 teaspoon ground cinnamon
1 teaspoon ground nutmeg
½ cup brown sugar
1½ cups grated carrot
½ cup oil
2 eggs, lightly beaten
½ cup sour cream
CREAM CHEESE FROSTING
60g packaged cream cheese, softened
30g soft butter
1 teaspoon grated lemon rind
1½ cups icing sugar
Grease a 20cm ring pan, line base with paper; grease paper.

Sift flours, soda, cinnamon and nutmeg into bowl, stir in sugar and carrot. Combine oil, eggs and sour cream, stir into flour mixture.

Pour mixture into prepared pan, bake in moderately slow oven for about 50 minutes. Turn on to wire rack to cool. When cold, spread with frosting, decorate with walnut halves.

Cream Cheese Frosting: Beat cream cheese, butter and lemon rind in small bowl with electric mixer until light and fluffy, gradually beat in sifted icing sugar; beat until combined.

Keeping time: 4 days.

CARROT AND ORANGE CAKE WITH ORANGE FROSTING

You will need to coarsely grate about 1 large carrot for this recipe. We made tiny carrots from almond paste; they were dried and painted with orange food colouring. The "leaves" were made from angelica.

125g butter
1 tablespoon grated orange rind
½ cup castor sugar
2 eggs
1 cup sultanas
1 cup coarsely grated carrot
1 cup self-raising flour
1 teaspoon ground nutmeg
1 teaspoon mixed spice
2 tablespoons orange juice
ORANGE FROSTING
60g butter
1 cup icing sugar
1 tablespoon orange juice
few drops orange food colouring
Grease a 14cm x 21cm loaf pan, line base with paper; grease paper.

Cream butter, rind and sugar in small bowl with electric mixer until light and fluffy; beat in eggs one at a time, beat until combined. Transfer mixture to large bowl, stir in sultanas and carrot, then sifted dry ingredients and orange juice. Spread into prepared pan, bake in moderately slow oven for 1½ hours. Stand 5 minutes before turning on to wire rack to cool. Top with frosting when cake is cold.

Orange Frosting: Beat butter in small bowl with electric mixer until light and fluffy, gradually beat in sifted icing sugar, then juice and a little colouring; beat until smooth.

Keeping time: 5 days.

MOIST CARROT AND RAISIN WALNUT LOAF

You will need to grate about 2 large carrots for this recipe.

125g butter
1 teaspoon vanilla essence
¾ cup castor sugar
2 tablespoons golden syrup
2 eggs
2 cups grated carrot
1 cup chopped raisins
1 cup chopped walnuts
1½ cups self-raising flour
½ teaspoon ground nutmeg
½ teaspoon ground cinnamon
Grease a 15cm x 25cm loaf pan, line base with paper; grease paper.

Cream butter, essence and sugar in small bowl with electric mixer until light and fluffy; beat in golden syrup, then eggs one at a time, beat until combined. Transfer mixture to large bowl. Stir in carrot, raisins and walnuts. Mixture will look curdled at this stage, but will reconstitute after the flour is added. Stir in sifted dry ingredients; stir until combined. Pour mixture into prepared pan. Bake in moderate oven for about 1¼ hours. Stand 5 minutes before turning on to wire rack to cool.

Keeping time: 1 week.

CARROT CAKE WITH ORANGE CREAM CHEESE FROSTING

You will need to grate about 2 large carrots for this recipe.

185g butter
1½ cups castor sugar
3 eggs
2 cups grated carrot
¾ cup chopped walnuts
¾ cup plain flour
¾ cup self-raising flour
1½ teaspoons mixed spice
ORANGE CREAM CHEESE FROSTING
60g packaged cream cheese
30g soft butter
1 teaspoon grated orange rind
1½ cups icing sugar
Grease a 20cm ring pan, line base with paper, grease paper.

Cream butter and sugar in small bowl with electric mixer until light and fluffy; beat in eggs one at a time, beat until combined. Transfer mixture to large bowl, stir in carrot and walnuts, then sifted dry ingredients. Spread into prepared pan. Bake in moderate oven for about 1 hour. Stand 5 minutes before turning on to wire rack to cool. Spread cold cake with frosting.

Orange Cream Cheese Frosting: Beat cream cheese, butter and rind in small bowl with electric mixer until light and fluffy, gradually beat in sifted icing sugar, beat until smooth.

Keeping time: 3 days.

RIGHT: back: Carrot and Orange Cake with Orange Frosting; centre: Sour Cream Carrot Cake; front: Moist Carrot and Raisin Walnut Loaf.

China is Albertina by Villeroy & Boch.

CARROT ALMOND CAKE

We used 2 large carrots for this recipe. We decorated this cake with tiny carrots made from almond paste. They were painted with orange food colouring; tops are made from angelica.

5 eggs, separated
1 teaspoon grated lemon rind
1¼ cups castor sugar
2 cups finely grated carrot
2 cups (250g) packaged ground almonds
½ cup self-raising flour

Grease a deep 23cm round cake pan, line base with paper; grease paper.

Beat egg yolks with lemon rind and sugar in small bowl with electric mixer until thick. Transfer to large bowl, stir in carrot, almonds and sifted flour. Beat egg whites in medium bowl until soft peaks form, fold lightly into carrot mixture. Pour mixture into prepared pan, bake in moderate oven for about 1 hour. Dust with sifted icing sugar before serving.

Keeping time: 2 days.

BOILED CARROT LOAF

You will need to grate about 1 large carrot for this recipe.

1 cup grated carrot
¾ cup chopped raisins
¾ cup water
¾ cup castor sugar
30g butter
½ teaspoon ground cinnamon
½ teaspoon ground nutmeg
¾ cup self-raising flour
¾ cup plain flour
½ teaspoon bicarbonate of soda
½ cup chopped walnuts

Grease a 14cm x 21cm loaf pan, line base and sides with paper; grease paper well.

Combine carrot, raisins, water, sugar, butter, cinnamon and nutmeg in saucepan, stir constantly over heat without boiling until sugar is dissolved. Bring to the boil, reduce heat, cover, simmer 10 minutes; cool to room temperature. Stir half the sifted flours and soda into cold mixture, then remaining flours and walnuts. Spread into prepared pan. Bake in moderately slow oven for about 1 hour. Stand 5 minutes before turning on to wire rack to cool. Serve sliced, with butter.

Keeping time: 3 days.

EASY-MIX CARROT CAKE

2 eggs
½ teaspoon bicarbonate of soda
½ teaspoon ground cinnamon
2 medium carrots, roughly chopped
185g butter, melted
¾ cup brown sugar, firmly packed
1 cup wholemeal self-raising flour
1 cup sultanas

Grease a 14cm x 21cm loaf pan, line base and sides with paper; grease paper well.

Combine eggs, soda, cinnamon and carrots in processor, process until carrots are finely chopped. Add butter and sugar, process until combined. Stir in sifted flour and sultanas. Pour into prepared pan, bake in moderate oven for about 50 minutes. Stand 5 minutes before turning on to wire rack to cool.

Keeping time: 4 days.

LEFT: back: Carrot Cake with Orange Cream Cheese Frosting (recipe previous page); front: Carrot Almond Cake.
BELOW: back: Easy-Mix Carrot Cake; front: Boiled Carrot Loaf.

Table and blind from Swatow Imports, Sydney; china is Albertina and Riviera by Villeroy & Boch.

Sour Cream

Cakes with sour cream as an ingredient are reliably moist and have good keeping qualities. Use the thick commercial cultured sour cream, fresh cream which has turned sour will not give you the same results as pictured.

BELOW: from left: Spicy Sour Cream Cake with Lemon Icing; Pecan Sour Cream Cake; Ginger Sour Cream Surprise Cake. RIGHT: Lemon Sour Cream Cake.

Background tiles from Country Floors, Woollahra, NSW; wooden stands and white platter from Vasa Agencies, Sydney; chair and table from House of Bambusit, Sydney; cake plate and mugs are Palmetto by Fitz & Floyd.

SPICY SOUR CREAM CAKE WITH LEMON ICING

125g butter
1¼ cups brown sugar, firmly packed
3 eggs
1¼ cups self-raising flour
1 teaspoon ground cinnamon
1 teaspoon ground cardamom
½ teaspoon ground ginger
½ teaspoon ground nutmeg
¼ cup finely chopped mixed peel
200g carton sour cream
LEMON ICING
1½ cups icing sugar
1 teaspoon soft butter
1 tablespoon lemon juice, approximately

Grease a 23cm square slab pan, line base with paper; grease paper.

Cream butter and sugar in small bowl with electric mixer until light and fluffy; beat in eggs one at a time, beat until combined. Transfer mixture to large bowl, fold in sifted dry ingredients, peel and sour cream, stir until mixture is smooth.

Pour mixture into prepared pan, bake in moderately slow oven for about 1¼ hours. Stand 5 minutes before turning on to wire rack to cool. Top cold cake with icing, sprinkle cake with cinnamon.

Lemon Icing: Sift icing sugar into small heatproof bowl, stir in butter and enough lemon juice to make a stiff paste. Stir over hot water until icing is spreadable.

Keeping time: 4 days.

Sour Cream

Cakes with sour cream as an ingredient are reliably moist and have good keeping qualities. Use the thick commercial cultured sour cream, fresh cream which has turned sour will not give you the same results as pictured.

BELOW: from left: Spicy Sour Cream Cake with Lemon Icing; Pecan Sour Cream Cake; Ginger Sour Cream Surprise Cake. RIGHT: Lemon Sour Cream Cake.

Background tiles from Country Floors, Woollahra, NSW; wooden stands and white platter from Vasa Agencies, Sydney; chair and table from House of Bambusit, Sydney; cake plate and mugs are Palmetto by Fitz & Floyd.

SPICY SOUR CREAM CAKE WITH LEMON ICING

125g butter
1¼ cups brown sugar, firmly packed
3 eggs
1¼ cups self-raising flour
1 teaspoon ground cinnamon
1 teaspoon ground cardamom
½ teaspoon ground ginger
½ teaspoon ground nutmeg
¼ cup finely chopped mixed peel
200g carton sour cream
LEMON ICING
1½ cups icing sugar
1 teaspoon soft butter
1 tablespoon lemon juice, approximately

Grease a 23cm square slab pan, line base with paper; grease paper.

Cream butter and sugar in small bowl with electric mixer until light and fluffy; beat in eggs one at a time, beat until combined. Transfer mixture to large bowl, fold in sifted dry ingredients, peel and sour cream, stir until mixture is smooth.

Pour mixture into prepared pan, bake in moderately slow oven for about 1¼ hours. Stand 5 minutes before turning on to wire rack to cool. Top cold cake with icing, sprinkle cake with cinnamon.

Lemon Icing: Sift icing sugar into small heatproof bowl, stir in butter and enough lemon juice to make a stiff paste. Stir over hot water until icing is spreadable.

Keeping time: 4 days.

CARROT ALMOND CAKE

We used 2 large carrots for this recipe. We decorated this cake with tiny carrots made from almond paste. They were painted with orange food colouring; tops are made from angelica.

5 eggs, separated
1 teaspoon grated lemon rind
1¼ cups castor sugar
2 cups finely grated carrot
2 cups (250g) packaged ground almonds
½ cup self-raising flour

Grease a deep 23cm round cake pan, line base with paper; grease paper.

Beat egg yolks with lemon rind and sugar in small bowl with electric mixer until thick. Transfer to large bowl, stir in carrot, almonds and sifted flour. Beat egg whites in medium bowl until soft peaks form, fold lightly into carrot mixture. Pour mixture into prepared pan, bake in moderate oven for about 1 hour. Dust with sifted icing sugar before serving.

Keeping time: 2 days.

BOILED CARROT LOAF

You will need to grate about 1 large carrot for this recipe.

1 cup grated carrot
¾ cup chopped raisins
¾ cup water
¾ cup castor sugar
30g butter
½ teaspoon ground cinnamon
½ teaspoon ground nutmeg
¾ cup self-raising flour
¾ cup plain flour
½ teaspoon bicarbonate of soda
½ cup chopped walnuts

Grease a 14cm x 21cm loaf pan, line base and sides with paper; grease paper well.

Combine carrot, raisins, water, sugar, butter, cinnamon and nutmeg in saucepan, stir constantly over heat without boiling until sugar is dissolved. Bring to the boil, reduce heat, cover, simmer 10 minutes; cool to room temperature. Stir half the sifted flours and soda into cold mixture, then remaining flours and walnuts. Spread into prepared pan. Bake in moderately slow oven for about 1 hour. Stand 5 minutes before turning on to wire rack to cool. Serve sliced, with butter.

Keeping time: 3 days.

EASY-MIX CARROT CAKE

2 eggs
½ teaspoon bicarbonate of soda
½ teaspoon ground cinnamon
2 medium carrots, roughly chopped
185g butter, melted
¾ cup brown sugar, firmly packed
1 cup wholemeal self-raising flour
1 cup sultanas

Grease a 14cm x 21cm loaf pan, line base and sides with paper; grease paper well.

Combine eggs, soda, cinnamon and carrots in processor, process until carrots are finely chopped. Add butter and sugar, process until combined. Stir in sifted flour and sultanas. Pour into prepared pan, bake in moderate oven for about 50 minutes. Stand 5 minutes before turning on to wire rack to cool.

Keeping time: 4 days.

LEFT: back: Carrot Cake with Orange Cream Cheese Frosting (recipe previous page); front: Carrot Almond Cake. BELOW: back: Easy-Mix Carrot Cake; front: Boiled Carrot Loaf.

Table and blind from Swatow Imports, Sydney; china is Albertina and Riviera by Villeroy & Boch.

LEMON SOUR CREAM CAKE

This is a moist buttery cake. It is delicious plain, or served with cream.

250g butter
2 teaspoons grated lemon rind
2 cups castor sugar
6 eggs
2 cups plain flour
¼ cup self-raising flour
200g carton sour cream

Grease a deep 27cm round cake pan, line base with paper; grease paper.

Cream butter, rind and sugar in large bowl with electric mixer until light and fluffy; beat in eggs one at a time, beat until combined. Stir in half the sifted flours with half the sour cream, then stir in remaining flours and cream, stir until smooth. Spread mixture into prepared pan; bake in moderately slow oven for about 1½ hours. Stand 5 minutes before turning on to wire rack to cool. Dust with icing sugar before serving.

Keeping time: 1 week.

PECAN SOUR CREAM CAKE

250g butter
1 teaspoon vanilla essence
¾ cup castor sugar
2 eggs
300g carton sour cream
1½ cups plain flour
½ cup self-raising flour
1 teaspoon bicarbonate of soda
½ cup finely chopped pecan nuts
2 tablespoons brown sugar
½ teaspoon ground cinnamon

Grease a deep 23cm round cake pan.

Cream butter, essence and sugar in small bowl with electric mixer until light and fluffy; beat in eggs one at a time, beat until combined. Transfer mixture to large bowl, stir in sour cream then sifted flours and soda.

Spread half the cake mixture into prepared pan; sprinkle with half the combined pecans, brown sugar and cinnamon. Spread evenly with remaining cake mixture, sprinkle with remaining pecan mixture; press gently into cake mixture. Bake in moderate oven about 1 hour. Stand 5 minutes before turning on to wire rack to cool.

Keeping time: 3 days.

GINGER SOUR CREAM SURPRISE CAKE

This cake is best eaten on the day it is made. It is important not to over beat this cake mixture, or the sour cream will slip to the base of the pan.

185g butter
1 cup brown sugar, firmly packed
3 eggs
1½ cups self-raising flour
2 teaspoons ground ginger
⅔ cup sour cream
1 tablespoon castor sugar

Grease a 20cm baba pan. Combine butter, brown sugar, eggs and sifted flour and ginger in large bowl, stir with wooden spoon until mixture is smooth. Spread mixture into prepared pan. Combine sour cream and castor sugar, spread evenly over mixture. Bake in moderate oven for about 45 minutes. Stand 2 minutes before turning on to wire rack to cool. Dust with icing sugar before serving.

Keeping time: 1 day.

FIG WALNUT AND GINGER CAKE

We used moist unsweetened dessert figs for this recipe.

185g butter
¾ cup castor sugar
3 eggs
½ cup finely chopped figs
⅓ cup finely chopped glace ginger
½ cup finely chopped walnuts
½ cup plain flour
½ cup self-raising flour
⅓ cup sour cream

Grease a 14cm x 21cm loaf pan, line base with paper; grease paper.

Cream butter and sugar in small bowl with electric mixer until light and fluffy; beat in eggs one at a time, beat until combined. Transfer mixture to large bowl. Stir in figs, ginger and walnuts, then sifted flours and sour cream.

Spread mixture into prepared pan. Bake in moderately slow oven for about 1¼ hours. Stand 5 minutes before turning on to wire rack to cool.

Keeping time: 1 week.

CITRUS SOUR CREAM CAKE

125g butter
1 cup castor sugar
3 eggs
½ cup mixed peel
¾ cup plain flour
¾ cup self-raising flour
½ cup sour cream

Grease a 14cm x 21cm loaf pan, line with paper; grease paper.

Cream butter and sugar in small bowl with electric mixer until light and fluffy. Beat in eggs one at a time, beat until combined. Transfer mixture to large bowl, stir in peel with half the sifted flours and half the sour cream, then stir in remaining flours and sour cream.

Spread mixture into prepared pan. Bake in moderately slow oven for about 1¼ hours. Stand 5 minutes before turning on to wire rack to cool. Dust with icing sugar before serving.

Keeping time: 2 days.

ABOVE: back: Citrus Sour Cream Cake; front, from left: Cherry and Sultana Loaf; Fig Walnut and Ginger Cake.

White plates are Pillivuyt from Hale Imports, Sydney; round plate and bowl are Copco from Vasa Agencies, Sydney.

CHERRY AND SULTANA LOAF

125g butter
2 teaspoons grated lemon rind
1 cup castor sugar
3 eggs
½ cup sliced glace cherries
½ cup sultanas
1½ cups self-raising flour
¾ cup plain flour
¾ cup sour cream
¼ cup lemon juice

Grease a 14cm x 21cm loaf pan, line base with paper; grease paper.

Cream butter, rind and sugar in small bowl with electric mixer until light and fluffy; beat in eggs one at a time, beat until combined. Transfer mixture to large bowl. Stir in fruit, then half the sifted flours with half the combined sour cream and lemon juice, then stir in remaining flours and lemon mixture. Pour into prepared pan. Bake in moderate oven for about 1¼ hours. Stand 5 minutes before turning on to wire rack to cool.

Keeping time: 3 days.

Coconut

Your search for the best coconut cake is over — we present a choice selection; the richest and most moist is the Moist Coconut Cake with Coconut Ice Frosting.

ABOVE: Moist Coconut Cake with Coconut Ice Frosting.

Board from Appley Hoare Antiques, Mosman, NSW.

MOIST COCONUT CAKE WITH COCONUT ICE FROSTING

125g butter
½ teaspoon coconut essence
1 cup castor sugar
2 eggs
½ cup coconut
1½ cups self-raising flour
300g carton sour cream
⅓ cup milk
COCONUT ICE FROSTING
2 cups icing sugar
1⅓ cups coconut
2 egg whites, lightly beaten
pink food colouring

Grease a deep 23cm round cake pan, line base with paper; grease paper.

Cream butter, essence and sugar in small bowl with electric mixer until light and fluffy; beat in eggs one at a time, beat until combined. Transfer mixture to large bowl. Stir in half the coconut and sifted flour with half the sour cream and milk, then stir in remaining ingredients; stir until smooth.

Pour mixture into prepared pan. Bake in moderate oven for about 1 hour. Stand 5 minutes before turning on to wire rack to cool. Top with frosting when cold.

Coconut Ice Frosting: Combine sifted icing sugar in bowl with coconut and egg whites; mix well. If desired, tint pink with a little colouring.

Keeping time: 1 week.

ORANGE COCONUT CAKE WITH ORANGE ICING

Best made on same day as serving.

½ cup coconut
1 cup milk
125g butter
1 tablespoon grated orange rind
1 cup castor sugar
2 eggs
1¾ cups self-raising flour
ORANGE ICING
1½ cups icing sugar
15g soft butter
2 tablespoons orange juice,
    approximately

Combine coconut and milk, stand at room temperature for 1 hour.

Grease a 14cm x 21cm loaf pan, line base with paper; grease paper.

Cream butter, rind and sugar in small bowl with electric mixer until light and fluffy; beat in eggs one at a time, beat until combined. Transfer mixture to large bowl, stir in half the coconut mixture and half the sifted flour, then stir in remaining coconut mixture and flour, stir until smooth.

Pour mixture into prepared pan. Bake in moderately slow oven for about 1½ hours, stand 5 minutes, before turning on to wire rack to cool. Spread cold cake with icing; decorate with orange wedges if desired.

Orange Icing: Sift icing sugar into bowl, stir in butter and enough juice to mix to a spreadable consistency.

Keeping time: 1 day.

RIGHT: back: Cherry Coconut and Orange Cake; front: Orange Coconut Cake with Orange Icing.
FAR RIGHT: Coconut and Date Loaf.

CHERRY COCONUT AND ORANGE CAKE

125g butter
2 teaspoons grated orange rind
¾ cup castor sugar
2 eggs, separated
½ cup coconut
¾ cup sliced glace cherries
2 cups self-raising flour
⅔ cup orange juice

Grease a 14cm x 21cm loaf pan, line base and sides of pan with paper; grease paper.

Cream butter, rind and sugar in small bowl with electric mixer until light and fluffy; beat in egg yolks, beat until combined. Transfer mixture to large bowl, stir in coconut and cherries. Stir in half the sifted flour with half the orange juice, then stir in remaining flour and orange juice.

Beat egg whites in small bowl until soft peaks form, fold into cake mixture. Spread into prepared pan. Bake in moderate oven for about 1 hour. Stand 5 minutes before turning on to wire rack to cool.

Keeping time: 2 days.

COCONUT AND DAT

1 cup chopped dates
½ cup boiling water
125g butter
½ cup castor sugar
1 egg
⅔ cup self-raising flour
¼ cup coconut

Grease a 14cm x 21cm loaf pan, line base with paper; grease paper.

Combine dates with boiling water; cover, stand 15 minutes.

Cream butter and sugar in small bowl with electric mixer until light and fluffy; add egg, beat until combined. Transfer mixture to large bowl, stir in sifted flour, coconut and undrained dates. Spread into prepared pan, bake in moderate oven for about 40 minutes. Stand 5 minutes before turning on to wire rack to cool.

Keeping time: 2 days.

AKE WITH

LOAF

nly packed

1½ cups self-raising flour
½ cup milk
CARAMEL ICING
60g butter
½ cup brown sugar
2 tablespoons milk
1½ cups icing sugar

Grease a 19cm x 29cm lamington pan, line base with paper; grease paper.

Stir coconut constantly over heat in heavy frying pan until light golden brown. Remove from pan to cool.

Cream butter and sugar in small bowl with electric mixer until light and fluffy, beat in eggs one at a time, add honey, beat until combined. Transfer mixture to large bowl, stir in toasted coconut, half the sifted flour and half the milk, then stir in remaining flour and milk.

Spread mixture into prepared pan. Bake in moderate oven for about 35 minutes. Stand 5 minutes before turning on to wire rack to cool. Spread cold cake with icing, sprinkle with extra coconut if desired.

Caramel Icing: Melt butter in saucepan, add sugar, stir constantly over heat without boiling for about 2 minutes. Stir in milk then gradually stir in sifted icing sugar; stir until smooth.

Keeping time: 2 days.

RIGHT: back: Pineapple Coconut Cake with Pineapple Frosting; centre: Honey Coconut Cake with Caramel Icing; front: Apricot Coconut Cake with Macaroon Topping.

Plates are Taitu Indian Summer from Lifestyle Imports.

APRICOT COCONUT CAKE WITH MACAROON TOPPING

90g butter
2 teaspoons grated lemon rind
½ cup castor sugar
2 egg yolks
1 cup self-raising flour
½ cup milk
2 tablespoons apricot jam
MACAROON TOPPING
2 egg whites
2 tablespoons castor sugar
½ cup coconut
¼ cup packaged ground almonds

Grease a 20cm ring pan, line base with paper; grease paper.

Cream butter, rind and sugar in small bowl with electric mixer until light and fluffy, add egg yolks, beat until combined. Stir in half the sifted flour with half the milk, then stir in remaining flour and milk, stir until smooth. Spread into prepared pan, drizzle with warmed sieved apricot jam. Bake in moderately slow oven 20 minutes, spread evenly with topping, bake further 20 minutes or until golden brown. Stand 5 minutes before turning on to wire rack to cool.

Macaroon Topping: Beat egg whites in small bowl until soft peaks form, gradually add sugar, beat until dissolved, fold in coconut and almonds.

Keeping time: 2 days.

PINEAPPLE COCONUT CAKE WITH PINEAPPLE FROSTING

We used a 250ml carton of pineapple juice for this recipe.

125g butter
2 teaspoons grated lemon rind
1 cup castor sugar
2 eggs
½ cup coconut
2 cups self-raising flour
¾ cup pineapple juice
PINEAPPLE FROSTING
30g butter
2 cups icing sugar
¼ cup pineapple juice

Grease a deep 20cm round cake pan, line base with paper; grease paper.

Cream butter, rind and sugar in small bowl with electric mixer until light and fluffy, add eggs one at a time, beat until combined. Transfer mixture to large bowl, stir in coconut, then half the sifted flour and pineapple juice, then remaining flour and pineapple juice; stir until combined. Spread mixture into prepared pan. Bake in moderately slow oven for about 1 hour, stand 5 minutes before turning on to wire rack to cool. When cold, spread with frosting. Decorate with extra canned pineapple and toasted shredded coconut if desired.

Pineapple Frosting: Combine butter and sifted icing sugar in bowl, gradually stir in pineapple juice until smooth.

Keeping time: 2 days.

51

Nut Rolls

Good old fashioned nut rolls are forever popular; they are all moist and keep and cut well; always serve buttered. The nut roll tins we used have a diameter of 8cm and are 17cm tall. Always grease the inside of the tins and ends well and evenly.

Divide the mixture evenly into the tins. Dropping the mixture from a spoon is the least messy way to do this. Don't overfill the tins — as a guide they should be only a little over half-full.

Stand the tins upright on an oven tray for easier handling. After the cooking time has expired, remove the tins from the oven, remove the top lid from one roll (be careful of hot steam) — then test the roll with a skewer. If it is cooked, put the lid back in position, and stand the rolls for 10 minutes. This gives the rolls time to become firm enough to handle. Remove the lids carefully from both ends of the tins, then gently shake the rolls out on to a wire rack to cool. Some of the older tins open down the side for easy removal.

The recipes in this section will make two nut rolls.

Back, from left: Banana Bran Rolls; Boston Bread. Front: Fig and Muesli Rolls; centre: Moist Apricot Rolls.

Dresser from Appley Hoare Antiques, Mosman, NSW; china is Vienna from Villeroy & Boch.

BANANA BRAN ROLLS

We used 3 bananas for this recipe.

90g butter
½ cup brown sugar
2 eggs
1 cup chopped dates
½ cup chopped walnuts
1 cup mashed banana
½ cup unprocessed bran
1¼ cups wholemeal self-raising flour
¼ cup milk
Grease 2 nut roll tins.

Cream butter and sugar in small bowl with electric mixer until light and fluffy; beat in eggs one at a time, beat until combined. Stir in dates, walnuts and banana, then bran, sifted flour and milk. Spoon mixture into prepared tins. Bake in moderate oven for about 1 hour. Stand rolls in tins, with lids on, for 10 minutes. Remove lids, turn on to wire rack to cool.

Keeping time: 3 days.

FIG AND MUESLI ROLLS

1½ cups water
1¼ cups (250g) chopped glace figs
125g butter
1 cup brown sugar, firmly packed
¼ cup honey
2 eggs, lightly beaten
½ cup toasted muesli
1½ cups self-raising flour
Bring water to boil in pan, add figs, reduce heat, simmer uncovered 5 minutes. Add butter and sugar, stir until butter is melted. Transfer mixture to large bowl, cool to room temperature.

Grease 2 nut roll tins. Stir honey, eggs and muesli into fig mixture, then sifted flour; stir until combined. Spoon mixture evenly into prepared tins. Bake in moderate oven for about 1 hour. Stand rolls in tins, with lids on, for 10 minutes. Remove lids, turn on to wire rack to cool.

Keeping time: 3 days.

BOSTON BREAD

1 cup wholemeal plain flour
1 cup rye flour
1 teaspoon bicarbonate of soda
1¼ cups cornmeal (polenta)
1 tablespoon castor sugar
¾ cup chopped raisins
1½ cups milk
½ cup treacle
1 teaspoon brown vinegar
Grease 2 nut roll tins.

Sift flours and soda into large bowl, stir in cornmeal, sugar and raisins. Stir in combined milk, treacle and vinegar (mixture should look coarse and grainy). Spoon mixture evenly into prepared tins. Bake in moderate oven for about 1 hour. Stand rolls in tins, with lids on, for 10 minutes. Remove lids, turn rolls on to wire rack to cool.

Keeping time: 3 days.

MOIST APRICOT ROLLS

⅔ cup chopped dried apricots
125g butter
¾ cup castor sugar
2 eggs
¾ cup plain flour
1 cup self-raising flour
⅓ cup milk

Cover apricots with hot water, stand 30 minutes; drain well.

Grease 2 nut roll tins. Cream butter and sugar in small bowl with electric mixer until light and fluffy; beat in eggs one at a time, beat until combined. Stir in half the sifted flours with half the milk, then stir in remaining flours and milk; stir in apricots. Spoon mixture evenly into prepared tins. Bake in moderate oven for about 1 hour. Stand rolls in tins, with lids on, for 10 minutes. Remove lids, turn on to wire rack to cool.

Keeping time: 3 days.

DATE AND WALNUT ROLLS

1 cup chopped dates
60g butter
1 cup brown sugar, firmly packed
¾ cup water
½ teaspoon bicarbonate of soda
1 egg, lightly beaten
½ cup chopped walnuts
1 cup self-raising flour
½ cup plain flour

Combine dates, butter, sugar and water in pan, stir constantly over heat without boiling until sugar is dissolved. Bring to the boil, remove from heat. Transfer mixture to large bowl, cool to room temperature.

Grease 2 nut roll tins. Stir soda, egg and walnuts into date mixture, then sifted flours. Spoon mixture evenly into prepared tins. Bake in moderate oven for about 1 hour. Stand rolls in tins, with lids on, for 10 minutes. Remove lids, turn on to wire rack to cool.

Keeping time: 3 days.

OVERNIGHT APRICOT AND BRAN ROLLS

1¼ cups All Bran
1¼ cups brown sugar, firmly packed
1¼ cups milk
1 cup chopped dried apricots
2 tablespoons honey
1¼ cups self-raising flour

Combine All Bran, sugar, milk, apricots and honey in large bowl, cover, stand overnight.

Grease 2 nut roll tins. Stir sifted flour into All Bran mixture; stir until combined. Spoon mixture into prepared tins. Bake in moderate oven for about 1 hour. Stand rolls in tins, with lids on, for 10 minutes. Remove lids, turn on to wire rack to cool.

Keeping time: 3 days.

BELOW: from left: Date and Walnut Rolls; Overnight Apricot and Bran Rolls.
RIGHT: Choc-Cinnamon Meringue-Topped Cake.

Baked-on-Toppings

There is always an advantage in cooking a cake with a baked-on- topping — it's ready to eat as soon as it's baked. These can all be served warm with cream, or cold — whichever you choose. Remember to gently, but quickly turn these cakes right way up to cool.

CHOC-CINNAMON MERINGUE-TOPPED CAKE

This cake is at its best eaten on the same day as baking.

125g butter
⅔ cup brown sugar, firmly packed
2 egg yolks
1 egg
100g dark chocolate, grated
1½ cups self-raising flour
1 teaspoon ground cinnamon
⅔ cup milk
MERINGUE
2 egg whites
½ cup castor sugar
TOPPING
1 teaspoon sugar
½ teaspoon ground cinnamon
1 tablespoon coconut
¼ cup slivered almonds

Grease a 23cm square slab pan, line base with paper; grease paper.

Cream butter and sugar in small bowl with electric mixer until light and fluffy; beat in egg yolks and egg, beat until combined. Transfer mixture to large bowl, stir in chocolate, then half the sifted dry ingredients with half the milk, then stir in remaining dry ingredients and milk; stir until smooth.

Spread mixture into prepared pan, spread carefully with meringue, sprinkle with topping. Bake in moderately slow oven for about 50 minutes. Stand 5 minutes before turning on to wire rack to cool.

Meringue: Beat egg whites until soft peaks form, gradually add sugar, beat until dissolved.

Topping: Combine all ingredients.

  Keeping time: 1 day.

APPLE ALMOND CAKE

125g butter
⅔ cup castor sugar
2 eggs
½ cup self-raising flour
½ cup plain flour
⅓ cup milk
1 apple, grated
¼ cup slivered almonds

Grease a deep 20cm round cake pan, line base with paper; grease paper.

Cream butter and sugar in small bowl with electric mixer until light and fluffy; beat in eggs one at a time, beat until combined. Transfer mixture to large bowl, stir in half the sifted flours with half the milk, then stir in remaining flour and milk, stir until smooth. Spread into prepared pan, sprinkle with apple and almonds, bake in moderate oven for about 45 minutes. Stand 5 minutes before turning on to wire rack to cool.

Keeping time: 2 days.

STREUSEL-TOPPED RICH BUTTER CAKE

125g butter
1 teaspoon vanilla essence
½ cup castor sugar
2 eggs
⅔ cup self-raising flour
½ cup plain flour
2 tablespoons milk
TOPPING
¾ cup plain flour
⅓ cup brown sugar
2 teaspoons ground cinnamon
90g butter

ABOVE: from left: Streusel-Topped Rich Butter Cake; Apple Almond Cake.
RIGHT: in descending order: Wholemeal Apricot Upside Down Cake; Pineapple Cake with Crunchy Coconut Topping; Butterscotch Raisin Cake.

Dresser, wooden board, spice jars, blue bowl and jug, tea towel from Appley Hoare Antiques, Mosman, NSW; plates, cup and saucer are Saturn by Sasaki from Dansab.

Grease a 19cm x 29cm lamington pan, line base with paper; grease paper.

Cream butter, essence and sugar in small bowl with electric mixer until light and fluffy, beat in eggs one at a time, beat until combined. Transfer mixture to large bowl, stir in half the sifted flours with half the milk, then stir in remaining flours and milk.

Spread mixture into prepared pan, sprinkle with topping. Bake in moderate oven for about 30 minutes. Stand 5 minutes before turning on to wire rack to cool.

Topping: Combine flour, sugar and cinnamon in bowl, rub in butter. Press into a ball, refrigerate for about 30 minutes. Grate coarsely when cold.

Keeping time: 2 days.

WHOLEMEAL APRICOT UPSIDE DOWN CAKE

½ cup dried apricots
60g butter, softened
½ cup brown sugar
⅓ cup chopped walnuts
CAKE
125g butter
1 teaspoon vanilla essence
⅔ cup brown sugar, firmly packed
2 eggs
1 cup white self-raising flour
½ cup wholemeal self-raising flour
½ cup milk

Cover apricots with boiling water, soak 30 minutes, drain.

Grease a 20cm ring pan, line base with paper; grease paper.

Combine butter and sugar in small bowl, stir until smooth. Spread mixture evenly over base of prepared pan, sprinkle with walnuts. Top with apricots, cut side up. Spread carefully with cake mixture. Bake in moderate oven for about 40 minutes, stand 15 minutes before turning on to wire rack to cool.

Cake: Cream butter, essence and sugar in small bowl with electric mixer until light and fluffy, beat in eggs one at a time, beat until combined. Transfer mixture to large bowl, stir in half the sifted flours with half the milk, then stir in remaining flours and milk.

Keeping time: 2 days.

PINEAPPLE CAKE WITH CRUNCHY COCONUT TOPPING

450g can crushed pineapple
125g butter
½ cup castor sugar
2 eggs
1½ cups self-raising flour
COCONUT TOPPING
½ cup brown sugar
½ cup plain flour
½ cup coconut
90g butter

Grease a 20cm ring pan, line base with paper; grease paper. Drain pineapple, reserve ½ cup syrup.

Cream butter and sugar in small bowl with electric mixer until light and fluffy, beat in eggs one at a time, beat until combined. Transfer mixture to large bowl, stir in half the sifted flour and half the reserved syrup, then remaining flour and syrup.

Spread half the mixture evenly over base of prepared pan, top with well-drained pineapple and half the topping. Spread with remaining cake mixture, sprinkle with remaining topping. Bake in moderate oven for about 50 minutes, stand 5 minutes before turning on to wire rack to cool.

Coconut Topping: Combine sugar, flour, coconut in bowl, rub in butter.

Keeping time: 3 days.

BUTTERSCOTCH RAISIN CAKE

90g butter
¾ cup brown sugar, firmly packed
1 tablespoon golden syrup
2 eggs
1 cup chopped raisins
1¼ cups self-raising flour
¼ cup milk
TOPPING
¼ cup plain flour
2 tablespoons brown sugar
30g butter
½ cup chopped walnuts

Grease a 20cm ring pan.

Cream butter and sugar in small bowl with electric mixer until light and fluffy; beat in golden syrup, then eggs one at a time, beat until combined. Stir in raisins, then sifted flour and milk. Spoon mixture into prepared pan. Sprinkle with topping. Bake in moderate oven for about 45 minutes. Stand 5 minutes before turning on to wire rack to cool.

Topping: Combine flour and sugar in bowl; rub in butter, stir in walnuts.

Keeping time: 2 days.

Banana

The bananas used for these cakes must be over-ripe — the sweeter and softer the better! It is usually best to mash them on a plate with a fork. You will need to mash about 3 large bananas to give 1 cup of banana pulp.

CARAMEL BANANA CAKE

You will need 3 bananas for this recipe.

125g butter
¾ cup brown sugar, firmly packed
2 eggs
1 cup mashed banana
1½ cups self-raising flour
1 teaspoon bicarbonate of soda
¾ cup sour cream
1 tablespoon milk
CARAMEL ICING
60g butter
½ cup brown sugar
2 tablespoons sour cream
1½ cups icing sugar

Grease a 14cm x 21cm loaf pan.

Cream butter and sugar in small bowl with electric mixer until light and fluffy, beat in eggs, one at a time; beat until combined.

Transfer mixture to large bowl, stir in banana. Stir in half the sifted dry ingredients with half the combined sour cream and milk then stir in remaining dry ingredients and sour cream mixture; stir until smooth. Pour mixture into prepared pan. Bake in moderate oven for about 1 hour, stand 5 minutes before turning on to wire rack to cool. When cold, spread with icing.

Caramel Icing: Melt butter and sugar in saucepan, stir constantly over heat without boiling for 2 minutes. Add sour cream, bring to the boil, remove from heat, stir in sifted icing sugar.

Keeping time: 4 days.

BANANA PINEAPPLE CAKE

You will need 3 bananas for this recipe.

1½ cups plain flour
1 teaspoon ground cinnamon
½ teaspoon bicarbonate of soda
1 cup castor sugar
¾ cup chopped pecan nuts
1 cup mashed banana
450g can crushed pineapple, drained
½ cup oil
2 eggs, lightly beaten

Grease a 20cm ring pan, line base with paper; grease paper.

Combine sifted dry ingredients, sugar and pecans in large bowl. Stir in banana, well drained pineapple, oil and eggs. Spoon mixture into prepared pan. Bake in moderate oven for about 1 hour. Stand 10 minutes before turning on to wire rack to cool.

Keeping time: 4 days.

RIGHT: back: Banana and Passionfruit Yoghurt Cake; front: Banana Coconut Cake with Coconut Honey Topping (recipes over page).
BELOW: back: Banana Pineapple Cake; front: Caramel Banana Cake.

Plates at right are Desert Rose by Franciscan from Wedgwood Australia Ltd.

BANANA AND PASSIONFRUIT YOGHURT CAKE

We used 2 bananas for this recipe.

125g butter
1 cup castor sugar
1 egg
¾ cup mashed banana
⅓ cup chopped walnuts
200g carton passionfruit yoghurt
1 cup wholemeal self-raising flour
1 cup white self-raising flour
PASSIONFRUIT ICING
1½ cups icing sugar
1 teaspoon soft butter
2 passionfruit

Grease a deep 20cm round cake pan; line base with paper; grease paper.

Cream butter and sugar in small bowl with electric mixer until light and fluffy, add egg, beat until combined. Transfer mixture to large bowl, stir in banana, walnuts and yoghurt, then sifted flours.

Spread mixture into prepared pan, bake in moderate oven for about 1 hour. Stand 5 minutes before turning on to wire rack to cool. Top cold cake with icing.

Passionfruit Icing: Sift icing sugar into small heatproof bowl, stir in butter and enough passionfruit pulp to make a stiff paste. Stir over hot water until icing is spreadable.

Keeping time: 2 days.

GINGER BANANA CAKE

We used 2 bananas for this recipe.

90g butter
2 tablespoons golden syrup
¼ cup castor sugar
¼ cup brown sugar
1 egg
⅔ cup mashed banana
1½ cups self-raising flour
½ teaspoon bicarbonate of soda
2 teaspoons ground ginger
1 tablespoon milk
LEMON FROSTING
1½ cups icing sugar
30g butter
2 tablespoons lemon juice, approximately
¼ cup chopped glace ginger

Grease a 20cm ring pan, line base with paper; grease paper.

Cream butter, golden syrup and sugars in small bowl with electric mixer until light and fluffy. Add egg, beat until combined, then beat in banana. Transfer mixture to large bowl, stir in sifted dry ingredients and milk.

Pour mixture into prepared pan. Bake in moderate oven for about 45 minutes. Stand 5 minutes before turning on to wire rack to cool. Spread cold cake with frosting, sprinkle with ginger.

Lemon Frosting: Combine sifted icing sugar with butter and enough juice to mix to a spreadable consistency.

Keeping time: 2 days.

BANANA COCONUT CAKE WITH COCONUT HONEY TOPPING

We used 3 bananas for this recipe.

¾ cup coconut
90g butter
½ cup castor sugar
2 eggs
¾ cup self-raising flour
¼ cup plain flour
1 teaspoon bicarbonate of soda
¼ cup milk
1 cup mashed banana
COCONUT HONEY TOPPING
30g butter
2 tablespoons honey
1 cup shredded coconut

Grease a 15cm x 25cm loaf pan, line base with paper; grease paper. Toast coconut on oven tray in moderate oven for about 5 minutes, cool.

Cream butter and sugar in small bowl with electric mixer until light and fluffy; beat in eggs one at a time, beat until combined. Stir in half the combined sifted dry ingredients and toasted coconut with half the combined milk and banana, then stir in remaining dry ingredients and banana mixture; stir until smooth. Pour into prepared pan, bake in moderately slow oven for 30 minutes. Spread evenly with topping, bake for about further 30 minutes. Stand 5 minutes before turning on to wire rack to cool.

Coconut Honey Topping: Place butter and honey in saucepan, heat until butter is melted, add coconut, stir 5 minutes or until lightly browned.

Keeping time: 2 days.

BANANA WALNUT BREAD

We used 3 bananas for this recipe.

125g butter
1 teaspoon vanilla essence
¾ cup castor sugar
2 eggs
1 cup mashed banana
¾ cup self-raising flour
¾ cup plain flour
½ teaspoon bicarbonate of soda
½ cup chopped walnuts

Grease 2 x 8cm x 26cm bar pans, line bases with paper; grease paper.

Cream butter, essence and sugar in small bowl with electric mixer until light and fluffy, add eggs one at a time; beat until combined. Stir in half the banana with half the sifted dry ingredients and half the walnuts, then stir in remaining banana, dry ingredients and walnuts; stir until combined. Spread mixture evenly into prepared pans. Bake in moderate oven for about 45 minutes. Stand 5 minutes before turning on to wire rack to cool. Serve buttered.

Keeping time: 2 days.

WHOLEMEAL BANANA DATE AND PEANUT LOAF

We used 3 bananas for this recipe.

1½ cups wholemeal self-raising flour
1 cup wheatgerm
½ cup raw sugar
1½ cups (250g) chopped dates
125g butter, melted
1¼ cups milk
2 eggs, lightly beaten
1 cup mashed banana
¼ cup unsalted roasted peanuts

Grease a 15cm x 25cm loaf pan, line base with paper; grease paper.

Sift flour into large bowl, mix in wheatgerm, sugar and dates. Stir in butter, milk, eggs and banana. Pour into prepared pan, sprinkle with nuts, bake in moderate oven for about 1¼ hours. Stand 5 minutes before turning on to wire rack to cool.

Keeping time: 3 days.

BANANA SOUR CREAM CAKE WITH CHOCOLATE FROSTING

We used 3 bananas for this recipe.

125g butter
1 teaspoon vanilla essence
1 cup castor sugar
2 eggs
1 cup mashed banana
⅓ cup sour cream
2 cups self-raising flour
¼ teaspoon bicarbonate of soda
CHOCOLATE FROSTING
125g packet cream cheese
30g butter
1½ cups icing sugar
60g dark chocolate, melted

Grease a deep 20cm round cake pan, line base with paper; grease paper.

Cream butter, essence and sugar in small bowl with electric mixer until light and fluffy, add eggs one at a time; beat until combined. Stir in half the banana with half the sour cream and half the sifted dry ingredients, then stir in remaining banana, sour cream and dry ingredients. Spread mixture into prepared pan. Bake in moderate oven for about 1¼ hours. Stand 5 minutes, before turning on to wire rack to cool. Spread cold cake with frosting.

Chocolate Frosting: Beat cream cheese and butter in small bowl with electric mixer until smooth. Gradually beat in half the sifted icing sugar, cooled chocolate, then remaining icing sugar. Beat until thick.

Keeping time: 2 days.

RIGHT: back, from left: Banana Sour Cream Cake with Chocolate Frosting; Ginger Banana Cake; front, from left: Wholemeal Banana Date and Peanut Loaf; Banana Walnut Bread.

Wooden board from Scanada Agencies; plates are Desert Rose by Franciscan from Wedgwood Australia Ltd.

Lamingtons

Our favourite lamington recipe is included in this section along with a delicious honey-flavoured variety and old fashioned jelly cakes. Day old or partly frozen pieces of cake are easier to handle when dipping the cake into the icing.

LAMINGTONS

This is our favourite recipe for lamingtons. The lamington bars (right) simply use a smaller quantity of this recipe.

6 eggs
¾ cup castor sugar
1 cup self-raising flour
⅓ cup cornflour
⅓ cup hot water
15g butter, melted
3 cups (250g) coconut, approximately
CHOCOLATE ICING
4 cups (500g) icing sugar
⅓ cup cocoa
15g butter, melted
½ cup milk
Grease a 23cm square slab pan.

Beat eggs in medium bowl with electric mixer until thick and creamy; gradually add sugar, beat until dissolved between each addition. Transfer mixture to large bowl, fold in sifted flours, then combined water and butter. Pour into prepared pan, bake in moderate oven for about 35 minutes. Stand 5 minutes before turning on to wire rack to cool. Trim crusts from cake, cut into 25 squares. Dip each piece in icing, toss in coconut, stand on wire rack to set.

Chocolate Icing: Sift icing sugar and cocoa into a heatproof bowl, stir in butter and milk, stir over hot water until icing is smooth.

Makes 25.

Keeping time: 2 days.

LAMINGTON BARS

4 eggs
½ cup castor sugar
¾ cup self-raising flour
¼ cup cornflour
15g butter, melted
¼ cup hot water
¼ cup apricot jam
½ cup thickened cream
CHOCOLATE ICING
2 cups (250g) icing sugar
2 tablespoons cocoa
2 teaspoons butter, melted
¼ cup milk
1 cup coconut, approximately
Grease 2 x 8cm x 26cm bar pans.

Beat eggs in medium bowl with electric mixer until thick and creamy; gradually add sugar, beat until dissolved between each addition. Transfer mixture to large bowl, fold in sifted flours, then combined butter and water. Pour mixture into prepared pans, bake in moderate oven for about 25 minutes. Stand 5 minutes before turning on to wire rack to cool.

Cut cakes in half lengthways; trim edges. Join layers together with jam and whipped cream. Spread icing over top and sides of cakes, sprinkle evenly with coconut.

Chocolate Icing: Combine sifted icing sugar and cocoa in heatproof bowl, stir in butter and milk. Stir over hot water until icing is smooth.

Keeping time: 2 days.

JELLY CAKES

Gem irons are made from cast iron and are available at kitchenware stores.

125g butter
1 teaspoon vanilla essence
½ cup castor sugar
2 eggs
1½ cups self-raising flour
½ cup milk
½ cup thickened cream
1 tablespoon icing sugar
100g packet raspberry jelly crystals
1 cup boiling water
1 cup cold water
2 cups coconut, approximately
Grease gem irons well.

Beat butter, essence and sugar in small bowl with electric mixer until light and fluffy; beat in eggs one at a time, beat until combined. Stir in sifted flour and milk. Drop tablespoons of mixture into prepared gem irons. Bake in moderately hot oven for about 15 minutes. Cool on wire rack. Cut rounded tops from cakes.

Beat cream with sifted icing sugar until firm peaks form. Dissolve jelly crystals in boiling water, add cold water; refrigerate until jelly is partly set. Join cakes with cream; dip in jelly, roll in coconut. Refrigerate 30 minutes.

Makes 18.

Keeping time: 2 days.

HONEY LAMINGTONS

125g dark chocolate, chopped
⅔ cup honey
185g butter
½ cup castor sugar
2 eggs
1¾ cups plain flour
½ teaspoon bicarbonate of soda
½ cup water
2 cups coconut, approximately
HONEY SYRUP
½ cup honey
1½ cups sugar
1 cup water
Grease a 23cm square slab pan, line base with paper; grease paper.

Melt chocolate in bowl over hot water, stir in honey, cool.

Cream butter and sugar in small bowl with electric mixer until light and fluffy. Beat in eggs one at a time, beat until combined. Transfer mixture to large bowl, stir in chocolate mixture, then half the sifted flour and soda with half the water, then remaining flour and water. Spread into prepared pan. Bake in moderate oven for about 30 minutes. Stand 5 minutes before turning on to wire rack to cool.

Trim crusts from cold cake, cut into 25 squares. Toss each square in honey syrup. Toss in coconut. Allow to set on wire rack.

Honey Syrup: Combine honey, sugar and water in saucepan, stir constantly over heat without boiling until sugar is dissolved. Bring to the boil, reduce heat, simmer without stirring uncovered for 10 minutes. Syrup will be slightly thickened; cool.

Makes 25.

Keeping time: 2 days.

RIGHT: back, from left: Lamington Bars; Lamingtons; centre: Jelly Cakes; front: Honey Lamingtons.

Fruit

Fruit cakes are always in demand; we've included light, dark and a whole host in between. Rich, economical, boiled — they are all here. We find fruit cakes of all types will cut better if they are stored in the refrigerator and cut when cold; however this is a matter of personal preference.
The important thing to remember when storing fruit cakes is to keep them as airtight as possible.

DELECTABLY RICH FRUIT CAKE

Fruit for soaking can be prepared up to 2 weeks ahead.

⅓ cup pitted prunes, halved
1½ cups (250g) sultanas
1½ cups (250g) currants
½ cup sweet sherry
½ cup brandy
125g butter
½ cup brown sugar
3 eggs
1 tablespoon dry instant coffee
¼ cup hot water
¼ cup plum jam
1 cup plain flour
¾ cup self-raising flour
1 tablespoon cocoa
1 teaspoon ground cinnamon
½ teaspoon mixed spice
½ teaspoon ground nutmeg
1½ cups (250g) glace cherries
1½ cups (250g) halved dates
1 cup mixed peel
2 cups (250g) walnut pieces

Combine prunes, sultanas and currants in bowl, mix in sherry and brandy, cover, stand overnight.

Grease a deep 23cm round cake pan, line with 3 layers of paper.

Cream butter and sugar in small bowl with electric mixer only until combined. Add eggs quickly, one at a time, beat only until combined between each addition. Transfer mixture to large bowl, stir in the combined coffee and water and jam, then the sifted dry ingredients in 2 lots. Drain prune mixture, reserve liquid. Add prune mixture, cherries, dates, peel and walnuts to cake mixture. Spread cake mixture into prepared pan. Bake in slow oven for about 2 hours. Brush reserved liquid over hot cake, cover, cool in pan.
Keeping time: 3 months.

RIGHT: Delectably Rich Fruit Cake.

China is Noel by Taitu from Lifestyle Imports, Sydney.

BRANDIED SULTANA CAKE

750g sultanas
250g butter
1 cup castor sugar
5 eggs
2½ cups plain flour
¼ cup self-raising flour
¼ cup brandy

Cover sultanas with warm water, stand 2 hours. Drain well, place on to tray covered with absorbent paper, stand overnight to dry.

Grease a deep 23cm round cake pan, line base and side with paper.

Cream butter and sugar in large bowl with electric mixer only until combined. Add eggs quickly, one at a time; beat until combined. Stir in half the sifted flours with half the brandy and half the sultanas, then stir in remaining flours, brandy and sultanas. Spread mixture into prepared pan. Bake in moderately slow oven for about 2 hours. Cover cake with foil; cool in pan.

Keeping time: 1 week.

CURRANT CHERRY CAKE

1kg currants
1½ cups (250g) halved glace cherries
½ cup brandy
250g butter
1 cup brown sugar, firmly packed
5 eggs
2 cups plain flour
1 teaspoon mixed spice
2 tablespoons brandy, extra

Line base and sides of deep 23cm round cake pan with 3 layers of paper.

Combine currants, cherries and brandy in large bowl.

Cream butter and sugar in small bowl with electric mixer only until combined. Add eggs quickly, one at a time, beat only until combined between each addition. Stir into fruit mixture, stir in sifted flour and spice. Spread evenly into prepared pan, bake in slow oven for about 2½ hours.

Brush with extra brandy, cover tightly with foil, leave to cool in pan.

Keeping time: 3 months.

CREAM CHEESE FRUIT CAKE

90g butter
125g packet cream cheese
2 teaspoons grated lemon rind
¾ cup castor sugar
2 eggs
1 cup (125g) sultanas
¾ cup chopped raisins
¾ cup currants
¾ cup chopped glace apricots
1 cup quartered glace cherries
¼ cup brandy
¾ cup plain flour
½ cup self-raising flour

Line a deep 20cm round cake pan with 2 sheets of paper.

Cream butter, cream cheese, rind and sugar in small bowl with electric mixer until light and fluffy. Beat in eggs quickly one at a time, beat only until combined. Transfer mixture to large bowl, stir in fruit and brandy then the sifted flours in 2 lots. Spread mixture into prepared pan, bake in moderately slow oven for about 1½ hours. Cover with foil, cool in pan. Remove foil and pan, wrap cake in plastic wrap. Store in cool dark place.

Keeping time: 1 month.

OVERNIGHT SHERRIED DATE AND WALNUT LOAF

1½ cups (250g) chopped dates
⅓ cup strong hot strained tea
½ teaspoon bicarbonate of soda
155g butter
½ cup castor sugar
2 eggs, separated
1 cup chopped walnuts
½ cup plain flour
2 tablespoons sweet sherry

Grease a 14cm x 21cm loaf pan, line base and sides with paper; grease paper well.

Combine dates, tea and soda in bowl; cover, stand overnight.

Cream butter and sugar in small bowl with electric mixer until light and fluffy, beat in egg yolks. Transfer to large bowl. Stir in walnuts, sifted flour and sherry; then date mixture. Beat egg whites until soft peaks form, fold into cake mixture. Pour into prepared pan. Bake in moderately slow oven for about 1 hour. Stand 5 minutes before turning on to wire rack to cool.

Keeping time: 3 days.

LEFT: Brandied Sultana Cake.
RIGHT: back: Cream Cheese Fruit Cake; centre: Currant Cherry Cake; front: Overnight Sherried Date and Walnut Loaf.

Table and dresser from The Welsh Pine Shop, Sydney; china from The Old Ark Antique Market, Sydney; cake stand from Kerry Trollope Antiques, Sydney; wooden board by Peter Sorensen from R. J. Phillips, Sydney; lace doily from Lace and Linen, Balmain, NSW.

DATE CAKE WITH PORT

Sweet sherry or madeira can be used instead of port if preferred.

250g butter
1 tablespoon grated lemon rind
1 cup castor sugar
4 eggs
1½ cups (250g) chopped dates
¼ cup mixed peel
1½ cups plain flour
¼ cup self-raising flour
¼ cup port

Line base and side of deep 20cm round cake pan with 2 layers of paper.

Cream butter, rind and sugar in small bowl with electric mixer until light and fluffy; beat in eggs one at a time, beat until combined. Transfer mixture to large bowl, stir in dates and peel, then sifted dry ingredients and port. Spread mixture evenly into prepared pan, bake in moderately slow oven for about 2 hours. Cover cake with foil, cool in pan. Dust with icing sugar.

Keeping time: 2 weeks.

RUM AND CITRUS FRUIT CAKE

1½ cups (250g) quartered red glace
    cherries
½ cup chopped glace apricots
¾ cup sultanas
¾ cup currants
½ cup chopped blanched almonds
1 tablespoon grated orange rind
2 teaspoons grated lemon rind
2 tablespoons rum
250g butter
¾ cup castor sugar
5 eggs
1½ cups plain flour
¼ cup self-raising flour

Combine fruit, almonds, rinds and rum in bowl, cover, stand overnight.

Grease a deep 20cm round cake pan, line base and side with paper; grease paper well.

Cream butter and sugar in large bowl with electric mixer only until combined. Add eggs quickly, one at a time; beat until combined. Stir in half the sifted flours with half the fruit mixture, then remaining flours and fruit mixture. Spread mixture into prepared pan. Bake in moderately slow oven for about 2 hours. Cover cake with foil; cool in pan.

Keeping time: 2 weeks.

MIXED GLACE FRUIT LOAF

185g butter
½ cup castor sugar
3 eggs
¾ cup finely chopped glace pineapple
1½ cups (250g) chopped glace
    cherries
½ cup finely chopped glace apricots
1½ cups plain flour
½ cup self-raising flour
½ cup milk
1 tablespoon sweet sherry

Grease a 15cm x 25cm loaf pan, line base and sides with paper; then grease the paper.

Cream butter and sugar in small bowl with electric mixer only until combined. Add eggs quickly, one at a time; beat until combined.

Transfer mixture to large bowl; stir in fruit, then half the sifted flours with half the combined milk and sherry, then stir in remaining flours and milk mixture. Spread mixture into prepared pan. Bake in moderately slow oven for about 2 hours. Cover cake with foil; cool in pan.

Keeping time: 2 weeks.

BOILED PASSIONFRUIT AND ORANGE FRUIT CAKE

You will need about 7 large passion-fruit for this recipe.

½ cup strained passionfruit juice
500g mixed fruit
¼ cup orange juice
1 cup sugar
125g butter
3 eggs, lightly beaten
¾ cup plain flour
¾ cup self-raising flour
1 teaspoon mixed spice

Combine passionfruit juice, mixed fruit, orange juice, sugar and butter in saucepan, stir constantly over heat without boiling until sugar is dissolved. Bring to the boil, reduce heat, simmer uncovered 3 minutes. Remove from heat; transfer to large bowl, cool to room temperature.

Grease a deep 20cm round cake pan, line base and side with paper.

Stir eggs and sifted dry ingredients into cold fruit mixture. Pour into prepared pan. Bake in moderately slow oven for about 1½ hours. Cover cake with foil, cool in pan.

Keeping time: 1 week.

FAVOURITE BOILED FRUIT CAKE

This boiled fruit cake is one of our favourites; it will cut and keep well and can be used for a wedding cake.

2¼ cups (375g) sultanas
1½ cups (250g) chopped raisins
1½ cups (250g) currants
½ cup mixed peel
¾ cup halved glace cherries
¼ cup chopped glace pineapple
¼ cup chopped glace apricots
250g butter
1 cup brown sugar, firmly packed
½ cup brandy
½ cup water
5 eggs, lightly beaten
1 tablespoon treacle
2 teaspoons grated orange rind
1 teaspoon grated lemon rind
1¾ cups plain flour `
⅓ cup self-raising flour
½ teaspoon bicarbonate of soda

Combine fruit, butter, sugar, brandy and water in saucepan. Stir constantly over heat without boiling until sugar is dissolved. Bring to the boil, reduce heat, simmer covered 10 minutes; Transfer to large bowl; cool to room temperature.

Grease a deep 23cm round (or deep 19cm square) cake pan, line base and side with 2 thicknesses paper, bringing paper 5cm above edge of pan.

Add eggs, treacle and rinds to fruit mixture, stir until combined. Stir in sifted dry ingredients. Spread mixture evenly into prepared pan. If desired, decorate with glace cherries and almonds. Bake in slow oven for about 2½ hours. Cover cake with foil, cool in pan.

Keeping time: 3 months.

BOILED APRICOT NECTAR CAKE

¾ **cup chopped dried apricots**
¾ **cup chopped raisins**
¾ **cup sultanas**
¼ **cup chopped dates**
¼ **cup chopped glace cherries**
1 **cup apricot nectar**
250g **butter**
1 **cup brown sugar, firmly packed**
5 **eggs**
2⅓ **cups plain flour**
⅓ **cup self-raising flour**
¼ **teaspoon bicarbonate of soda**
½ **teaspoon ground nutmeg**
¼ **teaspoon ground cinnamon**

Combine fruit with apricot nectar in saucepan, bring to the boil, reduce heat, cover, simmer 5 minutes. Remove from heat, cover, stand mixture overnight.

Line base and side of deep 23cm round (or deep 19cm square) cake pan with 3 layers of paper.

Cream butter and sugar in large bowl with electric mixer only until combined, add eggs quickly, one at a time, beat only until combined between each addition.

Stir in fruit mixture, then sifted dry ingredients. Spread mixture into prepared pan, bake in slow oven for about 2½ hours. Cover with foil, cool in pan.
Keeping time: 1 month.

LEFT: back: Boiled Apricot Nectar Cake; left: Boiled Passionfruit and Orange Fruit Cake (recipe previous page); front: Favourite Boiled Fruit Cake (recipe previous page).
BELOW: Layered Brandied Almond Cake (recipe over page).

LAYERED BRANDIED ALMOND CAKE

DARK LAYER
1 cup (250g) chopped glace
    pineapple
1½ cups (250g) sultanas
¾ cup currants
½ cup mixed peel
1 cup halved glace cherries
½ cup brandy
60g butter
¾ cup brown sugar, firmly packed
3 eggs
¾ cup chopped roasted hazelnuts
60g dark chocolate, grated
¾ cup plain flour
1 teaspoon ground cinnamon
½ teaspoon bicarbonate of soda
200g roll almond paste
LIGHT LAYER
125g butter
1 cup castor sugar
3 eggs
1½ cups plain flour
½ cup brandy
¾ cup sultanas
½ cup mixed peel
1 cup halved glace cherries
¼ cup (60g) chopped glace pineapple
½ cup chopped pecan nuts
¾ cup slivered almonds

Dark Layer: Combine fruit and brandy in large bowl, cover; stand overnight.

Grease a deep 23cm square cake pan, line base and sides with paper.

Beat butter, sugar and eggs in small bowl with electric mixer until creamy. Transfer mixture to large bowl. Stir in hazelnuts and chocolate, then sifted dry ingredients. Stir in fruit mixture. Spread into prepared pan. Roll out almond paste on lightly sugared sur-face large enough to cover dark layer, spread evenly with light layer. Bake in slow oven for about 2 hours. Cover tightly with foil; cool in pan.

Light Layer: Cream butter and sugar in small bowl with electric mixer until light and fluffy, beat in eggs, one at a time; beat until combined. Transfer mixture to large bowl, stir in half the sifted flour and half the brandy, then remaining flour, brandy, fruit and nuts.

Keeping time: 1 month.

BOILED BRANDIED APRICOT FRUIT CAKE

1¼ cups (250g) chopped dried
    apricots
1 cup chopped raisins
¾ cup chopped dates
¾ cup glace cherries
1 cup sultanas
¼ cup currants
½ cup mixed peel
185g butter
1 cup brown sugar, firmly packed
1 cup water
½ cup brandy
¼ cup apricot jam
3 eggs, lightly beaten
1½ cups self-raising flour
1½ cups plain flour

Line a deep 19cm square cake pan with 2 sheets of paper.

Combine fruit, butter, sugar and water in saucepan, stir constantly over heat until sugar is dissolved, bring to the boil, reduce heat, cover, simmer 10 minutes. Remove from heat, stir in brandy and jam, cover, cool to room temperature.

Stir eggs, then sifted flours into fruit mixture. Spread into prepared pan. Bake in moderately slow oven for about 2½ hours. Cover with foil, cool in pan.

Keeping time: 1 month.

HONEY BEER FRUIT CAKE

1½ cups (250g) chopped raisins
1½ cups (250g) chopped dates
1½ cups (250g) sultanas
½ cup mixed peel
½ cup chopped dried apricots
¼ cup chopped glace ginger
½ cup halved glace cherries
375ml can beer
250g butter
1¼ cups honey
3 eggs
1½ cups wholemeal self-raising flour
1½ cups white plain flour
1 teaspoon mixed spice
½ cup slivered almonds

Combine fruit with beer in large bowl, cover, stand overnight.

Line a deep 23cm square cake pan with 2 sheets paper.

Cream butter and honey in small bowl with electric mixer until light and fluffy, beat in eggs quickly one at a time, beat until just combined. Stir into fruit mixture. Stir in sifted flours and spice in 2 lots, then almonds. Spread into prepared pan. Bake in slow oven for about 3½ to 4 hours. Cover tightly with foil, cool in pan.

Keeping time: 1 month.

MOIST DATE CAKE

500g dates
1 cup water
½ teaspoon bicarbonate of soda
185g butter
⅔ cup castor sugar
3 eggs
1½ cups self-raising flour
¼ cup plain flour

Combine dates, water and soda in bowl, cover, stand overnight.

Grease a deep 19cm square cake pan, line base with paper; grease paper well.

Cream butter and sugar in small bowl with electric mixer until light and fluffy. Beat in eggs one at a time, beat until combined. Transfer mixture to large bowl, stir in half the sifted flours and half the undrained date mixture, then stir in remaining flours and date mixture. Spread into prepared pan. Bake in moderate oven for about 1¼ hours. Stand 5 minutes before turning on to wire rack to cool.

Keeping time: 1 week.

RIGHT: back, from left: Boiled Brandied Apricot Fruit Cake; Honey Beer Fruit Cake; front: Moist Date Cake.

Butler tray from Kerry Trollope Antiques, Sydney; china is Satin Rose by Royal Albert.

72

Ginger

Ginger Cakes are always a great favourite because they are moist, keep well and cut well; they are usually at their best when a day old. Be fussy about lining and greasing pans for these cakes as they have a tendency to stick. Most of the recipes result in a soft pouring mixture — this is correct for these cakes. Golden syrup, honey and treacle can all be substituted for each other in these recipes. The colour and flavour will change slightly according to what you choose.

MOIST TREACLE GINGERBREAD

¾ cup plain flour
¼ cup self-raising flour
½ teaspoon bicarbonate of soda
1 teaspoon ground ginger
¼ teaspoon ground cinnamon
¼ teaspoon mixed spice
½ cup castor sugar
1 egg, lightly beaten
½ cup milk
60g butter
½ cup treacle
LEMON FROSTING
60g butter
1 teaspoon grated lemon rind
1 cup icing sugar
2 teaspoons lemon juice,
    approximately

Grease a 14cm x 21cm loaf pan, line base and sides with paper; grease paper well.

Sift flours, soda and spices into large bowl, stir in sugar and combined egg and milk. Combine butter and treacle in saucepan, stir constantly over heat without boiling until butter is melted, stir hot mixture into flour mixture. Pour into prepared pan. Bake in moderate oven for about 50 minutes. Stand 5 minutes before turning on to wire rack to cool. When cold, spread cake with frosting.

Lemon Frosting: Beat butter and lemon rind in small bowl with electric mixer until creamy, gradually beat in sifted icing sugar and enough lemon juice to make frosting spreadable.

Keeping time: 3 days.

CINNAMON GINGER CAKE WITH CARAMEL ICING

125g butter
⅓ cup castor sugar
1 egg
¾ cup golden syrup
1¾ cups plain flour
2 teaspoons ground ginger
1 teaspoon ground cinnamon
½ teaspoon bicarbonate of soda
¾ cup hot water
CARAMEL ICING
60g butter
½ cup brown sugar
2 tablespoons milk
1½ cups icing sugar
1 teaspoon vanilla essence

Grease a deep 20cm round cake pan.

Cream butter and sugar in small bowl with electric mixer until light and fluffy; add egg, beat until combined, gradually add syrup, beat well. Transfer mixture to large bowl, stir in half the sifted dry ingredients with half the water, then stir in remaining dry ingredients with water; stir until smooth. Pour into prepared pan, bake in moderate oven for about 1 hour. Stand 5 minutes before turning on to wire rack to cool. Top cold cake with icing. Sprinkle with a little extra cinnamon.

Caramel Icing: Combine butter and sugar in saucepan, stir constantly over heat without boiling until butter is melted and sugar dissolved, add milk, stir further 2 minutes over heat. Transfer mixture to small bowl, gradually beat in sifted icing sugar and essence.

Keeping time: 3 days.

Back: Cinnamon Ginger Cake with Caramel Icing; front: Moist Treacle Gingerbread.

Table from Barbara's House and Garden; china is Apple by Franciscan from Wedgwood Australia Ltd.

GINGER BABA CAKE

125g butter
¾ cup brown sugar, firmly packed
2 eggs
¼ cup golden syrup
1½ cups self-raising flour
½ teaspoon bicarbonate of soda
3 teaspoons ground ginger
1 teaspoon ground cinnamon
¾ cup milk
Grease a 20cm baba pan.

Cream butter and sugar in small bowl with electric mixer until light and fluffy; beat in eggs one at a time, beat until combined. Beat in golden syrup.

Transfer mixture to large bowl, stir in half the sifted dry ingredients with half the milk, then stir in remaining dry ingredients and milk. Spread mixture into prepared pan, bake in moderate oven about 50 minutes. Stand 5 minutes before turning on to wire rack to cool. Serve dusted with sifted icing sugar if desired.

Keeping time: 2 days.

RIGHT: back at top: Chocolate Frosted Spicy Ginger Cake; back at bottom: Gingerbread Loaf; front: Ginger Baba Cake.
BELOW: Ginger Cake with Honey Cream and Chocolate.

Table from Barbara's House and Garden, Double Bay, NSW; china at right is Apple by Franciscan from Wedgwood Australia Ltd; china below is Eternal Beau by Johnson Bros.

CHOCOLATE FROSTED SPICY GINGER CAKE

1 cup golden syrup
¾ cup milk
185g butter
1 cup castor sugar
2 eggs
2½ cups plain flour
2 teaspoons ground cinnamon
1 tablespoon ground ginger
1 teaspoon bicarbonate of soda
¾ cup hot water
CHOCOLATE FROSTING
100g dark chocolate, chopped
125g butter
1½ cups icing sugar
1 egg yolk
Grease a 23cm square slab pan, line base with paper; grease paper.

Heat golden syrup and milk in saucepan, cool to room temperature.

Cream butter and sugar in small bowl with electric mixer until light and fluffy; beat in eggs one at a time, beat until combined. Transfer mixture to large bowl. Stir in the sifted dry ingredients with the syrup mixture and water. Pour into prepared pan, bake in moderately slow oven about 1¼ hours. Stand 10 minutes before turning on to wire rack to cool. Top cold cake with chocolate frosting.

Chocolate Frosting: Melt chocolate over hot water, cool; do not allow to set. Cream butter and sifted icing sugar until light and fluffy, beat in egg yolk and chocolate.

Keeping time: 2 days.

GINGERBREAD LOAF

¾ cup golden syrup
¾ cup water
½ cup brown sugar
185g butter
2¼ cups plain flour
1½ teaspoons bicarbonate of soda
1½ tablespoons ground ginger
1½ teaspoons mixed spice
Grease 2 x 8cm x 26cm bar pans, line bases with paper; grease paper.

Combine golden syrup, water, sugar and butter in saucepan, stir over low heat until butter is melted. Pour mixture into medium bowl, cool. Stir sifted dry ingredients into mixture. Beat with electric mixer on medium speed for about 2 minutes or until smooth. Pour mixture into prepared pans, bake in moderate oven for about 35 minutes. Stand 5 minutes before turning on to wire rack to cool. Serve loaf buttered.

Keeping time: 2 days.

GINGER CAKE WITH HONEY CREAM AND CHOCOLATE

⅔ cup honey
⅔ cup water
⅔ cup brown sugar, firmly packed
1½ cups plain flour
⅔ cup self-raising flour
½ teaspoon bicarbonate of soda
1 tablespoon ground ginger
250g butter, melted
HONEY CREAM
⅓ cup water
½ cup sugar
1 tablespoon honey
125g butter
60g dark chocolate, chopped
Grease a 23cm square slab pan.

Combine all ingredients in large bowl, beat on low speed with electric mixer until ingredients are combined. Increase speed to medium, beat for about 3 minutes or until mixture is changed in colour and smooth. Pour mixture into prepared pan, bake in moderately slow oven for about 1 hour. Stand 5 minutes before turning on to wire rack to cool. Melt chocolate over hot water, cool; do not allow to set. Spread cold cake with Honey Cream, drizzle with melted chocolate.

Honey Cream: Combine water, sugar and honey in saucepan, stir constantly over heat without boiling until sugar is dissolved. Bring to the boil, remove from heat, cool to room temperature, allow to become completely cold. Beat butter in small bowl with electric mixer until white and fluffy. Gradually add syrup, beating well after each addition.

Keeping time: 2 days.

Tea and Coffee

Teacakes and coffee cakes are meant to be eaten when freshly made; they do not keep well. Most of them are served with butter.
Tea or coffee are not necessarily ingredients in these cakes, which traditionally accompany these refreshments.

CINNAMON TEACAKE

60g butter
1 teaspoon vanilla essence
½ cup castor sugar
1 egg
1 cup self-raising flour
⅓ cup milk
15g butter, melted, extra
1 tablespoon castor sugar, extra
½ teaspoon ground cinnamon

Grease a deep 20cm round cake pan, line base with paper; grease paper.

Cream butter and essence in small bowl with electric mixer, gradually add sugar, then egg, beat until light and creamy. Stir in sifted flour and milk, beat lightly until smooth. Spread into prepared pan, bake in moderate oven for about 25 minutes. Stand 2 minutes before turning on to wire rack; brush with extra butter, sprinkle with combined extra sugar and cinnamon.

Keeping time: 1 day.

RIGHT: Lemon Fruit Twist.
BELOW: back: Cinnamon Teacake; centre: Walnut Cinnamon Teacake; front: Custard Teacake.

WALNUT CINNAMON TEACAKE

60g butter
⅓ cup castor sugar
1 egg
¾ cup self-raising flour
⅓ cup milk
CINNAMON TOPPING
¼ cup finely chopped walnuts
¼ cup brown sugar
¼ cup coconut
2 tablespoons plain flour
1 teaspoon ground cinnamon
15g butter

Grease a deep 17cm round cake pan; line base with paper; grease paper.

Cream butter and sugar in small bowl with electric mixer until light and fluffy, add egg, beat until combined. Fold in sifted flour and milk. Spread into prepared pan, sprinkle with topping, bake in moderate oven for about 30 minutes. Stand 5 minutes before turning on to wire rack to cool.

Cinnamon Topping: Combine all ingredients in bowl, mix well.

Keeping time: 1 day.

CUSTARD TEACAKE

This teacake usually sinks slightly due to the soft custard in the centre.

125g butter
⅓ cup castor sugar
1 egg
¾ cup self-raising flour
¼ cup custard powder
CUSTARD
1 tablespoon custard powder
1 tablespoon castor sugar
⅔ cup milk
15g butter
2 teaspoons vanilla essence

Grease a deep 17cm round cake pan; line base and side with paper; grease paper well.

Cream butter and sugar in small bowl with electric mixer until light and fluffy, add egg, beat until combined, stir in sifted flour and custard powder. Spread half the cake mixture into prepared pan, spread with cold custard, spread carefully with remaining cake mixture. Bake in moderate oven for about 35 minutes. Cool in pan. When cake is cold, carefully remove paper. Serve dusted with sifted icing sugar.

Custard: Blend custard powder and sugar with milk in saucepan. Stir constantly over heat until mixture boils and thickens, stir in butter and essence, cover, cool to room temperature.

Keeping time: 2 days.

LEMON FRUIT TWIST

2¼ cups self-raising flour
60g butter
1 tablespoon castor sugar
2 tablespoons sultanas
2 teaspoons grated lemon rind
1 egg, lightly beaten
½ cup milk, approximately
2 tablespoons mixed peel
2 tablespoons chopped glace cherries
SUGAR GLAZE
1 tablespoon sugar
2 tablespoons boiling water
LEMON ICING
¾ cup icing sugar
1 tablespoon lemon juice
15g butter
1 tablespoon boiling water, approximately

Lightly grease an oven tray.

Sift flour into bowl, rub in butter. Stir in sugar, sultanas and lemon rind, then egg and enough milk to mix to a soft pliable dough. Knead on lightly floured surface until smooth, divide mixture into 3, roll each third into a roll about 40cm long. Plait the 3 rolls firmly together. Place on to prepared tray, press ends of plait together to form a round shape.

Bake in moderately hot oven for about 20 minutes. Brush with sugar glaze, bake further 5 minutes. Lift on to wire rack to cool. Drizzle with icing, sprinkle with peel and cherries.

Sugar Glaze: Combine sugar and water in bowl, stir until sugar is completely dissolved.

Lemon Icing: Sift icing sugar into bowl, stir in lemon juice, butter and enough water to mix to a pouring consistency.

Keeping time: 1 day.

China at left is Quadratino by Sasaki from Dansab; china at right is Evesham by Royal Worcester; board is from R. J. Phillips; butter dish from Peter Sorensen.

DATE AND PINEAPPLE LOAF

1½ cups (250g) chopped dates
450g can crushed pineapple
125g butter
½ cup castor sugar
2 eggs, lightly beaten
2 cups self-raising flour

Grease a 15cm x 25cm loaf pan, line base with paper; grease paper.

Combine dates, undrained pineapple, butter and sugar in saucepan, stir constantly over heat without boiling until butter is melted. Bring to the boil, reduce heat, simmer uncovered 3 minutes without stirring; cool.

Stir in eggs, then sifted flour in 2 lots. Pour into prepared pan. Bake in moderate oven for about 1 hour. Stand 10 minutes before turning on to wire rack to cool.

Keeping time: 2 days.

CINNAMON COFFEE CAKE

185g butter
1 cup castor sugar
2 eggs
1½ cups self-raising flour
1 cup plain flour
½ teaspoon bicarbonate of soda
1½ cups buttermilk
CINNAMON TOPPING
90g butter
¼ cup brown sugar
¾ cup plain flour
2 teaspoons ground cinnamon

Grease a deep 23cm square cake pan, line base with paper; grease paper.

Cream butter and sugar in small bowl with electric mixer until light and fluffy. Beat in eggs one at a time, beat until combined. Transfer mixture to large bowl, stir in half the sifted flours and soda and half the buttermilk, then stir in remaining flours and buttermilk. Spread into prepared pan, sprinkle with topping. Bake in moderate oven for about 50 minutes. Stand 5 minutes before turning on to wire rack to cool.

Cinnamon Topping: Cream butter and sugar in small bowl with electric mixer until light and fluffy. Stir in sifted flour and cinnamon. Push mixture through coarse sieve.

Keeping time: 2 days.

FRUIT SALAD CAKE

We used a Granny Smith apple in this recipe. You will also need 1 medium over-ripe banana for this recipe.

¾ cup castor sugar
60g butter
½ cup chopped dried apricots
1 teaspoon grated orange rind
1 teaspoon grated lemon rind
¼ cup orange juice
¼ cup lemon juice
1 apple, grated
⅓ cup mashed banana
1 egg, lightly beaten
2 cups self-raising flour

Grease a 14cm x 21cm loaf pan, line base and sides with paper; grease paper well.

Combine sugar, butter, apricots, rinds and juices in saucepan. Stir constantly over heat without boiling until sugar is dissolved. Transfer to large bowl, stir in apple, banana and egg, then sifted flour in 2 lots. Pour into prepared pan. Bake in moderate oven for about 1¼ hours. Stand 5 minutes before turning on to wire rack to cool.

Keeping time: 1 day.

ABOVE: back: Cinnamon Coffee Cake; front: Date and Pineapple Loaf.

China is Scottish Thistle by Mikasa.

APPLE AND APRICOT LOAF

½ cup chopped dried apples
½ cup chopped dried apricots
¾ cup boiling water
90g butter
¾ cup castor sugar
2 eggs
½ cup coconut
¼ cup golden syrup
2 cups self-raising flour
¼ cup milk

Grease a 14cm x 21cm loaf pan, line base and sides with paper; grease paper well.

Combine apples, apricots and water in bowl, cool to room temperature.

Cream butter and sugar in small bowl with electric mixer until light and fluffy. Beat in eggs one at a time, beat until combined. Transfer mixture to large bowl, stir in undrained apple mixture, coconut and golden syrup. Stir in half the sifted flour and half the milk, then stir in remaining flour and milk. Pour into prepared pan. Bake in moderately slow oven for about 1¼ hours. Stand 5 minutes before turning on to wire rack to cool.

Keeping time: 2 days.

APRICOT AND ALMOND SHORTCAKE

2 cups self-raising flour
125g butter
½ cup castor sugar
1 egg, lightly beaten
1 tablespoon lemon juice,
  approximately
⅔ cup apricot jam
egg white, lightly beaten
¼ cup blanched almonds

Grease a round 20cm sandwich pan.

Sift flour into large bowl, rub in butter. Stir in sugar, then egg and enough lemon juice to mix to a firm dough, cover, refrigerate 30 minutes.

Divide dough in half, roll out half between 2 sheets of plastic wrap large enough to cover base and sides of pan. Heat jam, strain, spread over base. Roll out remaining dough large enough to cover jam, press edges together firmly. Brush lightly with egg white, decorate with almonds. Bake in moderate oven for about 30 minutes. Stand 10 minutes before turning on to wire rack to cool.

Keeping time: 3 days.

BELOW: back: Apricot and Almond Shortcake; front, from left: Fruit Salad Cake; Apple and Apricot Loaf.

Plates are Fleuri by Royal Worcester.

Health

All of these cakes are brimming with healthy, fibre-filled ingredients. Also included are several cakes suitable for people who have allergies to wheat products and eggs.

CRUNCHY-TOPPED FRUIT AND NUT HEALTH CAKE

Pepitas (pumpkin seed kernels) and sunflower seed kernels are available at health food stores.

30g butter
¾ cup raw sugar
1½ cups (250g) mixed fruit
¾ cup chopped raisins
1 teaspoon ground cinnamon
½ teaspoon ground cloves
½ teaspoon ground nutmeg
1½ cups water
2 eggs, lightly beaten
¾ cup chopped walnuts
½ cup chopped glace pineapple
½ cup sunflower seed kernels
⅓ cup water, extra
2 cups wholemeal self-raising flour
2 tablespoons pepitas
2 tablespoons sunflower seed
   kernels, extra

Combine butter, sugar, mixed fruit, raisins, cinnamon, cloves, nutmeg and water in saucepan. Stir over heat without boiling until sugar is dissolved. Bring to the boil, reduce heat, simmer uncovered for 3 minutes, transfer mixture to large bowl, cool mixture to room temperature.

Line base and side of greased deep 20cm round cake pan with paper.

Stir eggs, walnuts, pineapple, sunflower seed kernels and extra water into fruit mixture, stir in sifted flour.

Spread mixture into prepared pan, sprinkle with pepitas and extra sunflower seed kernels. Bake in moderately slow oven for about 2 hours. Cover with foil, cool in pan.

Keeping time: 4 days.

WHOLEMEAL APRICOT AND COCONUT CAKE

1 cup chopped dried apricots
1 cup hot milk
¼ cup honey
1 egg, lightly beaten
1 cup wholemeal self-raising flour
¾ cup coconut

Combine apricots, milk and honey in bowl, cover, stand 1 hour.

Grease a 14cm x 21cm loaf pan, line base with paper; grease paper.

Stir egg, then sifted flour and ½ cup of the coconut into apricot mixture. Spread mixture into prepared pan. Sprinkle with remaining coconut. Bake in moderate oven for about 1 hour. Stand cake in pan 5 minutes before turning on to wire rack to cool.

Keeping time: 2 days.

WHOLEMEAL FRUIT AND COCONUT LOAF

⅔ cup chopped dates
⅓ cup chopped dried apricots
¼ cup coconut
2 tablespoons brandy
⅔ cup brown sugar, firmly packed
125g butter
½ teaspoon bicarbonate of soda
¾ cup boiling water
2 eggs, lightly beaten
¾ cup wholemeal self-raising flour
¾ cup wholemeal plain flour
1 teaspoon mixed spice

Combine dates in bowl with apricots, coconut and brandy, stand overnight.

Grease a 15cm x 25cm loaf pan, line base with paper; grease paper.

Add sugar, chopped butter and soda to date mixture, stir in boiling water; cool 10 minutes. Stir in eggs, then sifted dry ingredients. Pour into prepared pan. Bake in moderate oven for about 50 minutes. Stand 5 minutes before turning on to wire rack to cool.

Keeping time: 3 days.

RIGHT: back, from left: Wholemeal Apricot and Coconut Cake; Crunchy-Topped Fruit and Nut Health Cake; front: Wholemeal Fruit and Coconut Loaf.

Plates and jug from Villa Italiana, Sydney.

SUNSHINE CAKE

Fruit medley is a combination of chopped dried fruit containing apricots, apples, sultanas etc. Any fruit of your choice can be substituted. Store cake covered in refrigerator.

375g fruit medley
1 cup orange juice
¼ cup apple juice
¾ cup grated apple
¾ cup grated raw pumpkin
¼ cup grated carrot
1¼ cups wholemeal self-raising flour
¼ cup skim milk powder
1 tablespoon cocoa
1 teaspoon mixed spice
2 egg whites, lightly beaten

Combine fruit with orange and apple juice in saucepan, bring to the boil, reduce heat, simmer uncovered 2 minutes, cool, cover, stand overnight.

Grease a 20cm ring pan.

Combine fruit mixture with apple, pumpkin and carrot in bowl. Stir in sifted dry ingredients and egg whites. Spread mixture into prepared pan. Bake in moderate oven for about 1¼ hours. Stand 5 minutes before turning on to wire rack to cool.

Keeping time: 1 week.

ALLERGY-FREE FRUIT CAKE

This cake is suitable for many allergy diets, as it does not contain wheaten flour, eggs, milk or butter; the only sugar is in the fruit. Store in refrigerator in airtight container. You will need to cook 500g pumpkin for this recipe.

1 cup sultanas
¾ cup currants
¾ cup chopped raisins
2 cups water
1½ cups cold mashed pumpkin
1 tablespoon grated lemon rind
¼ cup oil
1½ cups soy flour
1½ cups rice flour
3 teaspoons baking powder
1 teaspoon ground cinnamon
1 teaspoon ground nutmeg
½ teaspoon ground cloves
2 tablespoons sugarless apricot jam

Line a deep 20cm round cake pan, with 2 sheets of paper.

Combine sultanas, currants, raisins and water in saucepan, bring to the boil, remove from heat, stir in pumpkin, rind and oil; cool to room temperature. Stir sifted flours, baking powder, cinnamon, nutmeg and cloves into fruit mixture. Spread into prepared pan, bake in moderately slow oven for about 1½ hours. Cover, cool in pan. Turn out when cold, brush top with warmed, sieved jam.

Keeping time: 1 week.

SULTANA ORANGE CAKE

750g sultanas
1¾ cups boiling water
½ cup orange juice
3 eggs
1 tablespoon grated orange rind
1 cup brown sugar, firmly packed
½ cup oil
1¾ cups wholemeal self-raising flour
1 cup soy flour

Grease a deep 19cm square cake pan, line base with paper; grease paper.

Combine sultanas, water and orange juice in bowl, stand 1 hour.

Beat eggs, rind and sugar in small bowl with electric mixer until thick and creamy, gradually beat in oil. Transfer mixture to large bowl, fold in sifted flours and sultana mixture. Spread into prepared pan, bake in moderately slow oven for about 1¾ hours. Stand 10 minutes before turning on to wire rack to cool.

Keeping time: 1 week.

LEFT: back: Sunshine Cake; front: Allergy-Free Fruit Cake.
RIGHT: Sultana Orange Cake.

Trolley is Bodum from Vasa Agencies, Sydney; china at left is Vieux Luxembourg by Villeroy & Boch; china at right is Riviera by Villeroy & Boch.

BANANA ORANGE AND DATE HEALTH LOAF

We used 3 over-ripe bananas for this recipe.

90g butter
2 teaspoons grated orange rind
⅓ cup raw sugar
2 eggs
1 cup mashed bananas
¾ cup chopped dates
2 cups wholemeal self-raising flour
½ cup orange juice

WHOLEMEAL BOILED FRUIT AND WALNUT CAKE

250g butter
2 cups raw sugar
2 cups water
1½ cups (250g) sultanas
1½ cups (250g) chopped raisins
¾ cup chopped dried apricots
⅓ cup currants
3 eggs, lightly beaten
½ cup chopped walnuts
1 cup wheatgerm
2 cups wholemeal plain flour
1 cup wholemeal self-raising flour

Combine butter, sugar, water, sultanas, raisins, apricots and currants in saucepan, stir over heat without boiling until sugar is dissolved. Bring to the boil, reduce heat, simmer uncovered for 3 minutes; transfer to large bowl, cool to room temperature.

Line base and side of deep 23cm round cake pan with 3 layers of paper.

Stir eggs and walnuts into fruit mixture then wheatgerm and sifted flours. Spread into prepared pan. Bake in moderately slow oven for about 3 hours, cover with foil, cool in pan.

Keeping time: 1 month.

ABOVE: Wholemeal Boiled Fruit and Walnut Cake.
RIGHT: from left: Banana Orange and Date Health Loaf; Honey Date and Nut Cake.

Tiles from Country Floors, Sydney; plates above from Villa Italiana, Sydney; plates at right are Longchamp from Studio Haus, Sydney.

Grease a 14cm x 21cm loaf pan, line base and sides of pan with paper; grease paper.

Cream butter, rind and sugar in small bowl with electric mixer until light and fluffy, beat in eggs one at a time, add banana, beat until combined. Transfer mixture to large bowl, stir in dates, then half the flour and half the orange juice, then stir in remaining flour and orange juice; stir until smooth.

Spread mixture into prepared pan. Bake in moderate oven for about 1 hour. Stand 5 minutes before turning on to wire rack to cool.

Keeping time: 3 days.

HONEY DATE AND NUT CAKE

1 cup honey
1 cup water
1 tablespoon golden syrup
30g butter
1½ cups (250g) chopped dates
¾ cup chopped walnuts
¼ cup chopped almonds
2¼ cups wholemeal self-raising flour
1 teaspoon ground ginger
½ teaspoon mixed spice

Combine honey, water, golden syrup and butter in saucepan, stir constantly over heat without boiling until butter is melted. Remove from heat; cool to room temperature.

Grease a deep 19cm square cake pan, line base with paper; grease paper well.

Stir dates, walnuts and almonds, then sifted dry ingredients into honey mixture; stir until combined. Pour mixture into prepared pan. Bake in moderate oven for about 50 minutes. Cover cake with foil, cool in pan.

Keeping time: 2 days.

Butter

Here are some of our favourite recipes for butter cakes, including the versatile basic butter cake with delicious variations.

BASIC BUTTER CAKE

The basic butter cake can be cooked in a variety of cake pans. We have included a list of alternatives with approximate cooking times. All pans need to be greased, the base lined with paper, then the paper greased (baking paper does not require greasing). All the cakes are cooked in a moderate oven.

Patty cakes are an exception, if you prefer them "peaked", increase the temperature to moderately hot.

125g butter
1 teaspoon vanilla essence
¾ cup castor sugar
2 eggs
1½ cups self-raising flour
½ cup milk

Cream butter, essence and sugar in small bowl with electric mixer until light and fluffy; beat in eggs one at a time, beat until combined. Stir in half the sifted flour and half the milk, then stir in remaining flour and milk. Pour mixture into prepared pan.

CAKE PANS AND COOKING TIMES
20cm baba pan
40 minutes

20cm ring pan
40 minutes

14cm x 21cm loaf pan
1 hour

2 x 8 cm x 26cm bar pans
35 minutes

deep 20cm round cake pan
50 minutes

24 patty pans
15 minutes

VARIATIONS

Many variations are possible, we leave the choice of cake pan to you (see list).

APPLE CAKE: Spread ⅔ of the cake mixture into the prepared pan, spread evenly with ½ cup well-drained canned or stewed apple. Spread evenly with remaining cake mixture, bake as directed above. Stand 10 minutes before turning on to wire rack to cool. Spread cold cake with icing.

Passionfruit Icing: Sift 1 cup of icing sugar into heatproof bowl, stir in 1 teaspoon butter and enough passionfruit pulp to mix to a stiff paste (1 or 2 passionfruit). Stir constantly over hot water until icing is spreadable.

ORANGE AND DATE CAKE: Add 1 tablespoon grated orange rind to the butter when creaming the mixture. Stir ¾ cup finely chopped dates into the creamed mixture before the flour and milk are added. Spread into prepared pan, bake as directed at left. Stand 5 minutes before turning on to wire rack to cool. Top cold cake with frosting.

Orange Cream Cheese Frosting: Beat 90g packaged cream cheese in small bowl with electric mixer until creamy. Beat in 2 teaspoons grated orange rind, then ½ cup sifted icing sugar, then about 2 teaspoons orange juice; enough to make frosting spreadable.

BUTTERFLY CAKES: It is best to cook patty cakes used for butterfly cakes in a moderate oven to keep them as flat-topped as possible. When the cakes are cold, cut out a circle from the top, cutting down to a depth of about 2cm. Place a small amount of jam in the cavity, top with whipped cream then the "wings" made from the halved circles of cake. Dust with sifted icing sugar, decorate with strawberries.

These variations can also be used for the basic Cake Mix recipe in the Processor section — page 20.

Keeping time: 2 days.

QUICK-MIX SAND CAKE

185g butter
2 teaspoons vanilla essence
1¼ cups castor sugar
3 eggs
⅓ cup milk
1½ cups self-raising flour
⅓ cup cornflour

Grease a 23cm square slab pan, line base with paper; grease paper.

Combine butter, essence, sugar, eggs, milk and sifted flour and cornflour in medium bowl. Beat with electric mixer until combined, then beat on medium speed for about 3 minutes, or until smooth and changed in colour. Spread into prepared pan. Bake in moderate oven for about 45 minutes. Stand 5 minutes before turning on to wire rack to cool. Dust with sifted icing sugar if desired.

Keeping time: 2 days.

LEFT: back, from left: Apple Cake with Passionfruit Icing; Orange and Date Cake; front: Butterfly Cakes.
BELOW: Quick-Mix Sand Cake.

Plates below are Saturn by Sasaki from Dansab, Sydney.

BUTTER ALMOND CAKE

185g butter
¼ teaspoon almond essence
1 tablespoon grated orange rind
200g roll almond or marzipan paste, chopped
¾ cup castor sugar
3 eggs
½ cup plain flour
½ cup self-raising flour
¼ cup blanched almonds

Grease a 23cm square slab pan, line base with paper; grease paper.

Cream butter, essence, rind and almond paste in medium bowl with electric mixer until smooth. Add sugar, beat until light and fluffy. Beat in eggs, one at a time; beat only until combined; stir in sifted flours. Spread into prepared pan, decorate top with split almonds. Bake in moderate oven for about 40 minutes. Stand 2 minutes before turning on to wire rack to cool.
Keeping time: 3 days.

RIGHT: clockwise from right: Poppy Seed Cake; Caraway Seed Cake; Cardamom Almond Cake.
BELOW: back: Butter Almond Cake; front: Sour Cream Butter Cake.

SOUR CREAM BUTTER CAKE

125g butter
1 teaspoon vanilla essence
1 cup castor sugar
3 eggs
1¼ cups plain flour
⅓ cup sour cream
LEMON FROSTING
60g butter
1 teaspoon grated lemon rind
¾ cup icing sugar
2 tablespoons lemon juice

Grease a 14cm x 21cm loaf pan, line base and sides with paper; grease paper well.

Cream butter, essence and sugar in small bowl with electric mixer until light and fluffy. Beat in eggs one at a time, beat until combined. Transfer mixture to large bowl, stir in half the sifted flour and half the sour cream, then stir in remaining flour and sour cream. Spread into prepared pan. Bake in moderately slow oven for about 1¼ hours. Stand 5 minutes before turning on to wire rack to cool. Top cold cake with frosting.
Lemon Frosting: Cream butter and rind in small bowl with electric mixer until white and fluffy. Gradually beat in the sifted icing sugar and juice.
Keeping time: 2 days.

CARDAMOM ALMOND CAKE

185g butter
¾ cup brown sugar, firmly packed
2 eggs
2 cups self-raising flour
2 teaspoons ground cardamom
¼ cup ground almonds
½ cup golden syrup
½ cup milk

Grease a 20cm baba pan.

Cream butter and sugar in small bowl with electric mixer until light and fluffy; beat in eggs one at a time, beat until combined. Transfer to large bowl. Stir in half the sifted flour and cardamom, almonds and combined syrup and milk, then stir in remaining dry ingredients and syrup mixture.

Pour into prepared pan, bake in moderate oven for about 50 minutes. Stand 5 minutes before turning on to wire rack to cool. Dust with sifted icing sugar before serving.
Keeping time: 2 days.

CARAWAY SEED CAKE

125g butter
1 cup castor sugar
2 eggs
½ cup milk
1¼ cups self-raising flour
¼ cup custard powder
2 tablespoons caraway seeds

Grease a 14cm x 21cm loaf pan, line base and sides with paper; grease paper well.

Beat butter, sugar, eggs, milk and sifted flour and custard powder in small bowl with electric mixer on low speed until combined, then beat on medium speed for about 3 minutes or until changed in colour. Stir in caraway seeds. Spread mixture into prepared pan. Bake in moderately slow oven for about 1 hour. Stand 5 minutes before turning on to wire rack to cool.

Keeping time: 3 days.

POPPY SEED CAKE

⅓ cup poppy seeds
¾ cup milk
185g butter
2 teaspoons vanilla essence
1 cup castor sugar
3 eggs
2 cups self-raising flour

Grease a 14cm x 21cm loaf pan, line base and sides with paper; grease paper well.

Combine poppy seeds and milk in medium bowl, stand 1 hour.

Add butter, essence, sugar, eggs, sifted flour to poppy seed mixture. Beat on low speed with electric mixer until combined, then beat mixture on medium speed for about 3 minutes, or until mixture is changed in colour. Pour into prepared pan. Bake in moderate oven for about 1 hour. Stand 5 minutes before turning on to wire rack to cool.

Keeping time: 2 days.

Table and lace above from Janet Niven Antiques; Woollahra, NSW; china and cutlery above from Royal Copenhagen; china at left from Cottage Antiques, Glebe, NSW; silver stand at left from Goodmans Antiques, Sydney.

CHERRY AND ALMOND-TOPPED DATE CAKE

1½ cups (250g) chopped dates
¼ cup boiling water
185g butter
¾ cup castor sugar
3 eggs
1½ cups self-raising flour
½ cup slivered almonds
½ cup chopped glace cherries

Grease a 23cm square slab pan, line base and sides with paper; grease paper well.

Combine dates with water in bowl, cover, cool to room temperature.

Cream butter and sugar in small bowl with electric mixer until light and fluffy. Beat in eggs one at a time, beat until combined. Transfer mixture to large bowl, stir in sifted flour in 2 lots. Spread half the mixture evenly into prepared pan. Combine remaining mixture with undrained date mixture, spread into pan. Sprinkle with almonds and cherries. Bake in moderately slow oven for about 50 minutes. Stand 5 minutes before turning on to wire rack to cool.

Keeping time: 3 days.

CHERRY GINGER CAKE

250g butter
1 cup castor sugar
4 eggs
1 cup halved glace cherries
¾ cup sultanas
¾ cup chopped raisins
¼ cup chopped glace ginger
2 tablespoons brandy
2 cups plain flour
½ cup self-raising flour
¼ cup milk

Grease a deep 23cm round cake pan, line base with paper; grease paper.

Cream butter and sugar in medium bowl with electric mixer until light and fluffy; beat in eggs one at a time, beat until combined. Fold in fruit and brandy. Stir in half the sifted flours with half the milk, then remaining flours and milk. Pour into prepared pan, bake in moderately slow oven for about 1½ hours. Cover with foil, cool in pan.

Keeping time: 1 week.

LEFT: Cherry and Almond-Topped Date Cake.
BELOW: Cherry Ginger Cake.

Table from Janet Niven Antiques, Sydney; china, cake plate and cutlery from Kerry Trollope Antiques and Fine Arts, Sydney; doily from Linen and Lace, Balmain, NSW.

ORANGE YOGHURT CAKE

125g butter
1 tablespoon grated orange rind
1 cup castor sugar
3 eggs, separated
½ cup mixed peel
2 cups self-raising flour
¼ cup orange juice
1 cup plain yoghurt
ORANGE ICING
1½ cups icing sugar
30g soft butter
2 tablespoons orange juice,
    approximately

Grease a 14cm x 21cm loaf pan, line base and sides with paper; grease paper well.

Cream butter, rind and sugar in small bowl with electric mixer until light fluffy; beat in egg yolks one at a time. Transfer mixture to large bowl, stir in peel, then half the sifted flour and half the combined orange juice and yoghurt, then stir in remaining flour and yoghurt mixture.

Beat egg whites in small bowl until soft peaks form, fold lightly into mixture in 2 lots. Pour mixture into prepared pan. Bake in slow oven for about 2 hours. Stand 5 minutes before turning on to wire rack to cool, Spread cold cake with icing.

Orange Icing: Combine sifted icing sugar and butter in bowl. Stir in enough juice to mix icing to a spreadable consistency.

Keeping time: 4 days.

RAISIN WALNUT AND ORANGE SYRUP CAKE

125g butter
2 teaspoons grated orange rind
1 cup castor sugar
2 eggs
1 cup chopped raisins
½ cup chopped walnuts
1¼ cups self-raising flour
⅔ cup milk
SYRUP
½ cup orange juice
⅓ cup castor sugar
1 teaspoon grated orange rind

Grease a 15cm x 25cm loaf pan; line base with paper; grease paper.

Cream butter, rind and sugar in small bowl with electric mixer until light and fluffy, add eggs one at a time, beat until combined. Transfer mixture to large bowl, stir in raisins and walnuts, then fold in sifted flour and milk in 2 lots. Pour mixture into prepared pan, bake in moderate oven for about 1 hour. Stand 5 minutes before turning on to wire rack. Pour the hot syrup over hot cake.

Syrup: Combine all ingredients in saucepan, stir constantly over heat without boiling until sugar is dissolved; bring to the boil; remove from heat.

Keeping time: 3 days.

LEMON AND APRICOT CAKE

185g butter
1 tablespoon grated lemon rind
1¼ cups castor sugar
4 eggs
½ cup chopped glace apricots
¼ cup finely chopped glace ginger
¾ cup sour cream
2 cups plain flour
½ teaspoon bicarbonate of soda

Grease a 20cm baba pan, sprinkle with flour, shake out excess flour.

Cream butter, rind and sugar in small bowl with electric mixer until light and fluffy; beat in eggs one at a time, beat until combined. Fold in apricots, ginger and sour cream, then sifted flour and soda. Spread into prepared pan, bake in moderately slow oven for about 1 hour. Stand 10 minutes before turning on to wire rack to cool. When cold, dust with sifted icing sugar.

Keeping time: 4 days.

RIGHT: Lemon and Apricot Cake.
BELOW: from left: Orange Yoghurt Cake;
Raisin Walnut and Orange Syrup Cake.

Plates below are Taitu from Lifestyle Imports, Sydney; plates at right are Rouen by Wedgwood.

APPLE CAKE

185g butter
2 teaspoons grated lemon rind
⅔ cup castor sugar
3 eggs
1 cup self-raising flour
½ cup plain flour
⅓ cup milk
2 apples
1 teaspoon gelatine
2 tablespoons water
2 tablespoons strained apricot jam

Grease a 20cm springform pan.

Cream butter, rind and sugar in small bowl with electric mixer until light and fluffy. Beat in eggs one at a time, beat until combined. Transfer mixture to large bowl, stir in sifted flours and milk. Spread into prepared pan.

Peel apples, cut into quarters, remove cores. Make lengthways cuts into rounded sides of apple quarters, cutting about three quarters of the way through. Arrange quarters, rounded side up, around edge of cake. Bake in moderate oven for about 1 hour.

Sprinkle gelatine over water, dissolve over hot water, add jam. Spread half jam mixture over hot cake, cool cake in pan. Remove from pan, brush with remaining warmed jam mixture.

Keeping time: 2 days.

MOIST APPLE AND DATE CAKE

We used Granny Smith apples.

2 apples, finely chopped
1 cup chopped dates
½ teaspoon bicarbonate of soda
1 cup boiling water
185g butter
1 cup castor sugar
1 egg
2 cups plain flour

Grease a 23cm square slab pan, line base and sides with paper; grease paper well.

Combine apples, dates, soda and water in bowl, cover, cool.

Cream butter and sugar in small bowl with electric mixer until light and fluffly, beat in egg. Transfer mixture to large bowl, stir in the sifted flour and apple mixture. Pour into prepared pan. Bake in moderately slow oven for about 1¼ hours. Stand 5 minutes before turning on to wire rack to cool.

Keeping time: 2 days.

HAZELNUT APPLE CAKE

185g butter
¾ cup castor sugar
3 eggs
½ cup self-raising flour
2 tablespoons cocoa
1¾ cups (185g) packaged ground hazelnuts
1 apple, grated
¼ cup chopped roasted hazelnuts
LEMON ICING
60g butter
1 cup icing sugar
1 tablespoon lemon juice, approximately

Plates at left are Wild Apple by Wedgwood; table and chair from The Welsh Pine Shop, Sydney; china from The Old Ark Antique Market, Sydney; serviette and doily from Linen and Lace, Balmain, NSW; wooden board by Peter Sorensen from R. J. Phillips, Sydney; knife from Royal Copenhagen.

Grease a deep 20cm round cake pan.

Cream butter and sugar in small bowl with electric mixer until light and fluffy; beat in eggs one at a time, beat until combined; transfer mixture to large bowl. Fold in sifted dry ingredients, ground hazelnuts and apple.

Spread mixture into prepared pan, bake in moderate oven for about 55 minutes, stand 5 minutes before turning on to wire rack to cool. Spread with icing and decorate with hazelnuts.

Lemon Icing: Beat butter in small bowl with electric mixer until light and fluffy. Gradually beat in sifted icing sugar, then enough lemon juice to give a spreadable consistency.

Keeping time: 3 days.

LEFT: Apple Cake.
RIGHT: Moist Apple and Date Cake.

SPICY APPLE AND CURRANT YOGHURT CAKE

125g butter
2 teaspoons grated lemon rind
¾ cup castor sugar
2 eggs
200g carton plain yoghurt
½ x 410g can unsweetened pie apple
¾ cup currants
2 cups self-raising flour
½ teaspoon bicarbonate of soda
2 teaspoons mixed spice

Grease a 23cm square slab pan, line base with paper; grease paper.

Beat butter, rind and sugar in small bowl with electric mixer until light and fluffy; beat in eggs one at a time, beat mixture until combined, stir in yoghurt, apple and currants, then sifted dry ingredients.

Spread mixture into prepared pan, bake in moderate oven for about 55 minutes. Stand 5 minutes before turning on to wire rack to cool. Dust with sifted icing sugar before serving.

Keeping time: 4 days.

CARAMEL APPLE CAKE

We used Granny Smith apples.

1 cup plain flour
¼ cup self-raising flour
1½ teaspoons ground cinnamon
1½ cups brown sugar, firmly packed
1 teaspoon vanilla essence
60g butter
3 eggs
2 apples, grated
1 cup chopped walnuts
½ cup chopped raisins

Grease a deep 19cm square cake pan, line base with paper; grease paper.

Combine sifted dry ingredients, sugar, essence, chopped butter and eggs in large bowl, beat on low speed with electric mixer until ingredients are combined. Increase speed to medium, beat for about 3 minutes or until mixture is changed in colour and smooth. Stir in apples, nuts and raisins. Spread into prepared pan, bake in moderate oven for about 50 minutes. Stand 5 minutes before turning on to wire rack to cool.

Keeping time: 1 week.

CARAMEL BUTTER CAKE

125g butter
1 teaspoon vanilla essence
1 cup brown sugar, firmly packed
2 eggs
1 tablespoon golden syrup
1 cup plain flour
½ cup self-raising flour
1 teaspoon ground cinnamon
½ cup milk
CARAMEL ICING
1 cup brown sugar, firmly packed
60g butter
2 tablespoons milk
¾ cup icing sugar
2 teaspoons milk, extra

Grease a deep 20cm round cake pan, line base with paper; grease paper.

Cream butter, essence and sugar in small bowl with electric mixer until light and fluffy, add eggs one at a time, beat until combined; beat in golden syrup. Transfer mixture to large bowl, fold in sifted dry ingredients and milk. Pour mixture into prepared pan, bake in moderate oven for about 50 minutes. Stand 5 minutes before turning on to wire rack to cool. Top cold cake with icing before serving.

Caramel Icing: Combine sugar, butter and milk in saucepan, stir constantly over heat without boiling until sugar is dissolved. Bring to the boil, reduce heat, simmer 3 minutes uncovered without stirring, stir in sifted icing sugar. Stir in the extra milk to make a spreadable consistency.

Keeping time: 4 days.

WHOLEMEAL DATE AND CARAMEL CAKE

125g butter, melted
1½ cups (250g) chopped dates
½ cup raw sugar
2 tablespoons golden syrup
⅔ cup milk
1 egg, lightly beaten
1 cup wholemeal self-raising flour
1 cup white self-raising flour

Grease a 20cm ring pan.

Combine butter, dates, sugar, golden syrup, milk and egg in large bowl. Stir in the sifted dry ingredients in 2 lots.

Spread into prepared pan, bake in moderate oven for about 50 minutes. Stand 5 minutes before turning on to wire rack to cool.

Keeping time: 3 days.

LEFT: back: Hazelnut Apple Cake (recipe previous page); front: Spicy Apple and Currant Yoghurt Cake.
RIGHT: back: Caramel Apple Cake; centre: Wholemeal Date and Caramel Cake; front: Caramel Butter Cake.

Plates at right are Scottish Thistle by Mikasa. Cup, saucer, plate at left from Vasa Agencies, Sydney.

SLICES

Slices can be plain and homely, or glamorous enough to serve with coffee after dinner. Health slices are great for school lunches, and for taking to the office, since they keep well.

Unbaked

Biscuit crumbs are often used as a main ingredient in these recipes. We used a plain sweet biscuit such as Nice, however any plain variety can be used. Make sure they are finely crushed in a processor or blender, or in a bag with a rolling pin.
Be particularly careful to be accurate when measuring combining ingredients such as sweetened condensed milk. Store all these slices, covered, in the refrigerator.

CRUNCHY CHOC-BUBBLE SLICE

1½ cups Rice Bubbles
1 cup roasted unsalted peanuts
1 cup mixed fruit
1 cup coconut
100g packet white marshmallows
60g butter
CHOCOLATE ICING
1½ cups icing sugar
1 tablespoon cocoa
1 teaspoon soft butter
1 tablespoon milk, approximately

Grease a 25cm x 30cm Swiss roll pan.

Combine Rice Bubbles, peanuts, fruit and coconut in large bowl. Combine marshmallows and butter in saucepan, stir constantly over heat without boiling, until marshmallows and butter are melted; stir into Rice Bubble mixture. Press mixture evenly into prepared pan, spread with icing, sprinkle with crushed nuts if desired. Refrigerate until set before cutting.

Chocolate Icing: Sift icing sugar and cocoa into small heatproof bowl, stir in butter and enough milk to make a stiff paste. Stir over hot water until icing is spreadable.

Keeping time: 1 week.

FROSTED APRICOT CHERRY AND WALNUT SLICE

1 cup (125g) sweet biscuit crumbs
1 cup halved glace cherries
⅔ cup chopped dried apricots
¾ cup chopped walnuts
½ cup coconut
½ cup sweetened condensed milk
125g butter, melted
FROSTING
30g butter
1 teaspoon vanilla essence
1 tablespoon yoghurt
1 cup icing sugar
2 tablespoons coconut

Line base and sides of a 19cm × 29cm lamington pan with foil.

Combine biscuits, fruit, walnuts, coconut, milk and butter in large bowl; stir until combined. Press mixture evenly into prepared pan, spread with frosting. Refrigerate until set before cutting. Sprinkle with coconut.

Frosting: Beat butter, essence, and yoghurt in small bowl with electric mixer until smooth and creamy. Gradually beat in sifted icing sugar.

Keeping time: 1 week.

HONEY COCONUT CRUNCH

We used Butternut cookies for this recipe but any sweet biscuit will do.

2 cups (250g) sweet biscuit crumbs
125g butter, melted
TOPPING
30g butter
2 tablespoons peanut butter
½ cup honey
1 tablespoon sugar
3 cups Cornflakes
½ cup coconut
¼ cup finely chopped dried apricots
¼ cup finely chopped unsalted
    roasted peanuts

Combine biscuits and butter, press over base of 19cm × 29cm lamington pan; refrigerate while preparing topping. Press topping over base, refrigerate until set before cutting.
Topping: Combine butter, peanut butter, honey and sugar in large saucepan, stir constantly over heat without boiling until butter is melted and sugar dissolved. Stir in Cornflakes, coconut, apricots and peanuts.
    Keeping time: 1 week.

ABOVE: from left: Honey Coconut Crunch; Frosted Apricot Cherry and Walnut Slice; Crunchy Choc-Bubble Slice.

Tiles from Fred Pazotti Pty Ltd, Sydney; platter from Artiana Imports, Sydney.

CREME DE MENTHE SLICE

We used plain un-iced Golliwog biscuits and an Aero peppermint chocolate bar in this recipe. Creme de Menthe is a mint-flavoured liqueur.

1 cup (125g) crushed sweet
   chocolate biscuits
90g butter, melted
FILLING
3 teaspoons gelatine
⅓ cup cold water
2 eggs, separated
2 tablespoons castor sugar
2 tablespoons Creme de Menthe
   liqueur
2 tablespoons milk
2 tablespoons castor sugar, extra
⅔ cup thickened cream
30g peppermint chocolate bar,
   grated

Grease a 19cm x 29cm lamington pan.

Combine biscuits and butter, press evenly into prepared pan; refrigerate 30 minutes. Pour Creme de Menthe mixture over base, refrigerate several hours or until firm. Sprinkle with peppermint bar.

Filling: Sprinkle gelatine over water. Beat egg yolks and sugar in small bowl with electric mixer until thick and creamy. Place in saucepan, add gelatine mixture, stir constantly over heat without boiling until gelatine is dissolved and mixture slightly thickened. Remove from heat, stir in Creme de Menthe and milk, transfer to large bowl, refrigerate until partly set.

Beat egg whites in small bowl until soft peaks form, gradually add extra sugar, beat until dissolved between each addition. Fold into gelatine mixture, then fold in whipped cream.

Keeping time: 2 days.

ROCKY ROAD SLICE

125g butter
1½ tablespoons cocoa
½ cup castor sugar
1 egg, lightly beaten
1 cup coconut
½ cup chopped walnuts
2 cups (250g) sweet biscuit crumbs
400g packet milk chocolate, chopped
100g packet pink marshmallows,
   roughly chopped
2 x 100g packets white
   marshmallows, roughly chopped
⅓ cup flaked almonds
1 cup halved glace cherries

Grease a 19cm x 29cm lamington pan.

Combine biscuits, butter, coconut and spice in bowl, mix well. Press evenly over base of prepared pan, refrigerate 30 minutes. Pour filling over base, refrigerate several hours or until firm. Spread with topping, refrigerate until topping is set. Sprinkle with extra toasted shredded coconut if desired.

Filling: Process cream cheese until soft, add cream, marshmallows, strawberries, process until smooth. Add gelatine to cold water, stir over hot water until gelatine is dissolved, fold into cream mixture.

Topping: Combine marshmallows and milk in saucepan, stir constantly over low heat without boiling until marshmallows are melted, cool topping to room temperature.

Keeping time: 2 days.

PINEAPPLE CREAM SLICE

2 cups (250g) sweet biscuit crumbs
125g butter, melted
1 teaspoon ground cinnamon
TOPPING
450g can crushed pineapple
1 tablespoon gelatine
¼ cup castor sugar
1 cup cottage cheese
1 tablespoon lemon juice
200g carton sour cream
¼ cup crushed nuts

Grease a 19cm x 29cm lamington pan.

Combine biscuits, butter and cinnamon in bowl, reserve ¼ cup crumbs for topping. Press remaining crumbs evenly into prepared pan, refrigerate 30 minutes. Pour topping over base, sprinkle with reserved crumbs and crushed nuts, refrigerate until firm.

Topping: Drain pineapple, reserve ½ cup syrup. Combine syrup, gelatine and sugar in saucepan, stir constantly over heat without boiling until gelatine and sugar are dissolved, cool. Push cottage cheese through sieve into bowl, stir in lemon juice, pineapple, sour cream and gelatine mixture.

Keeping time: 2 days.

Grease a 19cm x 29cm lamington pan.

Combine butter, cocoa and sugar in saucepan, stir constantly over heat without boiling until sugar is dissolved; transfer to large bowl. Stir in egg, coconut, walnuts and biscuits. Press mixture evenly over base of pan. Refrigerate 30 minutes or until firm.

Melt half the chocolate over hot water; remove from heat. Stir in marshmallows and almonds, spread over base; sprinkle with cherries.

Melt remaining chocolate over hot water, drizzle over cherries; refrigerate until set before cutting.

Keeping time: 1 week.

STRAWBERRY MALLOW SLICE

2 cups (250g) sweet biscuit crumbs
125g butter, melted
½ cup coconut
1 teaspoon mixed spice
FILLING
250g packet cream cheese
300ml carton thickened cream
100g packet pink marshmallows
250g punnet strawberries
1 tablespoon gelatine
¼ cup cold water
TOPPING
100g packet white marshmallows
1 tablespoon milk

ABOVE: from left: Pineapple Cream Slice; Creme de Menthe Slice; Strawberry Mallow Slice.
LEFT: Rocky Road Slice.

Cane stand from House of Bambusit, Sydney; plates, cup and saucer are Aria by Villeroy & Boch.

STRAWBERRY JELLY SLICE

We used Honey Snap biscuits in this recipe but any sweet biscuit will do.

2 cups (250g) sweet biscuit crumbs
125g butter, melted
100g packet pink marshmallows
1 teaspoon gelatine
¼ cup milk
¼ teaspoon strawberry essence
⅔ cup thickened cream
250g punnet strawberries, halved
2 x 100g packets strawberry jelly
2 cups boiling water

Grease a 19cm x 29cm lamington pan.

Combine biscuits and butter in bowl. Press evenly over base of prepared pan; refrigerate until firm.

Combine marshmallows, gelatine and milk in saucepan, stir over low heat, without boiling, until marshmallows are melted. Transfer to large bowl, add essence; cool to room temperature. Whip cream until soft peaks form, fold into marshmallow mixture, pour over base. Place strawberries over marshmallow; refrigerate mixture 30 minutes.

Dissolve jelly in boiling water; cool to room temperature. Pour jelly over strawberries, refrigerate until firm before cutting.

Keeping time: 2 days.

EASY VANILLA SLICE WITH PASSIONFRUIT ICING

250g packet Morning Coffee biscuits
300ml carton thickened cream
1 cup milk
85g packet vanilla instant pudding
PASSIONFRUIT ICING
1 cup icing sugar
2 passionfruit
1 teaspoon soft butter

Cover base of 23cm square slab pan with biscuits, plain side down.

Combine cream and milk in large bowl, add pudding mix; beat with rotary beater for about 1 minute or until smooth. Pour pudding mixture over biscuits. Top with a single layer of biscuits, plain side down. Top with icing; refrigerate overnight before cutting.

Passionfruit Icing: Combine sifted icing sugar, passionfruit pulp and butter in small heatproof bowl. Stir over hot water until icing is spreadable.

Keeping time: 1 day.

PASSIONFRUIT AND LEMON MARSHMALLOW SLICE

1 cup (125g) sweet biscuit crumbs
½ cup finely chopped pecan nuts
90g unsalted butter, melted

FILLING
250g packet cream cheese
½ cup sweetened condensed milk
2 teaspoons grated lemon rind
¼ cup lemon juice
TOPPING
1 tablespoon gelatine
¾ cup water
1 cup castor sugar
¼ cup passionfruit pulp
yellow food colouring

Grease a 19cm x 29cm lamington pan.

Combine biscuits, pecans and butter in bowl, mix well. Press evenly into prepared pan, refrigerate 30 minutes. Pour filling over base, refrigerate until firm. Pour topping over filling, refrigerate until firm. Serve with extra passionfruit if desired.

Filling: Beat cream cheese in small bowl with electric mixer until smooth, beat in milk, lemon rind and juice.

Topping: Combine gelatine, water and sugar in saucepan, stir constantly over low heat without boiling until gelatine and sugar are dissolved. Bring to the boil, reduce heat, simmer gently uncovered for 5 minutes without stirring. Place mixture into large bowl, cool to room temperature. Beat with electric mixer on high speed until thick. Stir in passionfruit and a little colouring.

Keeping time: 2 days.

CARAMEL NUT CRUNCH

250g soft caramels
100g packet marshmallows
125g butter
3 cups Rice Bubbles
¼ cup chopped roasted unsalted
   cashew nuts
¼ cup chopped Brazil nuts
¼ cup chopped roasted hazelnuts
¼ cup chopped macadamia nuts
30g dark chocolate

Grease a 25cm x 30cm Swiss roll pan.

Combine caramels, marshmallows and butter in saucepan, stir constantly over hot water until mixture is smooth. Place Rice Bubbles and nuts in baking dish, bake in moderate oven for about 5 minutes or until lightly toasted. Combine caramel mixture with nut mixture, mix well. Press mixture quickly and evenly into prepared pan, refrigerate until firm before cutting into triangles.

Melt chocolate over hot water, cool, drizzle over triangles.

Keeping time: 1 week.

CHOC-TOPPED CRUNCHY SLICE

3 x 65g Mars Bars, chopped
90g butter
3 cups Rice Bubbles
TOPPING
200g milk chocolate, chopped
30g butter

Grease a 19cm x 29cm lamington pan.

Combine Mars Bars and butter in large saucepan, stir constantly over low heat without boiling until mixture is smooth; stir in Rice Bubbles. Press mixture evenly into prepared pan, spread with topping. Refrigerate until set before cutting.

Topping: Melt chocolate and butter in pan over hot water; stir until smooth.

Keeping time: 1 week.

LEFT: from left: Strawberry Jelly Slice; Easy Vanilla Slice with Passionfruit Icing; Passionfruit and Lemon Marshmallow Slice. BELOW: back, from left: Lemon Date Bubble Bars; Caramel Nut Crunch; front: Choc-Topped Crunchy Slice.

Coffee table from Artes Studio, Sydney; plates are Taitu from Lifestyle Imports.

LEMON DATE BUBBLE BARS

1½ cups (250g) chopped dates
60g butter
½ cup sugar
1 tablespoon lemon juice
½ cup coconut
3 cups Rice Bubbles
½ cup chopped roasted unsalted
   peanuts
40g butter, extra, melted
LEMON GLACE ICING
1½ cups icing sugar
1 teaspoon soft butter
2 tablespoons lemon juice,
   approximately

Grease a 19 × 29cm lamington pan, line base and sides with paper; grease paper well.

Combine dates, butter and sugar in large saucepan, stir constantly over heat without boiling for 5 minutes, or until smooth and pulpy. Remove pan from heat, stir in lemon juice, coconut, Rice Bubbles, peanuts and extra butter. Press mixture firmly into prepared pan, spread with icing, refrigerate until set before cutting.

Lemon Glace Icing: Combine sifted icing sugar and butter in bowl, stir in enough juice to give a stiff paste. Stir over hot water until spreadable.

Keeping time: 1 week.

CHOC-MINT WHEATMEAL SLICE

90g butter
¼ cup castor sugar
1 tablespoon cocoa
1 egg, lightly beaten
1 cup (125g) wheatmeal biscuit crumbs
½ cup coconut
¼ cup chopped walnuts
FILLING
60g butter
¼ teaspoon peppermint essence
2 cups icing sugar
1 tablespoon custard powder
2 tablespoons hot water
TOPPING
125g dark chocolate, chopped
30g butter

Grease a 19cm x 29cm lamington pan, line base and sides with paper; grease paper well.

Combine butter, sugar and cocoa in saucepan, stir constantly over heat without boiling until sugar is dissolved. Quickly stir in egg, then biscuits, coconut and walnuts. Press mixture evenly into prepared pan, refrigerate until set.

Spread base with filling, refrigerate until set, then spread with topping, refrigerate until set before cutting.

Filling: Cream butter and essence in small bowl with electric mixer until smooth, gradually beat in sifted icing sugar and custard powder alternately with water. Beat until light and fluffy.

Topping: Melt chocolate and butter over hot water, cool slightly.

Keeping time: 1 week.

FRUIT HONEY AND OAT BARS

1 cup rolled oats
1 cup Rice Bubbles
4 Weet-Bix, crushed
1 cup coconut
¼ cup chopped dried apricots
¼ cup chopped dried apples
¾ cup brown sugar, firmly packed
½ cup honey
½ cup peanut butter
125g butter

Grease a 19cm x 29cm lamington pan.

Combine oats, Rice Bubbles, Weet-Bix, coconut and fruit in large bowl.

Combine sugar, honey, peanut butter and butter in saucepan, stir constantly over heat without boiling until butter is melted and sugar dissolved. Bring to the boil, reduce heat, simmer, stirring constantly for 5 minutes, or until mixture thickens.

Stir honey mixture into dry ingredients, press evenly into prepared pan. Refrigerate until set before cutting.

Keeping time: 1 week.

NANAIMO BARS

This is a treat from Western Canada.

185g butter, chopped
100g dark chocolate, chopped
1 egg, lightly beaten
2 cups (250g) wheatmeal biscuit crumbs
1 cup coconut
⅔ cup finely chopped pecan nuts
FILLING
60g butter
1 teaspoon vanilla essence
2 cups icing sugar
2 tablespoons custard powder
¼ cup milk
TOPPING
30g dark chocolate, chopped
15g butter

Grease a 19cm x 29cm lamington pan.

Melt butter and chocolate over hot water. Remove from heat, cool 5 minutes; stir in egg. Combine biscuits, coconut and pecans in bowl, stir in butter mixture. Press mixture firmly over base of prepared pan. Spread evenly with filling. Refrigerate until firm.

Drizzle slice with topping, refrigerate until set before cutting.

Filling: Cream butter and essence in small bowl with electric mixer, gradually beat in sifted icing sugar and custard powder, then milk.

Topping: Melt chocolate and butter over hot water, cool slightly.

Keeping time: 2 weeks.

HEALTHY HONEY MUESLI BARS

¼ cup sesame seeds
1 cup toasted muesli
3 cups Rice Bubbles
½ cup coconut
¼ cup sunflower seed kernels
125g butter
⅓ cup honey
⅓ cup peanut butter
½ cup raw sugar

Grease a 19cm x 29cm lamington pan.

Toast sesame seeds on oven tray in moderate oven for about 5 minutes, cool to room temperature.

Combine muesli, Rice Bubbles, coconut, sunflower and sesame seeds in bowl. Combine butter, honey, peanut butter and sugar in saucepan, stir constantly over heat without boiling until butter is melted and sugar is dissolved. Bring to the boil, reduce heat, simmer uncovered without stirring for 5 minutes; stir into dry ingredients. Press into prepared pan, refrigerate until set before cutting.

Keeping time: 1 week.

LEFT: from back: Nanaimo Bars; Choc-Mint Wheatmeal Slice.
RIGHT: from back: Fruit Honey and Oat Bars; Healthy Honey Muesli Bars.

Glass top tables from Artes Studio, Sydney; china is Origo by Villeroy & Boch.

CHOC-COCONUT SLICE

This slice is sweet and rich. Serve in small pieces.

1½ cups coconut
1 cup finely crushed Cornflakes
1 cup sultanas
½ cup sweet biscuit crumbs
⅓ cup cocoa
⅓ cup chopped walnuts
400g can sweetened condensed milk
90g butter, melted
CHOCOLATE GLACE ICING
1½ cups icing sugar
1 tablespoon cocoa
1 teaspoon soft butter
1 tablespoon milk, approximately

Grease a 25cm x 30cm Swiss roll pan, line base with paper; grease paper.

Combine coconut, Cornflakes, sultanas, biscuits, sifted cocoa and walnuts in large bowl, stir in milk and butter. Spread mixture evenly into prepared pan, refrigerate until firm. Remove slice from pan, remove paper, spread slice with icing, refrigerate until icing is set before cutting. Decorate with walnut halves if desired.

Chocolate Glace Icing: Sift icing sugar and cocoa into small heatproof bowl, stir in butter and enough milk to make a stiff paste. Stir over hot water until icing is spreadable.

Keeping time: 1 week.

BRANDIED CHOCOLATE ALMOND SLICE

100g dark chocolate, chopped
½ cup sweetened condensed milk
2 tablespoons brandy
1 teaspoon dry instant coffee
2 cups (250g) sweet biscuit crumbs
½ cup chopped walnuts
½ cup sultanas
½ cup chopped glace cherries
ALMOND PASTE
2½ cups icing sugar
1 cup packaged ground almonds
1 egg, lightly beaten
2 teaspoons lemon juice
CHOCOLATE TOPPING
90g dark chocolate, chopped
30g butter

Grease a 19cm x 29cm lamington pan, line base and sides with paper; grease paper well.

Melt chocolate in bowl over hot water, stir in milk, brandy and coffee, then stir in biscuits, walnuts, sultanas and cherries. Press firmly into prepared pan.

Roll out almond paste large enough to cover base, press gently on to base, smooth surface with knife. Spread almond paste with topping, refrigerate until set before cutting.

Almond Paste: Combine sifted icing sugar and almonds, stir in egg and lemon juice. Knead lightly until smooth on surface which has been dusted with a little extra sifted icing sugar.

Chocolate Topping: Melt chocolate and butter in bowl over hot water.

Keeping time: 1 week.

LEFT: from back: Brandied Chocolate Almond Slice; Choc-Coconut Slice. RIGHT: Luscious Lemon Coconut Meringue Slice.

Coffee table at left from Artes Studio, Sydney; plates at left are Contour by Studio Nova from Mikasa. Plate and mug at right are Foulard Noir by Kosta Boda.

Baked

Most of these recipes are quick and easy and geared for the family, but we've also included several delicious special occasion slices.

LUSCIOUS LEMON COCONUT MERINGUE SLICE

This shortbread base requires kneading to make it crisp.

90g butter
2 tablespoons castor sugar
¾ cup plain flour
⅓ cup cornflour
400g can sweetened condensed milk
2 eggs, separated
2 teaspoons grated lemon rind
½ cup lemon juice
¼ cup castor sugar, extra
½ cup desiccated coconut
½ cup flaked coconut

Grease a 19cm x 29cm lamington pan, line base with paper; grease paper.

Cream butter and sugar in small bowl with electric mixer. Gradually add sifted flour and cornflour, turn on to lightly floured surface, knead for 5 minutes. Spread evenly over base of prepared pan. Bake in moderate oven 15 minutes or until lightly browned.

Combine condensed milk, egg yolks, lemon rind and juice in bowl, pour over base, bake further 10 minutes. Beat egg whites in small bowl until soft peaks form, gradually add extra sugar, beat until dissolved. Add desiccated coconut, spread over filling, sprinkle with flaked coconut, bake further 10 minutes or until golden brown. Cool in pan before cutting.

Keeping time: 2 days.

CHOCOLATE FRUIT SLICE

125g butter
1 cup self-raising flour
2 tablespoons cocoa
½ cup castor sugar
1 cup coconut
½ cup mixed fruit
¼ cup chopped pecan nuts
CHOCOLATE ICING
1½ cups icing sugar
¼ cup cocoa
2 teaspoons melted butter
2 tablespoons milk, approximately
2 tablespoons coconut

Grease a 19cm x 29cm lamington pan, line base and sides with paper; grease paper well.

Melt butter in saucepan, stir in sifted flour and cocoa, sugar, coconut, fruit and pecans. Press into prepared pan, bake in moderate oven for about 20 minutes.

Spread with icing, sprinkle with coconut. Cool in pan before cutting.

Chocolate Icing: Sift icing sugar and cocoa into bowl, stir in butter and enough milk to make a stiff paste.

Keeping time: 3 days.

PEANUT SLICE

1½ cups plain flour
125g butter
1 tablespoon water, approximately
¼ cup raspberry jam
TOPPING
1 egg white
¾ cup castor sugar
½ cup cake crumbs
1 tablespoon cocoa
1½ cups (250g) roasted unsalted
    peanuts
1 teaspoon vanilla essence

Grease a 19cm x 29cm lamington pan.

Sift flour into bowl; rub in butter. Add enough water to make ingredients cling together. Knead gently on lightly floured surface until smooth. Cover pastry; refrigerate 30 minutes.

Roll out pastry large enough to cover base of prepared pan; prick well with fork. Bake in moderate oven for about 15 minutes; cool 10 minutes; spread evenly with jam, then topping. Brush surface evenly with water. Bake in moderate oven for about 20 minutes. Cool in pan before cutting.

Topping: Beat egg white in small bowl until stiff, beat in sugar, fold in cake crumbs, sifted cocoa, peanuts and essence; mix well.

Keeping time: 4 days.

RIGHT: back, from left: Chocolate Fruit Slice; Peanut Slice; front: Parisienne Slice with Coffee Icing (recipe over page).

Coffee table from Artes Studio, Sydney; platters and plate are Kaleidoscope by Villeroy & Boch.

PARISIENNE SLICE WITH COFFEE ICING

1 cup plain flour
½ cup self-raising flour
125g butter
1 egg, lightly beaten
1 tablespoon water, approximately
2 egg whites
½ cup castor sugar
2 tablespoons strawberry jam
1 cup coconut
1 cup cake crumbs
red food colouring
COFFEE ICING
1½ cups icing sugar
1 teaspoon soft butter
1 tablespoon hot milk
3 teaspoons dry instant coffee
1 cup chopped walnuts
½ cup chopped glace cherries

Grease a 19cm x 29cm lamington pan.

Sift flours into bowl, rub in butter, add egg and enough water to mix to a firm dough. Press into prepared pan.

Beat egg whites in small bowl with electric mixer until soft peaks form, gradually beat in sugar, beat until dissolved. Transfer to large bowl. Stir in jam, coconut, cake crumbs and a little colouring if desired. Spread mixture over base, bake in moderate oven for about 30 minutes. Cool in pan, top with icing, walnuts and cherries.

Coffee Icing: Sift icing sugar into small heatproof bowl, stir in butter and combined milk and coffee. Stir constantly over hot water until spreadable.

Keeping time: 4 days.

CHOCOLATE CARAMEL SLICE

There is no substitute for liquid glucose in this recipe.

1½ cups self-raising flour
3 teaspoons cocoa
⅓ cup castor sugar
⅓ cup coconut
185g butter, melted
TOPPING
1 cup castor sugar
125g butter
2 tablespoons golden syrup
⅓ cup liquid glucose
⅓ cup water
400g can sweetened condensed milk
¾ cup finely chopped walnuts
300g dark chocolate, chopped

Grease a 25cm x 30cm Swiss roll pan.

Combine sifted flour and cocoa, sugar, coconut and butter in bowl; mix well. Press evenly over base of prepared pan. Bake in moderate oven for 20 minutes. Cool 5 minutes before spreading with topping. Sprinkle evenly with walnuts; cool to room temperature; spread with chocolate; refrigerate until set.

Topping: Combine sugar, butter, golden syrup, glucose, water and milk in heavy-based saucepan. Stir constantly over low heat without boiling until sugar is dissolved; increase heat, boil steadily, stirring constantly for about 10 minutes or until caramel in colour. Melt chocolate over hot water; cool slightly before using.

Keeping time: 4 days.

NO-BOWL CHOC-BIT SLICE

90g butter, melted
1 cup (125g) sweet biscuit crumbs
1½ cups (185g) Choc Bits
1 cup shredded coconut
1 cup chopped mixed nuts
400g can sweetened condensed milk

Grease a 23cm square slab pan, cover base with paper; grease paper.

Pour butter into prepared pan, sprinkle evenly with biscuits, Choc Bits, coconut and nuts. Drizzle with milk. Bake in moderate oven for about 30 minutes. Cool in pan before cutting; store in refrigerator.

Keeping time: 1 week.

MALTED MOCHA SLICE

1 cup plain flour
⅓ cup brown sugar
90g butter
FILLING
½ cup malted milk powder
2 tablespoons self-raising flour
2 teaspoons drinking chocolate
¼ cup castor sugar
⅓ cup coconut
⅓ cup chopped blanched almonds
2 eggs, lightly beaten
1 teaspoon vanilla essence
MALTED ICING
1 cup icing sugar
2 tablespoons malted milk powder
2 teaspoons drinking chocolate
½ teaspoon dry instant coffee
1 tablespoon hot water
1 teaspoon soft butter

Grease a 23cm square slab pan.

Sift flour into bowl, add sugar, rub in butter. Press evenly into prepared pan. Bake in moderate oven 15 minutes, spread with filling, bake further 25 minutes; cool in pan. When cold, spread with icing; cut when icing is set.

Filling: Sift milk powder, flour and drinking chocolate into bowl, stir in sugar, coconut, almonds, eggs and essence; mix well.

Malted Icing: Sift icing sugar, milk powder and drinking chocolate into small heatproof bowl, stir in combined coffee, water and butter. Stir over hot water until icing is spreadable.

Keeping time: 4 days.

CARAMEL WALNUT SLICE

1 cup self-raising flour
1 cup coconut
½ cup castor sugar
125g butter, melted
TOPPING
2 eggs, lightly beaten
1 teaspoon vanilla essence
1 cup coconut
¾ cup brown sugar, firmly packed
½ cup chopped walnuts

Grease a 19cm x 29cm lamington pan.

Combine sifted flour, coconut and sugar in bowl, stir in butter. Press mixture into prepared pan. Bake in moderate oven for 15 minutes, spread with topping, bake further 20 minutes. Cool in pan before cutting.

Topping: Combine eggs and essence in bowl, stir in coconut, sugar and walnuts; mix well.

Keeping time: 4 days.

RIGHT: back: No-Bowl Choc-Bit Slice; Malted Mocha Slice; centre: Caramel Walnut Slice; front: Chocolate Caramel Slice.

Coffee tables from Artes Studio, Sydney; plates are Cortina Corners by Studio Nova from Mikasa, Sydney; coffee cups and sugar bowl are Bodum from Vasa Agencies, Sydney.

CHOCOLATE BROWNIES WITH SOUR CREAM FROSTING

125g butter
185g dark chocolate, chopped
1 cup castor sugar
2 teaspoons vanilla essence
2 eggs, lightly beaten
1 cup plain flour
½ cup chopped pecan nuts
SOUR CREAM FROSTING
100g dark chocolate, chopped
¼ cup sour cream

Grease a deep 19cm square cake pan, line base with paper; grease paper.

Melt butter and chocolate in saucepan over hot water. Transfer mixture to large bowl. Stir in sugar and essence, then eggs, sifted flour and pecans. Pour mixture into prepared pan, bake in moderate oven for about 30 minutes, cool in pan. Turn brownies out, top with frosting; refrigerate until set before cutting. Store in refrigerator.

Sour Cream Frosting: Melt chocolate in heatproof bowl over hot water, stir in sour cream, stir constantly until mixture is smooth and glossy.

Keeping time: 4 days.

CHOC-CHEESE BROWNIE SLICE

185g dark chocolate, chopped
45g butter
2 eggs
¾ cup castor sugar
½ cup plain flour
¼ cup self-raising flour
few drops almond essence
½ cup chopped walnuts
FILLING
60g butter
1 teaspoon vanilla essence
185g ricotta cheese
¼ cup castor sugar
2 eggs
2 tablespoons plain flour

Grease a 19cm x 29cm lamington pan.

Melt chocolate and butter over hot water, cool; do not allow to set. Beat eggs in small bowl with electric mixer until thick, add sugar gradually, beat until sugar is dissolved. Transfer mixture to large bowl, stir in sifted flours, essence and chocolate mixture. Spread half the chocolate mixture into prepared pan. Top with filling, then remaining chocolate mixture. Run a knife in a zig-zag pattern through mixture, sprinkle evenly with walnuts. Bake in moderate oven for about 30 minutes. Cool in pan before cutting. Store in refrigerator until set.

Filling: Beat butter, essence and cheese together in small bowl with electric mixer until mixture is creamy. Add sugar, beat until fluffy, add eggs one at a time, beat until combined. Stir in sifted flour.

Keeping time: 4 days.

CHOCOLATE PEPPERMINT SLICE

⅔ cup self-raising flour
2 tablespoons cocoa
¼ teaspoon bicarbonate of soda
⅓ cup castor sugar
30g butter
⅓ cup water
1 egg
PEPPERMINT FILLING
2¼ cups icing sugar
1 tablespoon oil
2 tablespoons milk, approximately
peppermint essence
CHOCOLATE TOPPING
125g dark chocolate, chopped
90g unsalted butter

Grease a 25cm x 30cm Swiss roll pan, line base with paper; grease paper.

Sift flour, cocoa and soda into small bowl of electric mixer, add sugar, butter and water; beat on medium speed for 2 minutes. Add egg, beat until combined. Spread mixture into prepared pan. Bake in moderate oven for about 20 minutes; cool in pan.

Spread base with filling, refrigerate until set, spread with topping, refrigerate until set before cutting.

Peppermint Filling: Combine sifted icing sugar and oil in small heatproof bowl, stir in enough milk to make a stiff paste; flavour with essence. Stir over hot water until spreadable.

Chocolate Topping: Melt chocolate and butter over hot water.

LEFT: back: Chocolate Brownies with Sour Cream Frosting; front: Choc-Cheese Brownie Slice.
RIGHT: back: Chocolate Peppermint Slice; centre: Chocolate Cherry Slice; front: Chocolate Almond Squares (recipe over page).

Tiles at left from Fred Pazotti Pty Ltd, Sydney; china at left from Morgan Imports, Sydney. Coffee tables from Artes Studio, Sydney; china is Kosta Boda Cubique.

CHOCOLATE CHERRY SLICE

200g dark chocolate, chopped
¾ cup coconut
⅓ cup castor sugar
1 cup chopped glace cherries
1 egg white

Grease a 19cm x 29cm lamington pan, line base and sides with paper; grease paper well.

Melt chocolate in heatproof bowl over hot water. Spread over base of prepared pan; refrigerate until set.

Combine coconut, sugar, cherries and egg white in bowl, spread over chocolate; rough top lightly with fork.

Bake in moderate oven for about 15 minutes. Cool in pan, cut when cold. Store in refrigerator.

Keeping time: 4 weeks.

115

CHOCOLATE ALMOND SQUARES

90g butter
⅓ cup castor sugar
4 eggs, separated
90g dark chocolate, grated
1½ cups (185g) packaged ground almonds
⅓ cup plain flour
¼ cup brandy
¼ cup apricot jam
COFFEE CREAM
1 teaspoon dry instant coffee
1 tablespoon hot water
90g butter
¼ cup icing sugar
CHOCOLATE ICING
90g dark chocolate, chopped
30g butter

Grease a 23cm square slab pan, line base and sides with paper; grease paper well.

Cream butter and sugar in small bowl with electric mixer until light and fluffy. Beat in egg yolks one at a time. Transfer mixture to large bowl, stir in chocolate, then almonds and sifted flour. Beat egg whites in small bowl until soft peaks form, fold into chocolate mixture in 2 lots.

Spread mixture into prepared pan, bake in moderate oven for about 30 minutes, turn on to wire rack to cool.

Split slice in half, brush each half with brandy, then spread one half with strained warm apricot jam. Spread other half with coffee cream, join halves together; trim edges. Turn slice upside down, spread base with icing. Refrigerate until set before cutting.

Coffee Cream: Dissolve coffee in water, cool to room temperature. Cream butter and icing sugar in small bowl with electric mixer until light and fluffy, beat in coffee mixture.

Chocolate Icing: Melt chocolate and butter in heatproof bowl over hot water; stir until smooth.

Keeping time: 1 week.

CORNFLAKE HONEY SLICE

1½ cups Cornflakes
1⅓ cups rolled oats
1⅓ cups coconut
¾ cup castor sugar
125g butter
2 tablespoons honey

Lightly grease a 19cm x 29cm lamington pan.

Combine Cornflakes, oats, coconut and sugar in bowl. Melt butter in saucepan, add honey, stir into dry ingredients. Spread into prepared pan. Bake in moderate oven for about 20 minutes. Stand 15 minutes before cutting; cool in pan.

Keeping time: 1 week.

CHOCOLATE FRUIT SLICE WITH LEMON ICING

1 cup self-raising flour
1 teaspoon mixed spice
¾ cup castor sugar
1 cup mixed fruit
½ cup coconut
½ cup Choc Bits
2 eggs, lightly beaten
90g butter, melted
LEMON ICING
1½ cups icing sugar
1 teaspoon soft butter
1 tablespoon lemon juice, approximately

Grease a 23cm square slab pan.

Combine sifted dry ingredients, sugar, fruit, coconut and Choc Bits in large bowl. Stir in eggs and butter, press mixture evenly into prepared pan. Bake in moderate oven for about 25 minutes. Stand 10 minutes before spreading with icing. Cool in pan before cutting.

Lemon Icing: Sift icing sugar into small bowl, stir in butter and enough lemon juice to make a stiff paste.

Keeping time: 3 days.

CURRANT AND JAM SLICE

1 cup self-raising flour
90g butter
2 teaspoons milk, approximately
¼ cup raspberry jam
1 cup currants
TOPPING
60g butter
1 teaspoon vanilla essence
⅓ cup castor sugar
2 eggs
¾ cup self-raising flour
¼ cup milk
LEMON ICING
2 cups icing sugar
60g soft butter
1 tablespoon lemon juice,
    approximately

Grease a 19cm x 29cm lamington pan.

Sift flour into bowl, rub in butter. Add enough milk to make ingredients cling together. Knead gently on lightly floured surface until smooth. Roll dough large enough to cover base of prepared pan. Spread with jam, sprinkle with currants; spread with topping. Bake in moderate oven for about 25 minutes. Cool on wire rack. When cold, spread with icing, cut when icing is set.

Topping: Cream butter, essence and sugar in small bowl with electric mixer until light and fluffy; beat in eggs one at a time, beat until combined. Stir in sifted flour and milk.

Lemon Icing: Sift icing sugar into bowl, stir in butter and enough lemon juice to make icing spreadable.

Keeping time: 4 days.

COFFEE APPLE BARS WITH CARAMEL ICING

We used Granny Smith apples.

½ cup sultanas
1 tablespoon dry instant coffee
½ cup water
90g butter
1 teaspoon vanilla essence
1 cup brown sugar, firmly packed
1 egg
1½ cups self-raising flour
½ teaspoon ground cinnamon
½ teaspoon bicarbonate of soda
1 apple, grated
CARAMEL ICING
2 tablespoons brown sugar
30g butter
1 tablespoon milk
1 cup icing sugar
⅓ cup chopped walnuts

Grease a 19cm x 29cm lamington pan, line base and sides with paper; grease paper well.

Combine sultanas, coffee and water in saucepan, bring to the boil, remove from heat, cool to room temperature.

Cream butter, essence and sugar in small bowl with electric mixer until light and fluffy, beat in egg, beat until combined. Transfer mixture to large bowl, stir in half the sifted flour, cinnamon and soda with half the sultana mixture, then stir in remaining flour and sultana mixtures; stir in apple.

Spread mixture into prepared pan. Bake in moderate oven for about 25 minutes. Spread with icing, sprinkle with walnuts, cool mixture in pan before cutting.

Caramel Icing Combine sugar, butter and milk in saucepan, stir constantly over heat without boiling until smooth. Gradually stir in sifted icing sugar.

Keeping time: 3 days.

LEFT: back: Cornflake Honey Slice; front, from left: Chocolate Fruit Slice with Lemon Icing; Currant and Jam Slice.
BELOW: back: Coffee Apple Bars with Caramel Icing; front: Grated Apple Slice (recipe over page).

Trays at left are from Dansab, Sydney; plates and cups are Taitu from Lifestyle Imports, Sydney; coffee pot and sugar bowl are Bodum from Vasa Agencies, Sydney; glass plates below are Sasaki from Dansab, Sydney.

GRATED APPLE SLICE

We used Granny Smith apples.

125g butter
2 tablespoons icing sugar
1½ cups plain flour
¼ cup self-raising flour
250g packet cream cheese
½ cup castor sugar
2 tablespoons lemon juice
2 apples, grated
1 tablespoon castor sugar, extra

Grease a 25cm x 30cm Swiss roll pan.

Cream butter and sifted icing sugar in small bowl with electric mixer until light and fluffy. Stir in sifted flours in 2 lots. Knead pastry quickly and gently on lightly floured surface until just smooth. Spread ⅔ of the pastry evenly over base of prepared pan. Wrap remaining pastry in plastic wrap, refrigerate 30 minutes or until firm.

Beat cream cheese in small bowl with electric mixer until smooth, beat in sugar and lemon juice. Spread mixture over pastry, top with apple. Grate remaining pastry coarsely, sprinkle over apple, sprinkle with extra sugar.

Bake in moderately hot oven for 10 minutes, reduce heat to moderate, bake further 20 minutes or until golden brown, cool in pan before cutting.

Keeping time: 2 days.

ORANGE ALMOND SLICE

125g butter
¼ cup castor sugar
1 cup plain flour
90g butter, extra
1 tablespoon grated orange rind
⅓ cup castor sugar, extra
2 eggs
1½ cups (185g) packaged ground almonds
½ cup flaked almonds
¼ cup apricot jam

Grease a 19cm x 29cm lamington pan, line base and sides with paper; grease paper well.

Cream butter and sugar in small bowl with electric mixer until light and fluffy, stir in sifted flour in 2 lots, spread evenly into prepared pan.

Cream extra butter and orange rind with extra sugar in small bowl with electric mixer until just combined, quickly beat in eggs (mixture will curdle at this stage). Stir in ground almonds, spread over base, sprinkle with flaked almonds.

Bake in moderate oven for about 20 minutes. Brush with warm strained apricot jam; cool in pan before cutting.

Keeping time: 3 days.

ICED APRICOT ORANGE BARS

1 cup finely chopped dried apricots
125g butter
2 teaspoons grated orange rind
1 cup brown sugar, firmly packed
2 eggs
1 tablespoon orange juice
1½ cups self-raising flour
ORANGE ICING
1 cup icing sugar
15g butter
2 teaspoons grated orange rind
1 tablespoon orange juice, approximately
½ cup chopped walnuts

Soak apricots in boiling water for about 10 minutes or until soft; drain well.

Grease a 25cm x 30cm Swiss roll pan well.

Cream butter, rind and sugar in small bowl with electric mixer until light and fluffy; beat in eggs one at a time, beat until combined. Stir in orange juice and apricots, then sifted flour. Spread mixture into prepared pan.

Bake in moderate oven for about 20 minutes or until brown. Stand 10 minutes, spread with icing, sprinkle with walnuts. Cool in pan before cutting.

Orange Icing: Sift icing sugar into small heatproof bowl, stir in butter, rind and enough orange juice to make a stiff paste. Stir over hot water until icing is spreadable.

Keeping time: 4 days.

OATY COCONUT SLICE

1 cup rolled oats
1 cup plain flour
¾ cup coconut
¾ cup raw sugar
125g butter
2 tablespoons honey
2 tablespoons water
½ teaspoon bicarbonate of soda

Grease a 25cm x 30cm Swiss roll pan.

Combine oats, sifted flour, coconut and sugar in large bowl. Combine butter, honey and water in saucepan, stir over heat until butter is melted, stir in soda, pour into dry ingredients; stir until combined . Press mixture evenly into prepared pan. Bake in moderate oven for about 25 minutes, cool in pan before cutting.

Keeping time: 2 days.

RIGHT: back: Iced Apricot Orange Bars; centre: Oaty Coconut Slice; front: Orange Almond Slice.
Spiced Fruit and Apple Slice and Spicy Mixed Peel Slice are pictured over page.

Table from Artes Studio, Sydney; coffee pot and cup are Bodum from Vasa Agencies, Sydney; plates are Regency Grey and Regency Magic Noire from Dansab, Sydney.

SPICED FRUIT AND APPLE SLICE

We used a Granny Smith apple.

185g butter
½ cup castor sugar
1 egg
1 tablespoon lemon juice
1½ cups plain flour
1 cup self-raising flour
FILLING
750g mixed fruit
½ cup brown sugar
1 teaspoon ground nutmeg
1 teaspoon ground cinnamon
2 teaspoons grated lemon rind
¼ cup lemon juice
1 tablespoon cornflour
1 cup water
1 apple, grated

Grease a 19cm x 29cm lamington pan.

Cream butter, sugar, egg and lemon juice in small bowl with electric mixer until light and fluffy. Stir in sifted flours in 2 lots. Turn on to lightly floured surface, knead until smooth. Roll out ⅔ of the pastry large enough to line base and sides of the prepared pan. Spread evenly with cold filling, roll out remaining pastry large enough to cover filling. Press edges of pastry firmly together; trim neatly. Cut a few holes in pastry to allow steam to escape. Bake in moderately hot oven 10 minutes, reduce heat to moderate, bake further 30 minutes. Cool in pan; sprinkle with sifted icing sugar before cutting.

Filling: Combine fruit, sugar, nutmeg, cinnamon, rind and juice in saucepan. Blend cornflour with water, add to saucepan, stir constantly over heat until mixture boils and thickens, reduce heat, cover, simmer 3 minutes, stir in apple, cool to room temperature.

Keeping time: 3 days.

SPICY MIXED PEEL SLICE

2 eggs
½ cup castor sugar
90g butter
¼ cup golden syrup
¾ cup self-raising flour
1 teaspoon ground coriander
½ cup mixed peel

Grease a 19cm x 29cm lamington pan.

Combine eggs and sugar in a small heatproof bowl, beat with electric mixer or rotary beater over simmering water until thick and creamy. Melt butter and golden syrup in saucepan; stir into egg mixture. Fold in sifted flour and coriander and peel.

Spread mixture into prepared pan. Bake in moderate oven for about 30 minutes. Stand 5 minutes before turning on to wire rack to cool. Dust with icing sugar before cutting.

Keeping time: 2 days.

PEANUT AND SULTANA SLICE

This slice is best made the day before required, to allow for easier cutting.

185g butter
½ cup castor sugar
½ cup sultanas
1 cup raw unsalted peanuts
1 cup coconut
1 cup plain flour

Grease a 19cm x 29cm lamington pan.

Melt butter in saucepan, stir in sugar, sultanas, peanuts and coconut, then sifted flour.

Press mixture firmly into prepared pan, bake in moderate oven for about 30 minutes. Cool in pan, cut when cold.

Keeping time: 3 days.

WHOLEMEAL DATE SLICE

1½ cups wholemeal plain flour
1¼ cups wholemeal self-raising flour
155g butter
1 tablespoon honey
1 egg, lightly beaten
⅓ cup milk
FILLING
500g dates, chopped
¾ cup water
2 tablespoons grated lemon rind
2 tablespoons lemon juice

Grease a 19cm x 29cm lamington pan. Sift dry ingredients into bowl, rub in butter. Add enough combined honey, egg and milk to make ingredients cling together. Knead gently on lightly floured surface until smooth, cover, refrigerate 30 minutes.

Divide dough in half, roll half large enough to cover base of prepared pan. Spread with cold filling, cover with remaining rolled-out pastry. Glaze with a little extra milk or water, sprinkle with a little extra sugar. Bake in moderately hot oven for about 25 minutes. Cool in pan before cutting.

Filling: Combine all ingredients in saucepan, cook stirring constantly until mixture is thick and smooth; cool to room temperature.

Keeping time: 3 days.

RIGHT: back, from left: Peanut and Sultana Slice; Spiced Fruit and Apple Slice (recipe previous page); front, from left: Wholemeal Date Slice; Spicy Mixed Peel Slice (recipe previous page).

Tiles from Fred Pazotti Pty Ltd, Sydney; platters and plates are Taitu from Lifestyle Imports, Sydney.

OUR BEST COCONUT SLICE

90g butter
½ cup castor sugar
1 egg
⅓ cup self-raising flour
⅔ cup plain flour
½ cup raspberry jam
TOPPING
2 eggs
⅓ cup castor sugar
2 cups coconut

Grease a 19cm x 29cm lamington pan.

Cream butter, sugar and egg in small bowl with electric mixer until light and fluffy; stir in sifted flours in 2 batches. Spread mixture evenly over base of prepared pan. Spread evenly with jam, then topping. Bake in moderate oven for about 35 minutes. Cool in pan, cut when cold.

Topping: Beat eggs lightly with fork in bowl, beat in sugar and coconut.

Variation: Substitute apricot for raspberry jam, and use 1 cup of coconut and 1 cup packaged ground almonds instead of the 2 cups coconut.

Keeping time: 4 days.

CARAMEL COCONUT SLICE

125g butter
½ cup brown sugar
1 cup plain flour
TOPPING
2 eggs
2 teaspoons vanilla essence
1 cup brown sugar, firmly packed
2 tablespoons self-raising flour
1 cup coconut
1 cup chopped walnuts

Grease a 19cm x 29cm lamington pan.

Cream butter and sugar in small bowl with electric mixer until light and fluffy, stir in sifted flour in 2 lots. Press mixture evenly into prepared pan bake in moderate oven for about 15 minutes.

Spread with topping, bake further 25 minutes or until topping is set. Cool in pan before cutting.

Topping: Beat eggs and essence in small bowl with electric mixer until thick and creamy, gradually add sugar beat until combined. Stir in flour, coconut and walnuts; mix well.

Keeping time: 3 days.

ALMOND-TOPPED CREAM SLICE

½ cup cream
½ cup castor sugar
1 teaspoon vanilla essence
2 eggs
1 cup self-raising flour
ALMOND TOPPING
90g butter
⅓ cup castor sugar
¼ cup cream
1 tablespoon plain flour
1 cup flaked almonds

Grease a 25cm x 30cm Swiss roll pan, line base with paper; grease paper.

Combine cream, sugar, essence and eggs in bowl, whisk until combined, whisk in flour in 2 lots. Spread mixture into prepared pan. Bake in moderate oven for 15 minutes. Spread with topping, bake further 15 minutes or until golden brown. Cool in pan before cutting.

Almond Topping: Melt butter in saucepan, stir in sugar, cream and flour. Stir constantly over heat until mixture boils and thickens, remove from heat, gently stir in almonds.

Keeping time: 3 days.

CHERRY COCONUT BARS

90g butter
1 teaspoon vanilla essence
2 tablespoons castor sugar
1 egg
¾ cup plain flour
¼ cup self-raising flour
3 x 55g Cherry Ripe bars, grated
FILLING
2 cups coconut
2 tablespoons self-raising flour
¼ cup castor sugar
1 egg, lightly beaten
¾ cup milk

Grease a 19cm x 29cm lamington pan.

Cream butter, essence, sugar and egg in small bowl with electric mixer until smooth and creamy. Stir in sifted flours in 2 lots. Press mixture evenly into prepared pan. Bake in moderate oven for about 20 minutes.

Spread base evenly with filling, bake further 25 minutes. Sprinkle immediately with Cherry Ripe bars. Cool in pan before cutting.

Filling: Combine dry ingredients in bowl, stir in combined egg and milk.

Keeping time: 4 days.

ABOVE: back: Our Best Coconut Slice; front: Variation of Coconut Slice; Apricot Almond Slice.
RIGHT: back, from left: Caramel Coconut Slice; Cherry Coconut Bars; front: Almond-Topped Cream Slice.

Plates above are Taitu from Lifestyle Imports, Sydney; tiles, right, from Fred Pazotti Pty Ltd, Sydney; wooden platter right from Orrefors; white plate right from Vasa Agencies, Sydney.

Information

CAKE MAKING TIPS

● We do not advise mixing cakes in blenders or processors unless specified in individual recipes. Use an electric beater to mix cakes and slices, always have the ingredients at room temperature, particularly the butter. Melted or extremely soft butter will alter the texture of the cooked cake.

● Start mixing ingredients on a low speed and once the ingredients are combined, increase the speed to about medium and beat for the required time. Creamed mixtures for cakes can be done with a wooden spoon, but it takes a lot longer.

● When measuring dry ingredients, gently shake the ingredient into the measuring cup, level off the surface with the top of the cup. When measuring liquids always stand the cup on a flat surface and check at eye level for accuracy. Spoon measurements should be levelled off with a knife or spatula. Be careful when measuring ingredients such as honey or treacle.

● Testing Cakes: All the cooking times in this book are approximate. There are many factors to be considered when judging whether a cake is cooked or not. Providing the correct measurements, specified pan and oven temperature is used then testing is easy. Feel the surface of the cake or slice with fingertips, it should feel firm, and the cake or slice should look very slightly shrunken from the edges of the pan. Use a skewer and gently push it into the thickest part of the cake, withdraw it slowly and check to see if the skewer is coated with uncooked mixture; return it to the oven for further cooking if necessary.

OVENS

● The recipes in this book were tested in gas and electric ovens. We positioned cakes and slices so that the top of the cooked product was roughly in the centre of the oven. If in doubt, check the manual for your oven.

● Several cakes and slices can be cooked in the oven at one time, providing the pans do not touch each other, the sides of the oven or the door when it is closed. Alternate the positions of the pans halfway during the cooking time, this will not hurt the cake if it is done gently and quickly.

● Fan Forced Ovens: If using a fan forced oven, check your operating manual for best results. As a rule, reduce the temperature by 10° Celsius when using the fan during cooking; cakes might also take slightly less time to cook than specified.

● None of the recipes in this book have been tested in a microwave or microwave/convection oven, as the cooking time and result would be different from the conventionally cooked cakes and slices.

CAKE PANS

● We tested most of the recipes in this book using Namco aluminium cake pans. If using pans which have a non-stick coating, or are anodised, or are made from stainless steel or tin, best results will be obtained by reducing the oven temperature by 10° Celsius (25° Fahrenheit).

● These cake pans can all be substituted for each other, they have roughly the same capacity. The cooking times will need to be adjusted slightly:
20cm baba pan
20cm ring pan
14cm x 21cm loaf pan
2 x 8cm x 26cm bar pans
deep 20cm round cake pan

● It is important to grease pans evenly; we used a pastry brush dipped in melted butter. We have suggested lining the pans only when necessary.

● When lining cake pans, use greaseproof or baking paper, grease the greaseproof when it is in the pan; it is not necessary to grease baking paper.

● Cakes which are cooked in pans such as bar, ring, baba or loaf usually crack due to the confined area.

KEEPING CAKES

● We have suggested minimum keeping times at the end of each recipe.

● Make sure cakes are at room temperature before storing them in a container which is as close to the size of the cake as possible to minimise the air space around the cake.

● All the cakes and slices in this book are suitable for freezing. It is usually better to freeze them uniced, as the icing often cracks during thawing. Cakes and slices thaw best in the refrigerator overnight.

● Wrap or seal cakes and slices in freezer wrap or bags. It is important to exclude as much air as possible.

● We prefer to store fruit cakes in the refrigerator, simply because they cut well, and they soon return to room temperature once sliced.

1: 19cm x 29cm lamington pan; **2**: 15cm x 25cm loaf pan; **3**: 14cm x 21cm loaf pan; **4**: 25cm x 30cm Swiss roll pan; **5**: 2 x 8cm x 17cm nut roll tins; **6**: 23cm square slab pan; **7**: deep 19cm square cake pan; **8**: deep 23cm square cake pan; **9**: 21cm tube pan; **10**: deep 27cm round cake pan; **11**: 20cm springform pan; **12**: deep 17cm round cake pan; **13**: 20cm ring pan; **14**: deep 23cm round cake pan; **15**: 20cm baba pan; **16**: round 20cm sandwich pan; **17**: deep 20cm round cake pan; **18**: gem irons; **19**: 2 x 8cm x 26cm bar pans.

FACTS AND FIGURES

Wherever you live, you'll be able to use our recipes with the help of these easy-to-follow conversions. While these conversions are approximate only, the difference between an exact and the approximate conversion of various liquid and dry measures is but minimal and will not affect your cooking results.

DRY MEASURES

Metric	Imperial
15g	1/2oz
30g	1oz
60g	2oz
90g	3oz
125g	4oz (1/4lb)
155g	5oz
185g	6oz
220g	7oz
250g	8oz (1/2lb)
280g	9oz
315g	10oz
345g	11oz
375g	12oz (3/4lb)
410g	13oz
440g	14oz
470g	15oz
500g	16oz (1lb)
750g	24oz (11/2lb)
1kg	32oz (2lb)

LIQUID MEASURES

Metric	Imperial
30ml	1 fluid oz
60ml	2 fluid oz
100ml	3 fluid oz
125ml	4 fluid oz
150ml	5 fluid oz (1/4 pint/1 gill)
190ml	6 fluid oz
250ml	8 fluid oz
300ml	10 fluid oz (1/2 pint)
500ml	16 fluid oz
600ml	20 fluid oz (1 pint)
1000ml (1 litre)	13/4 pints

HELPFUL MEASURES

Metric	Imperial
3mm	1/8in
6mm	1/4in
1cm	1/2in
2cm	3/4in
2.5cm	1in
5cm	2in
6cm	21/2in
8cm	3in
10cm	4in
13cm	5in
15cm	6in
18cm	7in
20cm	8in
23cm	9in
25cm	10in
28cm	11in
30cm	12in (1ft)

MEASURING EQUIPMENT

The difference between one country's measuring cups and another's is, at most, within a 2 or 3 teaspoon variance. (For the record, 1 Australian metric measuring cup holds approximately 250ml.) The most accurate way of measuring dry ingredients is to weigh them. When measuring liquids, use a clear glass or plastic jug with the metric markings.

Note: North America and UK use 15ml tablespoons. Australian tablespoons measure 20ml. All cup and spoon measurements are level.

How To Measure

When using graduated metric measuring cups, shake dry ingredients loosely into the appropriate cup. Do not tap the cup on a bench or tightly pack the ingredients unless directed to do so. Level top of measuring cups and measuring spoons with a knife. When measuring liquids, place a clear glass or plastic jug with metric markings on a flat surface to check accuracy at eye level.

We use large eggs having an average weight of 60g.

OVEN TEMPERATURES

These oven temperatures are only a guide. Always check the manufacturer's manual.

	C° (Celsius)	F° (Fahrenheit)	Gas Mark
Very slow	120	250	1
Slow	150	300	2
Moderately slow	160	325	3
Moderate	180 - 190	350 - 375	4
Moderately hot	200 - 210	400 - 425	5
Hot	220 - 230	450 - 475	6
Very hot	240 - 250	500 - 525	7

Glossary

Here are some names, terms and alternatives to help you understand our recipes and use them perfectly.

Arrowroot:
A thickening ingredient; cornflour can be substituted.

Bicarbonate of soda:
Baking soda.

Butter:
We used butter for all recipes in this book; a good quality cooking margarine can be used, if preferred.

Buttermilk:
The liquid left from separated cream, slightly sour in taste; use skim milk as a substitute, if preferred.

Cornflour:
Cornstarch.

Cream:
We have specified thickened (whipping) cream when necessary in recipes. Cream is simply a light pouring cream also known as half 'n' half.

Custard powder:
Pudding mix.

Dark chocolate;
We used a good quality cooking chocolate.

Essence:
Extract.

Golden Syrup;
Maple/pancake syrup. Honey can be substituted.

Ground almonds/hazelnuts:
We used pre-packaged ground nuts in our recipes.

Liquid glucose (glucose syrup):
Made from wheat starch; available at health food stores and supermarkets.

Mixed peel:
A mixture of chopped crystallised citrus peel.

Mixed fruit:
A combination of sultanas, raisins, currants, mixed peel and cherries.

Mixed spice:
A finely ground combination of spices which includes caraway, allspice, coriander, cumin, nutmeg, ginger and cinnamon; almost always used in sweet recipes. Do not confuse mixed spice with allspice.

Oil:
We used a light polyunsaturated salad oil.

Plain flour:
All-purpose flour.

Rice Bubbles:
Rice Crispies.

Rice flour:
Ground rice can be substituted for rice flour.

Self-raising flour:
Substitute plain (all purpose) flour and baking powder in the proportion of ¾ metric cup plain flour to 2 level metric teaspoons baking powder. Sift together several times before using. If using an 8oz measuring cup, use 1 cup plain flour to 2 teaspoons baking powder.

Semolina:
Farina.

Sour cream:
A thick commercially cultured sour cream.

Sugar:
Use a coarse granulated table sugar.

Castor sugar:
Regular fine granulated table or Berry sugar. This is used when a fine texture is required for a recipe.

Icing sugar:
Confectioners' or powdered sugar. We used icing sugar mixture (not pure) throughout this book.

Raw sugar:
Natural light brown granulated sugar or "sugar in the raw" can be used.

Sultanas:
Seedless white raisins.

Sweet biscuits:
Any plain sweet biscuit (or cookie) can be used.

Treacle:
Maple/pancake syrup. Honey can be substituted.

Weet-bix:
Weetabix or Ruskets.

Wholemeal flour:
Wholegrain flour; see self-raising flour and baking powder proportions for wholemeal self-raising flour.

Zucchini:
Courgette.

Index